How to Find a Job in Canada

Common Problems and Effective Solutions

How to Find a Job in Canada
Common Problems and Effective Solutions

Efim Cheinis

Dale Sproule

OXFORD
UNIVERSITY PRESS

OXFORD
UNIVERSITY PRESS

70 Wynford Drive, Don Mills, Ontario M3C 1J9
www.oup.com/ca

Oxford University Press is a department of the University of Oxford.
It furthers the University's objective of excellence in research, scholarship,
and education by publishing worldwide in

Oxford   New York
Auckland   Cape Town   Dar es Salaam   Hong Kong   Karachi
Kuala Lumpur   Madrid   Melbourne   Mexico City   Nairobi
New Delhi   Shanghai   Taipei   Toronto

With offices in
Argentina   Austria   Brazil   Chile   Czech Republic   France   Greece
Guatemala   Hungary   Italy   Japan   Poland   Portugal   Singapore
South Korea   Switzerland   Thailand   Turkey   Ukraine   Vietnam

Oxford is a trade mark of Oxford University Press
in the UK and in certain other countries

Published in Canada by
Oxford University Press

Library and Archives Canada Cataloguing in Publication

Cheinis, Efim, 1931-
How to find a job in Canada : common problems and effective solutions / Efim
Cheinis, Dale Sproule.

(Canadian newcomer series)
Includes bibliographical references and index.
ISBN 978-0-19-542795-0

1. Immigrants—Employment—Canada.   2. Job hunting—Canada—Handbooks,
manuals, etc.   I. Sproule, Dale, 1953-   II. Title.   III. Series.

HF5382.75.C3C44 2008   650.14086'9120971   C2007-905955-4

Cover design: Sherill Chapman
Cover images: **(top, left to right)** iStock International Inc; Andrew Penner/iStock International Inc;
Naheed Choudhry/iStock International Inc; Timothy Babasade/iStock International Inc
(bottom, left to right) Amanda Rhode/iStock International Inc; Willie B. Thomas/iStock
International Inc; blackrec/iStock International Inc; Diana Lundin/iStock International Inc

Printed and bound in Canada.

1 2 3 4 – 11 10 09 08

Dedication

This book is dedicated to my son Joseph, daughter Evguenia, and their families, who, with their hard work and optimism, overcame all of the immigration barriers and achieved well-deserved success in this remarkable country.

Acknowledgements

I want to thank everyone who helped me in the creation of this book. These people include, first of all, newcomers who turned to me for assistance with finding jobs in Canada. They also discussed their concerns, and shared their failures and successes with me. I am proud of the determination and strength that they used to achieve their goals, and I am thankful for their trust.

Secondly, I am very grateful to the Lawrence Square Employment Resource Centre staff, and especially to Sue Sadler, Monica Fellin, and Glenda Roy. They introduced me to job placement programs and workshops, and convinced me that Canada always welcomes new immigrants and helps them achieve a successful future in this country.

I'd like to express special gratitude to *Bonus Magazine* publisher, Simon Beker; *The Yonge Street Review* editor, Gennady Dertkin; *Russian Express* publisher, Maia Master; and *Canadian Newcomer Magazine* publisher, Dale Sproule. All of these individuals enabled me to publish various materials for newcomers.

And finally, I am very happy that I am fortunate enough to have such an excellent life-long partner, friend, and assistant as my lovely wife Alla. She not only released me from all of my domestic duties during the creation of this book, but also directly participated in the preparation of the manuscript. Thank you for all of your help, as well as the time you devoted to this book.

Efim Cheinis

Dedication

I would like to dedicate this book to my partner Laura, my beautiful daughters, Lauren and Sheena, and everyone in my extended family.

Acknowledgements

Acknowledgements must be paid to the many people in my life who came to Canada from around the world and helped me understand what I can do as a Canadian to welcome newcomers, make them feel at home, and help them succeed here. Foremost among them are Efim Cheinis, Mehdi Zahed, and Syed Ahmed. I would like to give an additional thanks to everyone who has supported and inspired *Canadian Newcomer Magazine*—especially Irena Nikolova and the late Elizabeth Gryte at Citizenship and Immigration Canada.

Dale Sproule

Both authors thank Oxford University Press for the appealing structure and visual appearance of this book. Special thanks to Julie Wade for her interest in publishing this book, and Jason Tomassini and Stephanie Kewin for their enthusiasm and hard work.

Table of Contents

Note on the language: As English is the second language of many newcomers to Canada, this book was written in straightforward language. In addition, at the end of each chapter readers will find a Key Words section that defines some of the important words and terms for that topic. For clear definitions at the appropriate language level the **Oxford ESL Dictionary** was used.

Foreword

Finding a job in Canada. It sounds simple enough, and yet finding the right job can be a complicated and challenging process, especially if you are new to the country and not familiar with the landscape that is the Canadian labour market.

Every day, hundreds of people from all corners of the globe arrive in different cities across Canada. They speak many different languages, have degrees and qualifications in a broad array of disciplines, and bring with them a world of experience. They share one very passionate and focused goal: to become a Canadian—to work, live, and raise their families in Canada. And the most important first step in achieving that goal is to find meaningful employment.

Canada continues in its commitment to building the nation through immigration because immigration offers Canada growth, prosperity, and opportunity—our future depends on it. And yet as a country, we still have much to learn and get better at in order to take full advantage of the opportunity that immigration offers. A key part of this is making it easier for new immigrants to connect with the right jobs more quickly and more effectively.

There is much work underway in this regard. Governments at all levels are working on this issue, and they are increasingly collaborating more with employers and other institutions that have a role to play in the issue. But while solutions and better systems of economic inclusion are being developed, new immigrants continue to arrive every day who need to find their way to work, right away.

For each immigrant to Canada, the story will be different. Each path to the right job will have its own unique turns and bumps on the road. Each person will need to use a variety of approaches and tools to find their way. *How to Find a Job in Canada* is one of these tools—much like a compass to help navigate the job search. A compass orients, provides direction, and empowers users to make decisions about the choices to which it leads them. This book will guide readers to the resources, opportunities, and supports that will hopefully lead them successfully to the right job in Canada.

Elizabeth McIsaac
Executive Director
TRIEC (Toronto Region Immigrant Employment Council)

Why This Book Was Written

Most immigrants you talk to will tell you that the search for suitable employment is the biggest challenge any newcomer to Canada will face. This search will take up more of your time than any other activity, not to mention much of your physical strength, emotional health, and money.

For the most part, newcomers are not properly prepared to enter the Canadian job market. They aren't often aware of the barriers they will face until they run into them.

- They are not sure whether they need a professional licence in order to practise in their field.
- They don't know enough about the duties and responsibilities of their occupation.
- They are not informed about which provinces offer the most openings in their occupational field.
- They underestimate the value of Canadian education and experience in the Canadian workforce.

By the time newcomers begin to understand these aspects of the Canadian job market, several months may have passed and the money they immigrated with may be almost at an end. Feeling uneasy, anxious, and uncertain, these newcomers are forced to accept survival jobs as new careers, or return home.

This book will help you to avoid these problems by ensuring that you are prepared for what lies ahead.

The Promise of the Future

Canada has found effective ways of responding to the problems newcomers face. A support network has been created for newcomers through immigrant-serving agencies to help substitute for the family and friends left behind.

Through these agencies, this book, and your own research on the Internet, even before you arrive many of you will know the basics.

- Are your international credentials sufficient for a career in your field in Canada?
- In what ways does Canada help newcomers prepare for entry into the Canadian workforce?

- What quality government and public educational programs are available for newcomers?
- What are the most effective methods of finding employment in Canada?
- How should you seek out help in your native language?

Numerous newcomer information centres, employment resource centres (ERCs), and Service Canada centres offer a wide range of special programs for internationally educated professionals (IEPs) and tradespeople. Great support for immigrants is also offered by professional associations. In many educational centres, there are co-op programs where you can gain Canadian experience and find reliable references, which will help you find suitable employment.

One of the best ways to socially and economically integrate into Canadian society is to use all of the opportunities and resources that are offered to you in Canada. This book will point you toward many of these opportunities. Once you are on the right track, with hard work and determination you will likely be among the majority who eventually reach or surpass their goals for life in Canada.

What Will You Learn from This Book?

The main goal of this book is to help you overcome some of the barriers you will face. You will learn how to do the following:

- How to assess your readiness for the Canadian job market.
- How to create a career plan.
- How to find the government and public organizations that help newcomers with employment.
- How to find the educational and training programs that are offered for newcomers.
- How to assess your international documents and diplomas.
- How to assess your international qualifications.
- How to improve your English language skills.
- How to choose your Canadian province or territory of residence.
- How to gain Canadian experience.
- How to receive a Canadian education.
- How to find the kinds of financial support you can receive.
- How to effectively search for work.
- How to create a professional resume and cover letter.
- How to prepare for a job interview.
- How to find a survival job.
- How to find the rights you have when you do begin working.

Reading this book will reduce the time it will take you to find a job—all of the important information you'll need has been organized in one place!

Who Will Benefit from This Book?

This book is for three groups of people:

- The first is people who are thinking about immigrating to Canada or have already started the process and want to prepare for the Canadian job market before they arrive.
- The second is newly arrived immigrants who can use the book to ease their transition period.
- The third is immigrants to Canada who are working at jobs that are below their training level and can use the book to reach their full potential.

How is This Book Different?

One of the main advantages of this book is that its simple language makes it accessible for newcomers with English as a second language. It looks at specific mistakes commonly made by newcomers during their job search and explains how to avoid them. This book also has a comprehensive unit on the Internet, today's most powerful source of information, to help with your job search. Moreover, you will learn about specific services and programs for newcomers that are offered by Canadian public, social, and government organizations. Finally, the book includes specific Canadian addresses, phone numbers, and Internet sites to aid you in all areas of your job hunt.

How to Read This Book

The structure of this book allows you to find the answers you're seeking in short, self-contained chapters. So jump back and forth between chapters, or read it from beginning to end for a more complete picture of the Canadian job market for newcomers.

Every effort has been made to ensure that the Internet pages in this book are correct and accurate. However, Internet sites are similar to living creatures: they are born, grow, become old (sometimes quite quickly), and die. Therefore, it is possible that you will find a few websites that are no longer correct. If that should occur, use the Internet searching tips found in the Creating Your Canadian Experience section (at the end of each unit) to seek out new, reliable websites.

Section 1

Preparation

By failing to prepare, you are preparing to fail.
—Benjamin Franklin

Before You Arrive

In This Unit

- Newcomers and the Canadian Job Market
- Making a Pre-departure Plan
- Evaluating Your Credentials
- Create an Inventory of Your Skills

1.1 Newcomers and the Canadian Job Market

Problem

Canada welcomes newcomers like you. That's why the Canadian immigration system is designed to attract highly educated and skilled immigrants. But many new Canadians encounter serious barriers once they start looking for employment. Why does this happen, and what can you do about it?

Solution

Competing with Canadians

It's not surprising that most of your competition for jobs comes from people born and educated in Canada. They have Canadian education and experience, and they're more comfortable with the language and working environment. They also have a wider circle of business contacts and acquaintances (networks).

But newcomers like you have a few advantages as well. According to Statistics Canada, 36 percent of immigrants aged 25 to 54 have at least a bachelor's degree, compared to only 22 percent of Canadians.

Although you might think this should solve your problem, you are likely to encounter other barriers:

- Many employers are anxious about hiring immigrants because it's difficult to verify foreign diplomas and international experience. About 20 percent of all Canadian occupations are **regulated**, so you will need a Canadian licence to work in those fields. This usually requires studying and passing difficult examinations, so more time and money will need to be spent as a result.
- Employers may also be concerned that newcomers will not have the language skills necessary for the job. They may also be worried that a newcomer's cultural background will prevent them from fitting into a working team.

Taking It Online	
Website Name	**Website Address**
Statistics Canada	www.statcan.ca/Daily/English/070910/d070910a.htm

These barriers are just a couple of reasons why skilled immigrants (such as engineers, doctors, and teachers) may start out working as taxi drivers, janitors, or factory workers. In most cases, these jobs are not permanent. They are temporary survival jobs. While working at survival jobs, newcomers can improve their skills. For instance, a newcomer might consider taking English and computer skills courses or enrolling in college or university to prepare for certification in a **professional** field.

Employment Statistics for New Canadians

According to one Canadian immigrant labour market study based on 2006 statistics, the national unemployment rate for immigrants who have been in Canada five years or less was 11.5 percent. This is more than double the rate of 4.9 percent for those born in Canada, but the situation improved for immigrants who had been in Canada between five and ten years. Their unemployment rate was 7.3 percent. The figures have also improved dramatically since the last study in 2002, suggesting that many newcomers may simply need time to adjust to their new life in Canada.

You Can Succeed!

You are not alone in facing the challenges of entering the Canadian job market. Approximately 250,000 newcomers are in this situation every year. Those who work hard to adapt to their new country can overcome the barriers. The Government of Canada, businesses, and other organizations are working on solutions to make it easier for immigrants to find work that matches their level of expertise.

Source: "Canada's Immigrant Labour Market," The Daily (Statistics Canada, 2007).

Tip: Success will not come easily in your new homeland. But if you use the Canadian support systems described in this book, your chances of success will increase dramatically.

1.2 What Are Your Pros and Cons?

Situation
As a newcomer, you will have both advantages and disadvantages as you enter the Canadian job market.

Advice and Action Plan
All workers, including newcomers, can be considered "goods" on the Canadian job market. Only the best-quality goods will attract "buyers"—in other words, employers. Many new Canadians have personal and professional qualities that satisfy (or even exceed) the requirements of the Canadian job market. Other qualities may not attract employers.

Put a check mark beside each pro or con that applies to you.

Assessing Your Pros and Cons	
Pros	**Cons**
☐ You are well-educated. You have a diploma or degree from a respected college or university.	☐ People have difficulty understanding your spoken English or French.
☐ You have at least two years of work experience in your area of expertise.	☐ Your written English needs improvement.
☐ You know one or more languages in addition to English or French.	☐ You do not know much professional English **terminology** relating to your field.
☐ You are healthy, and you have no criminal record.	☐ You have no Canadian experience (usually listed as a requirement in job advertisements).
☐ You are an energetic and enterprising person.	☐ Your occupation is regulated in Canada, and you do not have the necessary certificates or licences.
☐ You will accept lower wages in exchange for the opportunity to prove yourself to an employer, and potentially earn more in the future.	☐ You lack knowledge of Canadian standards, rules, and regulations.
☐ You have a strong network of business associates and industry knowledge in your native country.	☐ You are not familiar with Canadian **technologies** and materials.
	☐ You need more computer training.
☐ You have brought some inventions, discoveries, new ideas, or knowledge with you to Canada.	☐ You are not familiar with Canadian workplace culture.
	☐ You have no business network in Canada.

Immigrant Experience

Akm worked for ten years as a pharmaceutical chemist in Bangladesh. Then he changed to a career in pharmaceutical marketing. He knew that he would likely have to change his career yet again when he moved to Canada.

During his first year here, he looked for jobs with the same level of responsibility he'd had back home. He had no luck. Companies didn't want to take a chance on him because he had no Canadian experience.

Akm considered returning to school for a year to upgrade his skills, but realized that he couldn't afford it. Instead, he decided to become a **quality-control** worker for a pharmaceutical company. Akm knew that by staying in his original field (pharmaceuticals), he could demonstrate his knowledge and impress his superiors, giving him a good chance at success.

Taking It Online

Website Name	Website Address
CIC point system	www.cic.gc.ca/english/immigrate/skilled/apply-factors.asp

Using the checklist on the opposite page, imagine a set of scales where one side contains your pros and the other side, your cons. Which side is heavier? For more details, look at the point system on the Citizenship and Immigration Canada (CIC) website. This system is used for qualifying immigrants as skilled workers. There are six variables on which points are awarded, and the system helps you to estimate how many points you would receive for each variable. To receive a passing mark, you must have at least 67 points. If you are below or close to this passing mark, identify weaknesses you can work on to improve your score.

Tip: For help in **evaluating** your strengths (pros) and weaknesses (cons), visit an employment assessment centre as soon as you arrive in Canada.

1.3 Making Your Pre-departure Plan

Situation

After submitting your application for immigration, you should start to study the Canadian job market and prepare for work in Canada. There will be time for this before your departure, and this chapter will tell you how to prepare.

Advice and Action Plan

Learn the Language

The most valuable skill you can bring to Canada is **fluency** in one or both official languages—English and French. You will need to be fluent in French only if you settle in Quebec (and in some cases, New Brunswick or Manitoba). However, French can be an asset anywhere in Canada.

Spend as much time or money as you can in order to master the language. Here are some important tips for studying English:

- Take courses where the teacher's native language is English (North American English is best).
- Use language textbooks published in Canada or the United States (US).
- Listen to English-language radio.
- Use every opportunity to listen to, and speak in, English.
- Read English books and magazines, and watch English movies.

Become Computer Literate

Do as much as you can to acquire or improve computer skills. They are essential in order to work in Canada. Here are some points to consider:

- If you can afford to buy a computer, buy one.
- If you can't afford to buy a computer, use the computer of a friend or relative, stay after-hours and use one at work, or go to an Internet café.
- Become familiar with any **software** that might be valuable in your current or future occupation.

Taking It Online

Website Name	Website Address
NOC	www5.hrsdc.gc.ca/NOC-CNP/app/index.aspx?lc=E
Foreign Credentials Referral Office	www.credentials.gc.ca

Obtain a Driver's Licence

If you do not have an International Driver's Licence, obtain one before you leave. Although you will eventually have to take driving tests to get your Canadian licence, your International Driver's Licence will allow you to drive for several months in some Canadian provinces.

Know the Requirements of Your Occupation

Your professional certificates and diplomas from your native country will be evaluated before you are allowed to have a Canadian visa. But passing this evaluation does not necessarily make you ready to work in Canada. If your profession is regulated, Canadian certificates or diplomas will be needed.

Therefore, connect with the appropriate regulating body through the Internet to find out how to obtain the Canadian certificate or diploma that you need. A good way to begin your research is by finding your profession online using the National Occupational Classification (NOC) website (see 1.4).

Understand the Job Market

Research the Canadian job market to learn about your occupation. It's important, for example, to find out which cities or provinces in Canada have the greatest demand for workers such as yourself.

Study job ads with vacancies in your occupation. You can find these ads online at job banks and in the Classified sections of Canadian newspapers. Take notes on companies that could potentially become your employer.

E-mail Your Resume

If you are confident with your written language skills, it is never too early to work on your resume and cover letter. E-mail these documents to companies in Canada. However, do not expect responses from all of them. At best, potential employers will thank you for your resume and ask you to visit them for an interview after you have arrived in Canada.

But remember, resumes in Canada may differ from those in your native country (see Unit 9), so do your research before sending your resume to potential Canadian employers.

Tip: Does the Canadian consulate in your country offer information sessions for potential immigrants? If so, attend a session. These sessions will give you important information, and an opportunity to ask questions.

1.4 How Your Occupation Is Classified in Canada

Situation

Most Canadian immigrants are university, college, or **trade** school graduates and have years of work experience. If you're in this position, you won't have to start your professional career in Canada from the very beginning. However, you may have to obtain new, Canadian, **qualifications**.

Advice and Action Plan

First, find out how your occupation is classified in Canada and learn about any new qualifications you may need. To do this, look at the official Canadian trade **directory**—the National Occupational Classification (NOC) website (www23.hrdc-drhc.gc.ca).

Once you are on the NOC website, look for two major resources:

- The Index of Titles, which lists almost 40,000 Canadian occupations alphabetically. Each occupation is followed by a unique, four-digit code. If you know your exact job title, use it to search for your occupational code.
- After you've found your occupational code, look for the second resource, Occupational Descriptions. The Occupational Descriptions resource includes information on the industries or workplaces where various occupations are needed, examples of job titles, the most significant duties, and the employment requirements of different occupations.

Understanding the NOC Classification System

Each digit in an occupational code has a particular meaning:

- The first digit represents the skill type that best suits you. You can choose from ten types of skills—for example, management, health, sales and service, and trades.

Tip: The NOC was created, and is managed, by Human Resources and Social Development Canada (HRSDC) in partnership with Statistics Canada. The HRSDC produces NOC books and other books found in libraries or at employment resource centres.

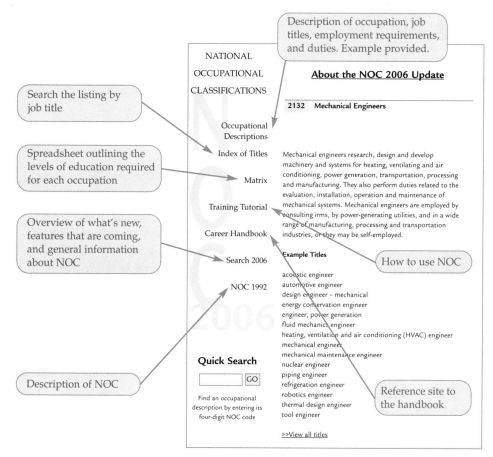

Search the listing by job title

Spreadsheet outlining the levels of education required for each occupation

Overview of what's new, features that are coming, and general information about NOC

Description of NOC

NATIONAL
OCCUPATIONAL
CLASSIFICATIONS

Occupational Descriptions

Index of Titles

Matrix

Training Tutorial

Career Handbook

Search 2006

NOC 1992

Quick Search

[   ] GO

Find an occupational description by entering its four-digit NOC code

Description of occupation, job titles, employment requirements, and duties. Example provided.

About the NOC 2006 Update

2132   Mechanical Engineers

Mechanical engineers research, design and develop machinery and systems for heating, ventilating and air conditioning, power generation, transportation, processing and manufacturing. They also perform duties related to the evaluation, installation, operation and maintenance of mechanical systems. Mechanical engineers are employed by consulting irms, by power-generating utilities, and in a wide range of manufacturing, processing and transportation industries, or they may be self-employed.

Example Titles

acoustic engineer
automotive engineer
design engineer – mechanical
energy conservation engineer
engineer, power generation
fluid mechanics engineer
heating, ventilation and air conditioning (HVAC) engineer
mechanical engineer
mechanical maintenance engineer
nuclear engineer
piping engineer
refrigeration engineer
robotics engineer
thermal design engineer
tool engineer

>>View all titles

How to use NOC

Reference site to the handbook

Source: National Occupational Classification.

- The second digit indicates your skill level, including secondary school, college, **occupation-specific** training, apprenticeship, and university.
- The third digit of your occupational code represents groups of occupations.
- The fourth digit represents a job title.

Example: An industrial electrician's job title is represented by NOC occupational code 7242.

This means skill type 7 (trades, transport, and equipment operators), skill level 2 (college education or apprenticeship training), occupational group 4 (electrical trades and telecommunication occupations), and job title 2 (industrial electricians).

1.5 Regulated Occupations in Canada

Situation

About 20 percent of occupations in Canada are regulated. This means that special licences are required to work in these fields. What types of occupations are regulated in Canada?

Solution

What Is a Regulated Occupation?

Two types of occupations are regulated in Canada: professions and trades. Physicians, nurses, teachers, veterinarians, and lawyers are in regulated professions. Plumbers, welders, and electricians are in regulated trades. These occupations are controlled by provincial or federal law and are **governed** by regulatory bodies, usually through professional or trade **associations**. The government controls these occupations because they are closely connected with the health and safety of Canadians.

Canadian occupational standards and regulations are often different than the standards and regulations in other countries. So, internationally educated professionals and tradespeople must meet Canadian standards.

Find Out if Your Occupation Is Regulated

You will usually find out whether or not your occupation is regulated in Canada during the immigration process. If not, you can easily find this information on the Internet by searching the National Occupational Classification (NOC) website. Using the NOC search engine (or the process described in 1.4), look up the title of your occupation. In a section called Employment Requirements, you will see whether or not your occupation requires registration for regulation.

If your occupation is regulated, find the provincial regulatory body where you can obtain your licence by searching the Work Destinations website. If necessary, contact the appropriate regulatory body of the appropriate province and begin the licensing procedure.

Taking It Online

Website Name	Website Address
NOC	www23.hrdc-drhc.gc.ca/ch/e/docs/ch_welcome.asp
Red Seal	www.red-seal.ca
Work Destinations	www.workdestinations.org

Exceptions

In some occupations, you may actually be allowed to practise without a licence if you are under the supervision of someone who is licensed. For example, you may be allowed to work as a mechanical engineer without a licence in some engineering companies, but you will not have the job title or **salary** of a professional engineer. Your licensed manager will also be considered responsible for your work.

Note, too, that if you work in a trade industry and move from your province or **territory** to another province or territory, you may have to earn a new certificate. However, the federal government has made the transition easier through the Red Seal Program. This program gives you a seal of approval on your certificate after you have successfully completed an Interprovincial Standards Examination. Once you have the Red Seal, you will be allowed to practise your trade in any province or territory without having to write further exams. To find out if your trade occupation is covered by the Red Seal Program, visit the Red Seal website.

Tip: It is a serious crime to act as if you have a Canadian licence or certificate if, in fact, you do not.

1.6 Evaluating Your Credentials

Problem

Most immigrants come to Canada with diplomas, certificates, or other **credentials** they have earned outside of Canada. As a newcomer, you will need to know if these documents are recognized in Canada. Do they allow you to continue your studies or find a job in your field? How can you find out if your credentials fit with Canadian standards?

Solution

To find out if your credentials are equal to those expected in Canada, contact an evaluation service such as International Credential Assessment Service (ICAS); International Credentials Evaluation Service (ICES); International Qualifications Assessment Service (IQAS); or World Education Services (WES). Each of these can be accessed on the Internet, through their own websites or the website of the Canadian Information Centre for International Credentials (CICIC). Some of these services relate specifically to certain provinces, and some do not have offices across Canada. Each service will have its own procedure. Most charge a fee.

After assessing your degree, diploma, certificate, or other credentials, the evaluation service might give you a certificate stating that your credentials are equivalent to a Canadian university degree. If they tell you that your credentials are *not* equal to those expected in Canada, you will need to take courses to become qualified.

Taking It Online

Website Name	Website Address
CICIC	www.cicic.ca/en/index.aspx
ICAS	www.icascanada.ca
ICES	www.bcit.ca/ices
IQAS	employment.alberta.ca/cps/rde/xchg/hre/hs.xsl/4512.html
WES	www.wes.org

Why Should You Have Your Credentials Evaluated?

- You are looking for a job, and you need to present your credentials to a potential employer.
  - Send your documents to one of the evaluation services you'll find on the Canadian Information Centre for International Credentials (CICIC) website.
- You want to continue your studies at a Canadian college or university, and you must provide proof of your credentials in your application. If your international diploma is recognized by a Canadian institution, you may be allowed to take fewer courses.
  - Contact the institute's admissions department to find out what documents you need to send, where you should send them, and when.
- You have to be licensed to work in your field.
  - Present your diploma to the regulatory body (usually a **professional association** or educational institution). This body will decide whether or not you are ready to write the qualification exams or if you require further education.

As soon as you have had your credentials evaluated, contact the regulatory body that issues licences for your occupation. Submit your international diplomas, lists of programs and courses taken (and your marks if you have them), references from your previous employers, and any other relevant documents requested. Documents that have been assessed by a recognized evaluation service can help to reduce the time needed to obtain a licence.

Tip: Before sending your diploma to an evaluation service, make sure it is the appropriate service for your purpose.

1.7 Organize Your References

Problem

As part of the hiring process, Canadian employers will ask for **references**. References are people who know you and can say positive things about you. They are usually former employers, co-workers, or teachers, but they can also be classmates or friends. How can you make sure that your references will help you get a job?

Solution

Make a List of Potential References

- It's extremely important to have excellent references. To make sure this happens, make a list of people you think would give you a good reference.
- Most of the time, you will need to provide three references. You may use the same three references for all of your interviews.
- For each reference, include their name, job title, phone number, fax number, e-mail address, the name and address of their company, and how you know them. *It is illegal in Canada to use a false or non-existent reference.*
- First on your list of potential references should be former managers and co-workers. If you did not have a good relationship with your former employer, you can choose another manager at the same company or a colleague or client.

Notify Your References

- Before you send any names to a potential employer, notify your references. Contact them by phone or e-mail, or meet with them personally.
- Ask if they are willing to act as a reference for you. If you give their name to a potential employer without telling them, the employer might phone them and catch them unprepared, causing your reference to say something negative. You could then fail to get the job because of a bad reference!
- Many potential employers prefer to contact a reference by phone. When you contact your references, tell them that they might receive a phone

References should be people who can speak positively about your ...

1. Career accomplishments
2. Educational achievements
3. Work ethic
4. Interpersonal skills

Nina's Personal Experience

In China, when you apply for a job, companies seldom ask you to provide references. Things are different in Canada. When I started to look for work here, I learned that almost all companies require references or letters of reference. Some companies ask you to provide both work-related references from employers who have known you for more than three years and non-work-related references (personal references). It is a pity I wasn't aware of this before I immigrated. It would have been helpful if I had asked my former supervisors and co-workers for reference letters before I left my home country because it's been difficult to get references from overseas.

call. Ask them for their phone number and for times when a potential employer might call them. Always take your list of references to a job interview. Make sure that your name appears at the top of the page, and include complete information about your references (a neatly typed reference list is best). Give this list to the interviewer only if requested.

Obtain Letters of Reference

- Canadian employers will accept references from abroad, so before you leave for Canada, ask for letters of reference. It's best if the letter is written in English or French (depending on where you are seeking work). If this is not possible, have it translated by a professional service that will guarantee the accuracy of their translation.
- To be sure that the letter of reference is effective, write a rough draft yourself and offer it to the person who has agreed to be a reference. Let them know that they can change the text in any way they want to. If you are unsure if your reference will like this, ask in advance, "Do you mind if I prepare a draft copy or rough outline for you?"

Tip: It is best to have references from Canada. If you have arrived only recently and have never worked in Canada, consider asking your Canadian ESL teachers, a job counsellor, or a trusted landlord to be a reference.

1.8 Create an Inventory of Your Skills

Situation

Soon after you arrive in Canada—or even before—prepare to sell your skills on the Canadian job market. Start by creating an inventory of your language skills, employability skills, and **professional skills**.

Advice and Action Plan

You may have had a successful career in your native country, but it may not be possible to continue with it immediately in Canada. You likely have a great deal to learn about this new country, including its languages and the job market. You will probably need to develop your language skills and become familiar with Canadian style and vocabulary, as well as improve your job-searching and professional skills.

Language Skills

Unless you came as a refugee, you almost certainly studied English in your homeland. But Canadian employers demand much more knowledge of the language than immigration law requires. By visiting a Language Instruction for Newcomers to Canada (LINC) assessment centre, you can find out if your language skills are strong enough for you to start looking for a job (free English classes are offered in all provinces but are sometimes called by different names). The advisors at the centre will evaluate your English and recommend schools and classes for improving your reading, writing, grammar, listening, and speaking skills. According to the Canadian language benchmarking system, you are not ready for the **workforce** until you reach level 6.

Taking It Online	
Website Name	**Website Address**
CICIC	www.cicic.ca/en/index.aspx
LINC	www.cic.gc.ca/english/resources/publications/ welcome/wel=22e.asp
Service Canada	www.servicecanada.gc.ca
Canadian Language Benchmarks	www.language.ca

Job-Search Skills

Are you ready for a job? Before you come to Canada, you should find out whether your occupation is in demand and which province has the most need of people in your field. Start building a network in Canada and investigate both the visible and the hidden job markets (see Units 5 and 6). Find out what makes a resume great (see Unit 9) and how to prepare for a successful interview (see Unit 10). You should also have enough money to spend time looking for work. If this isn't the case, apply for financial assistance or look for a survival job. Use the resources of an employment assessment centre. They will evaluate your employability skills and answer your questions about searching for a job. Service Canada (see Unit 7) can help you find an employment assessment centre near you.

Professional Skills

You may discover that the job you held in your homeland exists in Canada. The duties in Canada for that same job, however, may not match the ones in your native country. This means you will have to find out how to make your education, work experience, and skills match the requirements of Canadian employers. You may need to take courses or programs from a college or university to obtain a licence to work in your occupation in Canada. To find out whether your professional skills match the ones required, contact the professional association that governs your occupation. Names of these associations can be found at the Canadian Information Centre for International Credentials (CICIC) website (see also 1.6).

Prepare for the Job of Getting a Job

Start a notebook and write down everything you think you should learn, study, and master in order to improve your skills. Keep detailed lists of organizations and people that might help you later on in your job search. Your notebook will help you prepare for the job of getting a job!

Tip: Employment assessment centres not only give advice, they can also offer you the opportunity to enter a government-funded study program.

1.9 Upgrade Your Skills with Distance Education

Problem

Having a Canadian education will definitely help you find a job. And, fortunately, you don't have to be in Canada to obtain Canadian credentials because Canada has developed excellent computer-based distance education programs. The country is so large and many people live in remote areas, so they cannot attend classes in person. For these reasons, you can also study from your own remote location, your homeland. But how can you enroll in a distance education program?

Solution

In Canada, distance education is offered by many colleges and universities. It is possible to take almost any subject through distance education. For example, over 4,000 students per year take distance education from the University of Manitoba because it offers over 120 degree credit courses from 11 faculties. This includes a Bachelor's degree program for Registered Nurses. Many other colleges and universities in Canada offer a wide variety of distance education courses as well. Be sure to investigate your options before signing up for a course!

You may decide to take a course for your own interest, or you may need to take a course as a **prerequisite** for entry into a special program or as part of a certificate or diploma program. Conduct some research before you enroll in a course. Make sure it will improve your chances of getting a job.

Advantages of Distance Education

- You can choose to study at home and spend approximately ten hours a week doing so.
- You may use manuals and audio- and videocassettes. You will submit completed work to your instructors through a website on the Internet. This site will often also allow you to communicate with your instructor and fellow students. So when you move, your "classroom" moves with you.

- You can take your time completing a program. You could take two courses a year for five years or even one course a year for ten years, depending on the program.
- You may decide to take separate, unrelated courses, rather than courses that are all part of the same degree program. If you do this, you may be able to apply credits from these courses to a later degree. However, be sure to check if this is possible with the institution you are attending. Also, find out whether or not you will be able to continue your education in person once you arrive in Canada.
- If you have already studied abroad, you may be able to receive credit for those courses in Canada. (To do this, have your credentials evaluated— see 1.6.) If some of your courses cannot be applied to a Canadian certificate, diploma, or degree, you could use distance education to obtain the needed credits and bring your degree to Canadian standards.

Sign Up for Distance Education

- After you have chosen a college, university, or other educational institution, look at their website. Here, you will find descriptions of all their distance education programs and the rules for enrolling.
- An institution's website will likely provide application forms and information about the cost of courses.
- Once you start a course, you will receive information about manuals and other instructional materials, lesson-by-lesson instructions, and possibly access to other educational websites.

Tip: Take time to research distance education courses. Make sure that you take courses only from a respected college, university, or other institution. This way, you'll be sure that your certificate, diploma, or degree will be recognized in the Canadian job market.

1.10 The Canadian Immigration Integration Project

Situation

The Canadian government has set up a new initiative—the Canadian Immigration Integration Project (CIIP)—to help potential immigrants receive better information, earlier, about the Canadian job market. The CIIP also works to help immigrants obtain evaluation of their credentials (diplomas, certificates, and degrees). Anyone who applies for immigration to Canada can now receive this kind of employment assistance from Canadian officials before they leave their home country. What is CIIP exactly, and how can you benefit from it?

Advice and Action Plan

The CIIP is managed by the Association of Canadian Community Colleges (ACCC) together with Citizenship and Immigration Canada (CIC). It is funded by the Foreign Credential Recognition (FCR) program at Human Resources and Social Development Canada (HRSDC).

The CIIP was created for two main reasons:

- It helps new immigrants coming to Canada under the Federal Skilled Worker Program to prepare to work upon arrival.
- It helps Canada increase its qualified workforce as quickly as possible.

CIIP: In China, India, and the Philippines

If you live in China, India, or the Philippines and you have applied for immigration to Canada under the Federal Skilled Worker Program, you might be able to receive help from CIIP. If you are eligible, you will receive a CIIP registration form from CIC during the final stages of your immigration process.

You should note that, at present, there are *only* CIIP offices in China, India, and the Philippines. However, offices may be set up in other countries in the future.

Taking It Online	
Website Name	**Website Address**
CIIP	ciip.accc.ca
FCRO	www.credentials.gc.ca

Three Kinds of Help from the CIIP

- A one-day group session (with approximately 20 people) to learn about trends in the Canadian job market, employment requirements in particular occupations, and how to search for a job in Canada.
- A one-hour, one-on-one meeting with a counsellor to create your own integration plan. The plan will outline what you must do to prepare for a job in Canada.
- Help in contacting Canadian organizations that can assist you with credential evaluation and licensing, language and skills testing, and skills upgrading.

After obtaining assistance from the CIIP, you will have a more realistic understanding of the opportunities and challenges you will find in Canada. With this new understanding, you can adjust your employment plans if necessary. For example, you may decide to move to a different province and city because you've discovered that there is more demand for your occupation in that location.

The Foreign Credentials Referral Office

The CIIP also works directly with the Foreign Credentials Referral Office (FCRO) (see 8.8) to help internationally trained professionals obtain faster assessment and recognition of their credentials.

    The FCRO is part of CIC. You can ask questions from within Canada by phoning the FCRO at 1-888-854-1805 or from abroad by browsing their website.

Source: Canadian Immigration Integration Project.

Tip: You are not required to participate in CIIP. If you do not participate, your immigration will not be affected negatively. However, it's a great idea to take advantage of the help you can receive from this project.

1.11 Helpful Guides for Newcomers

Problem

Before considering immigrating to Canada, most people do a lot of research. They speak with people at the Canadian consulate, embassy, or other official office in their country. They also read brochures and booklets supplied by the Canadian government. If your questions are not answered through these sources, where *can* you go for answers?

Solution

Once you arrive in Canada, you will find helpful information in printed publications at libraries, **settlement agencies**, employment resource centres, bookstores, and on the Internet. In your home country, you can find plenty of excellent information on the Internet.

Print Resources

Below are two excellent print publications.

- Here are some of the great features of *Canadian Newcomer Magazine*:
  - The magazine is free of charge.
  - It can be found in libraries, settlement agencies, ESL classes, and employment resource centres throughout Ontario.
  - To help make your settlement and integration easier, the magazine is filled with useful articles.
  - The magazine is equipped with an annual directory of Ontario settlement and employment agencies.
  - It is also available online. To find the website, just enter the keyword "CNMag."

Taking It Online

Website Name	Website Address
Canada Prospects	www.careerccc.org/ccw
CIC	www.cic.gc.ca/english/index.asp
HRSDC	www.hrsdc.gc.ca
Settlement.org	www.settlement.org

- Some of the features of *The Canadian Immigrant Magazine* are listed below:
  - The magazine is free of charge.
  - It can be found at retail outlets in Vancouver, the southern mainland of BC, and in Toronto.
  - The magazine can be enjoyed by all immigrants.
  - It is also available online.

Resources on the Internet

Here are some excellent online resources:

- Settlement.org
  - This website was created to help immigrants to Ontario but contains information useful to immigrants anywhere in Canada.
  - It allows you to join forums (online discussion groups), where you can ask questions about work, housing, and almost any other settlement issue you can imagine.
  - With nearly 1,000 links to well-proven resources, including PDF files such as *Your First Days in Ontario* (how to obtain your Social Insurance [SIN] card, how to register in language courses, and how to have your credentials evaluated properly) and *The Canadian Labour Market Online: An Internet Guide for Internationally Trained Professionals and Trades People* (developed by the New Canadians' Centre in Windsor, Ontario), the site is very valuable to newcomers.
- Government websites
  - Human Resources and Social Development Canada (HRSDC) is a site where you can find answers to Frequently Asked Questions (FAQs) about such issues as employment, foreign diplomas, getting employment insurance, and how to receive loans for education.
  - Citizenship and Immigration Canada (CIC) has links to such sites as the Foreign Credentials Referral Office (FCRO) and access to a wide range of information to help you through your first days in Canada.
  - The websites for the provincial and territorial immigration ministries, including Ontario Immigration, Alberta Immigration, and others are excellent. Just enter the keyword "immigration" and the name of the province or territory to find these websites.

Tip: Nearly all of these resources can be found by entering the name of the publication, ministry, or company as keywords in a reliable search engine. For longer titles, put the entire title inside quotation marks.

1.12 Making Your Arrival Plan

Situation

Searching for a job can be a long and difficult process. Canadians take an average of between three and nine months to find a job—immigrants usually need more time. How can you make sure that your job search is as brief as possible?

Advice and Action Plan

Although it's safe to predict that the job-search process will take a long time, you can make that time shorter by planning. Each person's plan will be different, but there are some general ideas that most newcomers should include in their own plan.

Browse the list below and check off any items that you feel will help you conduct an efficient job search.

- ❏ Improve your English (and/or French, depending on the province).
- ❏ Research details about your occupation in Canada.
- ❏ Conduct informational interviews (see 10.3).
- ❏ Contact professional associations.
- ❏ Obtain a Canadian licence or certificate if you work in an occupation that is regulated in Canada (see 1.5).
- ❏ Prepare your portfolio (including work samples).
- ❏ Build a professional network.
- ❏ Create or join a support group.
- ❏ Search for job ads in your field.
- ❏ Improve your professional skills, including computer literacy, to meet Canadian standards.
- ❏ Gain Canadian experience by doing volunteer jobs or working through co-op programs.
- ❏ Attend workshops and programs at employment resource centres to learn effective techniques for finding a job in Canada.
- ❏ Write your resume and cover letter.
- ❏ Do practice job interviews.

Taking It Online

Website Name	Website Address
Job Futures	www.jobfutures.ca
Service Canada	www.servicecanada.gc.ca
HRSDC	www.hrsdc.gc.ca

It Takes Time!

On average, job hunters should spend 40 hours per week looking for a job, so the job-*searching* process is like having a full-time job. If you've made an arrival plan, it will take between six and twelve months to find a job. In the meantime, keep working on your plan:

- Write, revise, and update your job-hunting plan every day.
- Set up a weekly schedule of all the tasks that should be done when you arrive in Canada. This should include who you are going to contact for jobs or as part of your network, research that needs to be done, follow-up phone calls that need to be made, and job ads that you should apply to.
- Don't forget to set weekly goals and to reward yourself for meeting them.

Tip: The average job hunter makes 47 contacts to get one interview and 62 contacts to get a single job offer.

Source: Sonnenblock Caroll, Michaele Basciano, and Kim Grabbe. Job Hunting Made Easy *(New York: Learning Express, 1997).*

1.13 Unit Summary

Key Words

association: a group of people or organizations who join or work together for a particular purpose

credentials: the experience, knowledge, or education that show that a person is qualified or suitable for a certain job

directory: an alphabetical list of names, addresses, telephone numbers, etc.

evaluation: the act of giving your opinion about the meaning of something, or about how good something is, after thinking about it carefully

fluency: the ability to speak and write a language easily and accurately

governed: ruled, managed, or controlled

occupation-specific: relevant to a particular job

prerequisite: something that is necessary before something else can happen, exist, or be done

profession: a job that requires a lot of training and are respected by other people

professional association: a group of people or organizations that govern or regulate professional jobs

professional skills: abilities that allow you to do something well, especially because of training, practice, etc.

qualifications: skills or qualities that make you suitable to do something, such as a job

quality-control: making sure that a product or work environment is of a high standard, or is useful, productive, etc.

reference: a statement or letter written by somebody who knows you, giving information about your character and abilities, especially to a new employer

regulated: controlled by laws, governing organizations, etc.

salary: the money that a person receives regularly for the work he/she has done

settlement agency: an organization that helps immigrants get used to living in their new communities

software: programs that you use to operate a computer

technologies: the different areas of scientific knowledge that are used in practical ways in industry, etc.

terminology: the special words and expressions that are used in a particular profession, subject, or activity

territory: a region that has not been recognized as a province and is given its powers by the federal government

trades: jobs for which you need a special skill, especially with your hand

workforce: the total number of people who work in a particular place

Note: Entries taken or adapted from the Oxford ESL Dictionary.

Creating Your Canadian Experience

1. Search the Internet for the unemployment rate of each Canadian province. Find out what the unemployment rate is in the province you are thinking of living in. Use the table below to compare it with the unemployment rate in three other provinces.

Province	Unemployment Rate

2. Search the Internet for the average income by Canadian province. Find out what the average income is in the province you are thinking of living in. Compare it with the average income in three other provinces.

Province	Average Income

3. Search the Internet for the Canadian immigration points system, and calculate your score (a score of at least 67 is needed to pass).

_____

4. Write down three ways that you could improve your score before applying.
   Tip: Look at the areas that are changeable and the questions that are worth the most points.

   a. _____

   b. _____

   c. _____

5. Use the categories in 1.3 to create your own pre-departure plan. Use the chart below as a guideline.

Pre-departure Activity	Action Plan
Learn the Language	
Become Computer Literate	
Obtain a Driver's Licence	
Know the Requirements of Your Occupation	
Understand the Job Market	
Get Feedback	

6. Read 1.4 and become familiar with the NOC website to answer the following three questions.

a. What is the NOC number for your profession?

Profession: _____ NOC Number: _____

b. What are the employment requirements for your profession in Canada?

i. _____

ii. _____

c. What are the main duties?

i. _____

ii. _____

iii. _____

7. Read 1.5 to find out if your profession is regulated in Canada. If it is, search the Internet using the keywords "[your profession]" and "[your province]" to find out what the regulatory body is.

Name: _____

Address: _____

Contact Information: _____

8. According to 1.6, which of your credentials will you need to have evaluated? What steps will you take to get these credentials evaluated?

Credentials to Be Evaluated	Steps to Take for Evaluation

9. List three people you will contact to ask if they can give you a reference (see 1.7).

a. _____

b. _____

c. _____

10. Search the Internet to find out the province in which your job is in most demand.
Tip: The Canada Job Futures website is a good place to start looking.

_____

11. What is the average income for your occupation?
Tip: The Canada Job Futures website is a good place to start looking.

_____

Preparing for Your Job Search

In This Unit

- The Art of Job Searching in Canada
- Understanding Employability Skills
- Obtaining a Professional Licence in Canada
- Gain Canadian Experience

2.1 The Art of Job Searching in Canada

Problem

It's not always the most qualified person who finds a job quickly, it's often the one who is best at searching for jobs. How can you become skilled in the art of job searching?

Solution

Before you start searching for a job, make sure that you have done the following (see Unit 1):

- It is important for you to have studied English.
- You should be familiar with the job market in your field.
- You should make sure your professional knowledge meets Canadian requirements.
- Any necessary certificates or licences should be obtained.
- Your resume and cover letter should be excellent.
- You should have learned how to prepare for an interview.

Another term for "job search" is "job hunt." Just like a hunter, you will have to chase after many possibilities and opportunities before you succeed.

It's difficult to know, in advance, how long you will be looking for a job because so many different factors will affect your search. On average, the well-prepared newcomer spends between six and twelve months looking for work. You will need to prepare yourself both mentally and financially to survive for that period of time.

Why Do Some People Find a Job Faster than Others?

Some people find a job faster than others because they actively look for work and spend a lot of time doing so. **Employment professionals** recommend that you spend eight hours a day, five days a week job searching. Just as a full-time Canadian worker spends an average of 40 hours a week at their workplace, job hunters in Canada should spend that much time looking for work.

The Visible Job Market

About 20 percent of all jobs are found through the visible job market (see Unit 5). This market includes job ads in newspapers, magazines, and the Internet, including online job banks. If at least half of your skills, education, and experience match the employer's request, send in your resume. Then follow up with them until you receive an answer. (But, do not phone or email too often. You do not want the potential employer to think you are a pest.) If you have mastered both English and French (both of Canada's official languages), consider finding a job with the government.

The Hidden Job Market

Did you know that approximately 80 percent of job vacancies in Canada are not published or advertised anywhere? That is why this job market is referred to as the "hidden job market" (see Unit 6). In order to gain access to it, look for companies that may require your skills and then connect with them in person or by telephone. Even if a job is not advertised, send in your resume. The potential employer may then contact you if an appropriate job does come up. Or, you may then contact the employer for an informational interview (see 10.3).

Success in the hidden job market requires hard work and frequent use of your personal network, which you should begin setting up soon after you arrive in Canada—if not before.

Other Options ...

You may also use employment agencies or recruiting services to help you find a job. These services have access to large job databases. However, these agencies work for potential employers, not for you. Therefore, if your skills do not match perfectly with the needs of the employers, they likely won't work with you. Note, too, that legitimate employment agencies and recruiters are paid by employers, so do not trust any agency that asks you to pay them for their services.

Tip: Use a special notebook to record all your job-search actions. Sum up your daily successes and failures so that you can learn from your mistakes.

2.2 The Art of the Follow-Up

Situation
You should be following up after every job tip you receive, resume you send, and interview you attend. This way, you'll be sure to create, and improve upon, important connections.

Advice and Action Plan
In a notebook or on a computer, prepare a chart like the sample shown below. Use it to keep track of your job-searching steps and contacts you've made. This will help you make sure you don't forget to follow up on all your actions. You can also record failures and problems you've encountered. In doing this, you'll learn from your mistakes and find out more about how the Canadian job market works.

Date	Company	Contact	Action	Result	Follow-Up	Notes
Sept. 28	ABC Inc.	Regan Ray	E-mailed about employment	Set up a meeting on Oct. 6	Confirm meeting	I was referred to Regan by Dil Sengupta, a mutual friend.
Sept. 28	Professional Association	General inquiry	E-mailed regarding certification	Waiting for reply	If no response, follow up in two weeks	I contacted them about the status of my application.

When Should I Follow Up?
Follow Up on Job Tips
Whenever someone tells you about a possible job opening, send them a **follow-up** letter thanking them for their advice, telling them what action you took, and describing any results you've obtained. This makes a good impression on the person who helped you, and they will probably be more likely to help you again in the future.

Follow Up on Resumes
Dozens or even hundreds of resumes are often received for a single job opening. If you don't follow up, your resume might be overlooked. If you do follow up, the potential employer may be more likely to give you an interview. They may also realize that your resume has been lost or that it was never received. Another reason for following up is to demonstrate that you are eager to get the job and that you know how to take initiative.

You may follow up in person, by mail or e-mail, or by telephone. If you decide to send a follow-up letter (no more than one page) or e-mail, be sure to follow the tips listed below:

- Remind the employer who you are.
- State when, and to whom, your resume was sent.
- Ask if the employer has received your resume.
- Enclose or attach another copy of your resume.
- Ask if a meeting would be possible.

Send follow-up letters five to seven days after you've sent in a resume. Your follow-up letter should not be a **"form" letter**, that is, it should not be a generalized letter. Be sure to include specific details about the employer you are sending your letter to.

If you follow up by phone, you might have an unexpected telephone interview. You should prepare for this before you make the phone call.

Follow Up after an Interview

After an interview, send a follow-up letter (no more than one page) on the same day. In the follow-up letter, include the important points listed below:

- Begin by thanking the employer for the interview.
- Present new information you learned during the interview about why you are suitable for the job. Tell the potential employer that this information made you even more interested in the job.
- At the end of the letter, thank the interviewer and express hope for a prompt reply. Use a sentence like "I look forward to hearing from you soon."

Your follow-up letter should include specific details about the interviewer and items that were discussed during the interview.

The interviewer should have given you a date by which they'd decide whether or not to hire you. If you do not receive an answer to your follow-up letter by that time, it is perfectly acceptable to phone the potential employer. You may discover, when you do this, that you did not get the job. If this happens, simply ask politely why you were refused and request advice about how to increase your chances for future success.

Tip: Don't be shy! Remind yourself that persistence is a business practice that is not only accepted, but admired in Canada.

2.3 Applying for a Social Insurance Number or Work Permit

Problem

Everyone in Canada must have a Social Insurance Number (SIN) in order to work in the country. When you apply from outside of the country for a temporary job in Canada, you will need to obtain both a work permit and a SIN. Where and how can you obtain these documents?

Solution

If you already have permanent resident status, obtain a SIN card right away. This will give you the right to work in any province or territory in Canada. Without a SIN card, it is illegal to work in Canada. SIN cards contain your full name and the nine-digit number that has been assigned to you. They do not have photographs. Penalties for working without a SIN, or for using someone else's SIN to obtain a job, are deportation, a fine of up to $1,000, or a year's imprisonment. Any employer who hires someone without a SIN faces fines of up to $50,000 and two years' imprisonment.

Obtaining a SIN

If you are living in Canada permanently, take all of your immigration documents to the nearest Service Canada Centre to obtain a SIN card. To find your nearest office, look in the phone book or on the Internet. Application forms, instructions, and rules governing SIN cards are available on the Service Canada website. If all of your documents are in order, you should be able to receive your SIN within three weeks.

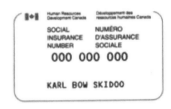

Source: Service Canada.

Taking It Online	
Website Name	**Website Address**
CIC	www.cic.gc.ca
Service Canada	www.servicecanada.gc.ca

Obtaining a Work Permit

For almost any temporary job in Canada, workers from abroad will need a work permit, as well as a SIN. The Citizenship and Immigration Canada (CIC) website will give details on how to obtain a work permit for a temporary job.

Source: Wish

To obtain a work permit, you must first find an employer who is willing to hire you. It's best to apply to work in an occupation that has a shortage of employees in Canada. Often, firms looking for high-quality programmers, scientists, or other experts will hire from abroad. Universities will invite experts to be paid through grants. But Canada has invited people to work in many occupations—from nannies, construction workers, and farm workers to singers and dancers.

Even if a company is willing to hire you, however, you still may not be able to receive a work permit. When companies offer temporary employment to workers from abroad, they must apply to Human Resources and Social Development Canada (HRSDC) for permission. If your occupation is not suffering from employment shortages, the company must prove that they were unable to find a suitable person for that job from within Canada. Otherwise, CIC will not issue a work permit.

In some fields with critical shortages, such as the software industry, the Canadian government has simplified the entry process for specialists with skills that are in demand. The permit process is also different for live-in caregivers and businesspeople who are covered by the North American Free Trade Agreement (NAFTA). There is actually a long list of categories of workers who do not need to have work permits. Most of these are people working in Canada for foreign employers. Details are available on the CIC website.

Tip: The Government of Canada has issued a fraud advisory that asks people to beware of any agency claiming that you can get a work permit or special treatment from the Canadian government by using, and paying for, their services. All necessary forms for obtaining a work permit are available *free of charge* through the CIC website.

2.4 Understanding Employability Skills

Situation

Most Canadian employers are looking for similar sorts of skills when hiring their employees. The Conference Board of Canada has developed a list of three categories of employability skills: **fundamental**, personal management, and teamwork skills. As a newcomer, it is essential that you understand and develop these skills.

Information

Fundamental Skills

You will be better prepared to progress in the world of work when you can communicate, manage information, use numbers, and solve problems.

- Communicate
    - Read and understand information presented in words, graphs, charts, and diagrams; write and speak so others pay attention and understand; listen and ask questions to understand and appreciate the points of view of others; share information using voice, e-mail, and computers.
- Manage Information
    - Locate, gather, and organize information from various **disciplines** such as the arts, languages, science, technology, mathematics, and social sciences; use appropriate technology and information systems.
- Use Numbers
    - Decide what needs to be measured or calculated; observe and record data using appropriate methods, tools, and technology; make estimates and verify calculations.
- Think and Solve Problems
    - Assess situations and identify problems; recognize the human, interpersonal, technical, scientific, and mathematical dimensions of a problem; identify the root cause of a problem; and evaluate solutions to make recommendations or decisions.

Tip: If an employer asks you about your strengths during an interview, apply your knowledge of the employability skills. Tell them which of these skills you have, and be specific.

Personal Management Skills

Possible work opportunities will be greater when you have a positive attitude, are responsible, are adaptable, and when you work safely.

- Demonstrate Positive Attitudes and Behaviours
  - Feel good about yourself and be confident; deal with people, problems, and situations with honesty, integrity, and personal ethics; recognize your own and other people's good efforts; take care of your personal health; and show interest, initiative, and effort.
- Be Responsible
  - Set goals and priorities balancing work and personal life; plan and manage time, money, and other resources to achieve goals; act in a socially responsible way; and contribute to your community.
- Be Adaptable
  - Work independently or as part of a team; be innovative and resourceful (identify and suggest alternative ways to achieve goals and get the job done); learn from your mistakes and accept feedback; cope with uncertainty; learn continuously; be willing to grow; assess personal strengths and areas for development; as well as identify and access learning sources and opportunities.
- Work safely
  - Be aware of personal and group health, and safety practices and procedures, and act in accordance with these.

Teamwork Skills

You will be better prepared to add value to a project or team when you can work with others and participate in projects and tasks.

- Work with Others
  - Understand and work within the dynamics of a group; ensure that a team's purpose and objectives are clear; respect the thoughts, opinions, and contributions of others in a group; contribute to a team by sharing information and expertise; and manage and resolve conflict when appropriate.
- Participate in Projects and Tasks
  - Plan, design, or carry out a project or task from start to finish with well-defined objectives and outcomes; work to agreed quality standards and specifications; and continuously monitor the success of a project or task and identify ways to improve it.

Source: The Conference Board of Canada, Employability Skills 2000+.

2.5 Upgrading Your Skills and Qualifications

Situation

Newcomers sometimes have difficulty finding jobs because Canadian employers think they are lacking in skills and qualifications. How familiar are you with the standards, regulations, skills, and qualifications you need to get a job in your chosen field in Canada?

Advice and Action Plan

The best way to increase your qualifications is to study, study, study! In Canada, most people continue studying even after they are working, and employers value employees who want to learn more. The more courses and programs you can list on your resume—that are relevant to your occupational field—the better your chances of getting a job.

> **Tip:** Before applying to a course, make sure that the school is registered by the provincial ministries of education and that the certificate you will be earning is recognized by your industry or professional association.

Newcomers who want to work in their chosen careers in Canada might have to learn new technologies or software programs in order to find employment or to become certified. In licensed trades and professions, the chances of finding a job will sharply increase once having received accreditation from your professional association. For example, you must be registered as a Chartered Accountant (CA), Certified General Accountant (CGA), or Certified Management Accountant (CMA) to be considered for a well-paid job in accounting.

Taking It Online

Website Name	Website Address
NOC	www23.hrdc-drhc.gc.ca

Nina's Personal Experience

I think that people bring different skills to the workplace and that jobs have different requirements. However, I'd say that certain basic skills are essential for success in any job.

Communication skills, for one, are absolutely critical. We need to be able to communicate well with our superiors and co-workers. I do everything I can to improve my English: I listen to the radio at home to develop my listening skills, I read the paper on the subway to expand my vocabulary, and I talk to people at the park to improve my conversation skills. This has helped me improve my English and develop my confidence.

I'd say that computer skills are also extremely important in the workforce. I don't have my own PC right now, so I book computer time at my local library. I've taken several courses there in word processing and one on using the Internet (they're free!). I'm inputting all the details of my work experience so far and am going to draft a resume using MS Word. I've also learned to use e-mail, so now I can communicate a lot easier with my family and friends back home.

Each field of study uses its own specific computer programs and standards. For example, draftspeople might need to be familiar with SolidWorks or the latest version of AutoCAD, while bookkeepers and accountants should know one or more of the specialized software on the market for their occupation. You can find out what subjects you need to study or skills you have to improve upon after you get acquainted with the description of your occupation in the National Occupational Classification (NOC) of Canada.

If you are considering becoming a **tradesperson**, enroll in a training program known as an apprenticeship. These provide you with on-the-job training under the supervision of a registered tradesperson. You can get information about these by contacting the regulatory bodies in your field.

Tip: Some employers will fund job-related studies to improve the qualifications of their staff. There is also government support available to assist in the studies of someone on income support or employment insurance.

2.6 Improve Your Language Skills

Problem

Do you have high-level English writing, reading, speaking, and listening skills? If you are having trouble writing your resume and cover letter in proper English, or if you are uncomfortable at the thought of negotiating with a potential employer, you will need to improve your language skills. How can you, as a newcomer, go about doing this, and what resources are available to help you?

Solution

Most newcomers study at least one of Canada's official languages (English and French) before they come to Canada. However, Canadian employers usually demand much greater fluency than the levels accepted by immigration law. There are many stories of internationally trained professionals forced to work in unskilled jobs because of poor language skills.

Canadian Language Courses and Evaluation

Types of Courses

Many free English as a Second Language (ESL) courses are available in Canada, as well as courses that require payment. Note that some **fee-based** courses can be quite expensive, so it's wise to consider taking the free courses first. Free courses, however, sometimes accommodate the weakest students in the class. They also occasionally have no definite term or end date. This means that progress can be slow. Arrange a meeting to speak with the coordinator of a language program or course to find out whether the classes are suitable for you before you enroll.

Have Your Language Evaluated before You Start

Before you start any course, go for a language assessment at the nearest Language Instruction for Newcomers to Canada (LINC) assessment centre (or at a free, provincially funded ESL class in your area). Once your English ability is evaluated, you will be guided to an appropriate school where you

Tip: To improve your English, try doing a volunteer job in an English-speaking environment.

Immigrant Experience

Before Rozalina left Bangladesh, she felt quite confident about her proficiency in English. She was one of the best students in her English class, which was the second-highest level in her school.

Upon arriving in Canada, however, Rozalina noticed that her pronunciation was poor compared to native speakers. People who share a common language often have the same pronunciation problems in a new language. This means that they have no difficulty understanding each other, but communicating with people who speak different native languages can be a challenge. Rozalina enrolled in an English class with students from around the world.

In her new class of students with different language backgrounds, everyone had to focus very carefully on their pronunciation in order to be understood. As a bonus, Rozalina met interesting people who came to Canada from many different parts of the world.

can upgrade your reading, grammar, writing, speaking, and listening skills to the necessary level. (According to the Canadian benchmarking system, you need to be assessed at a benchmark level 6 or higher.)

In the year 2000, the Centre for Canadian Language Benchmarks established three levels of English proficiency for LINC and ESL classes: Basic, Intermediate, and Advanced. This new system is now accepted as the Canadian standard.

To find a language assessment centre near you, look in the phone book or go to the Citizenship and Immigration Canada (CIC) website. Make an appointment for an evaluation; at your appointment, language specialists will offer you a simple English test. You will also have to answer some questions and speak with the **assessor**. The assessor will then evaluate your English levels in listening, speaking, reading, and writing and direct you to ESL classes where your English can be improved.

Taking It Online

Website Name	Website Address
Centre for Canadian Language Benchmarks	www.language.ca/display_page.asp?page_id=253
CIC	www.cic.gc.ca
LINC information	www.settlement.org/sys/faqs_detail.asp?faq_id=4000331

2.7 Obtaining a Professional Licence in Canada

Problem

If your occupation is regulated in Canada, you will need to obtain a Canadian licence before looking for a job. How can you obtain a professional licence in Canada?

Action Plan

You will need to take three steps to obtain a professional licence in Canada.

Step One

Show the regulatory body governing your occupation any degrees, diplomas, and licensing documents you obtained in your home country. Include a detailed description of the subjects you studied, including the number of lecture hours you attended.

If the licensing body feels your qualifications are not equivalent to Canadian standards, you will be asked to take Canadian courses.

Step Two

The regulatory body will want to confirm that your experiences are valid, so they will ask you to show them documents proving that you have been employed in that field abroad or in Canada. Some occupations allow for some of the experience to be from abroad. However, at least part of your experience must have taken place in Canada under the direction of a licensed professional.

If you do not have enough Canadian experience, you will be required to find a job in Canada under the direction of a licensed expert. Once you have worked the required number of hours, months, or even years, you may apply for **certification**.

Taking It Online

Website Name	Website Address
Canadian Information Centre for International Credentials (CICIC)	www.cicic.ca/en/index.aspx
Immigration.ca	www.immigration.ca

Step Three—Professions

Finally, you will have to pass Canadian licence examinations. For professionals educated outside of Canada, examinations may include a language test, a **professional ethics** test, a Canadian law and regulations test, and/or a professional skills test. Contact your regulatory body to learn specific details about the exams.

During examinations, you will be required to speak or write in English (or perhaps French if you are in Quebec or applying for a governmental position in Ottawa). Using dictionaries during the examination is not permitted. Questions are often written as problems that may occur in your profession, and you'll be asked to solve them in sentence form. Your answers must be detailed and the solutions must be conclusive.

The response time for exam results depends on your occupation and its licensing body. Once you pass, you are permitted to pay the licence fee and be certified. But if you fail, you may apply to repeat the examination.

Step Three—Trades

The certification and licensing process is different for some of the trades. The regulatory body governing your trade may require you to provide documents such as a diploma from an educational institution, an apprenticeship trade certificate, or records verifying your work history or hours of experience. If the regulatory body is satisfied with your credentials, you will receive a permit for temporary work in Canada. Depending on the occupation, these permits can certify you for up to six months. During or after that time period, you must pass an examination to obtain a permanent certificate of qualification. In some trade examinations, you will be allowed to use a dictionary or even an interpreter.

If your regulatory body is not satisfied with your credentials, however, you will be required to enroll in a Canadian apprenticeship program with an appropriate employer.

Tip: When you are applying for your licence or certificate, ask about programs or assistance that may be available for immigrants.

2.8 Changing Your Occupation

Problem

Perhaps since you've arrived in Canada you have decided to change your occupation. How should you choose a new career that is suitable for you?

Solution

List Your Reasons

Before you start your search for a new occupation, write down all the reasons that have led you to the decision to change careers. Discuss these reasons with your family and friends. This will help you later on, when you have to explain your decision to a potential employer.

List Your Transferable Skills

Begin your career transition by choosing an industry you like, whether it is manufacturing, teaching, construction, medicine, care of seniors, or another field.

Then, make a list of the education and skills you have that can be used for a new occupation. These are referred to as "transferable skills" (skills that can be used in many jobs). Knowing your transferable skills can help you decide which direction to take in your career. Transferable skills include those listed below:

- Good social skills can be used in sales, human resources, public relations, and administration.
- The ability to work with your hands can be applied in the skilled trades.
- The ability to work with data will help you find jobs in calculating, data entry, computing, and research.

Choosing a New Occupation

If you are not sure which occupation you'd like to pursue, visit the nearest employment assessment centre. They can help you find an occupation that matches your skills, education, experience, and interests. The employment assessment centre will help you to do the following tasks:

- The centre may help you to gradually narrow your search and make a list of occupations that seem most suitable for you.
- You will be able to learn everything you can about these occupations by arranging informational interviews (see Unit 10) with people who are currently working in that field.
- You could consider taking introductory lectures at a business school, college, or university.

Research the Job Market

At the library and on the Internet, research the job market.

- Learn which industries are hiring and which ones will likely be hiring in the future. On the Internet, use keywords such as "job futures" or "labour market information."
- Find out which **regions** have the most jobs. Some jobs (such as nursing) have openings throughout Canada, but for others, the demand for workers varies between provinces.
- Find out what kind of education you will need for your new field. Much of this research can be done on the Internet.

Career transition is not a simple process. If your first choice turns out to be unreasonable, be prepared to go back to your list of occupations to choose something else.

Start Your Own Business

You might also want to start your own business. Consider this option if you have business management skills, some starting capital, and an idea for a business venture.

Tip: Do not be afraid to change your career. Many Canadians change their careers three to four times during their working lives.

2.9 Human Resources in Canada

Problem

In order to successfully adapt to Canada, you need accurate information about the Canadian job market. If you know its rules and regulations, it will be easier to find a job. But how can you find this information?

Solution

Begin by visiting the website for Human Resources and Social Development Canada (HRSDC); enter the keyword "HRSDC" in any Internet search engine.

HRDSC is responsible for helping Canadians find the government services they need within their own communities. On the HRSDC website, you will find addresses, phone numbers, and e-mail addresses of

---

You will find the following information on the HRSDC website:

- Look for job bank and labour market information (LMI), as well as information about potential employers, volunteer work, and youth employment (on the Employment Opportunities page).
- There will be lists of employers who have hired specialists from your industry in the past.
- The website also presents the rules and regulations governing foreign workers' employment, including how to get a Canadian work permit.
- Information about programs and funding opportunities, including apprenticeship, internship, career counselling, and youth employment will be featured.
- Do not miss the information on successful Canadian job-search techniques.
- Make sure you read the articles discussing topics such as obtaining student loans, Canadian pension plans, children's benefits, disability benefits, and childcare.

Service Canada Centres, employment resource centres, and employment assessment centres across the country. The site also provides valuable information about a wide range of subjects including employment, labour standards, social insurance numbers, workplaces, and employers. Spend as much time as you can exploring this excellent resource.

Discovering the information available to you on the HRSDC website will give you a full overview of the Canadian job market and job-search opportunities.

Adapted from: Human Resources and Social Development Canada.

Tip: The HRSDC website contains hundreds of pages. Don't try to read every page! Instead, search only for information that is important to you.

Problem

Public libraries have excellent sources of information about the job market—free of charge! But sometimes the large amount of information available can be overwhelming. How can you use libraries effectively to find out more about the job market?

Solution

Get a Library Card

Every city in Canada has at least one public library. Branch locations can be found in phone books, in brochures, and on the Internet. Once you arrive at the library, you'll find books, magazines, newspapers, videos, CDs, and other resources. You do not need any documents to visit a public library and use these materials, but if you want to borrow items by taking them home, you must obtain a library card.

To get a library card, you'll need to provide identification. A valid passport or driver's licence is usually all you need. You must also prove

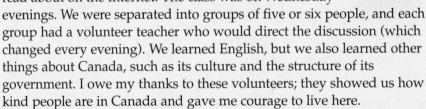

Peter's Personal Experience

I visit libraries for two reasons: to borrow books and to attend ESL classes. The first time I went to a library in Canada, it was to take part in a conversation circle that I read about on the Internet. The class was on Wednesday evenings. We were separated into groups of five or six people, and each group had a volunteer teacher who would direct the discussion (which changed every evening). We learned English, but we also learned other things about Canada, such as its culture and the structure of its government. I owe my thanks to these volunteers; they showed us how kind people are in Canada and gave me courage to live here.

In my country I never went to public libraries because they didn't have many new books or services and it wasn't easy for me to get there. But in Canada, I go often because I think libraries are wonderful places. They are clean and bright and offer many programs for people of different ages. You can borrow books, use the Internet, and search for useful information in reference materials—and almost all of their services are free. You can stay all day and not feel the least bit bored.

that you live in the city in which you're applying for a card. For this you will need a utility bill or other official letter showing your address.

Learning How to Use a Library

Most libraries in Canada have large computer **databases** that you can access in the library itself, or on the Internet. These databases show the resources available in the library. Once you've found something useful, you can go to the library to use the resources you've already identified. Or you can simply go to the library and use the computer databases there.

Resources about employment, such as career transition books, resume and interview guides, and job-searching manuals, are usually kept in one place.

Every Canadian college and university has a library, and most of their resources can be used by anyone. However, you need to be enrolled as a student there to take books home.

Remember, too, that all public libraries provide free access to computers and the Internet.

Information You'll Find for Your Job Search

- Some libraries publish their own booklets containing lists of useful resources on how to find a job, and many libraries have a selection of information about employment specifically for newcomers.
- Unfortunately, many books about employment in Canadian libraries have been published in the US. Although there is helpful advice in these books, the websites and contact information do not apply to Canada. Be sure to check where the book has been published, because there are similar books about Canada.
- Most libraries have Canadian business directories. These contain names and contact information for the Canadian companies you'll need to find to get into the hidden job market (see Unit 6).
- Local and national newspapers and magazines are kept in the periodicals section. Use these resources to find job ads in the visible job market (see Unit 5).
- Libraries sometimes have videotapes or DVDs that will teach you how to study the job market, how to write resumes, and how to succeed in interviews.

Tip: Never hesitate to ask for help from librarians! They are eager to help, and they can save you valuable time by directing you to information you would likely have trouble finding on your own.

2.11 Canadian Job Market Futures

Problem

A key to your job search will be understanding the present **trends** and future possibilities of different occupations. How and where can you find this information?

Solution

The most effective way to begin educating yourself is by using Service Canada's Job Futures website (www.jobfutures.ca). On the site, you will have access to plenty of information about current and possible future trends in the Canadian job market.

What You Will Find

This website lists all of the occupations in the National Occupational Classification (NOC). **Click** on the "I want to be…" tab and choose your occupation, or any others that you are interested in. This will bring you to a screen that has visuals explaining the average hourly income, the future outlook, and the average unemployment rate for that occupation (see the image below for more detail). Clicking on one of these will give you more details.

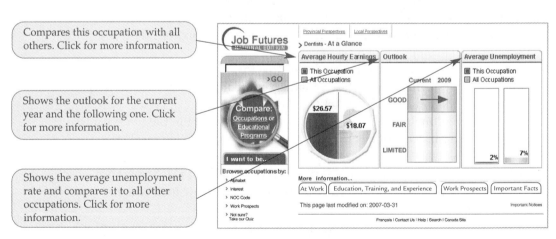

Source: Service Canada's Job Futures.

Just below the visuals there are four tabs that explain more about the occupation. On the following page is a chart that explains what each one offers.

Tab	What It Tells You
At Work	Explains the duties of the job, gives some related jobs, and tells where people in that occupation typically find work.
Education, Training, and Experience	States any regulations, educational requirements, useful skills, and useful secondary school subjects to take.
Work Prospects	Describes the current condition of the job market for the occupation, the outlook for the following year, and what to do to excel in the field.
Important Facts	Discusses salary, unemployment rate, full-time and part-time forecast, the possibility of self-employment, and the age and gender division of the current market.

Career Transition Help

If you are thinking of changing occupations, a good place to start may be the Know Yourself quiz. This has a number of questions about your likes and dislikes that are designed to help you better understand what career you should consider. At the end of the quiz you will be given a list of possible careers. By checking these careers you can see which ones will be in demand in the coming years.

Trends in Canada

Some of the fastest growing fields in Canada include Health, Biotechnology, Engineering, and Environment.

Managers will soon be in high demand in many fields, including construction, finance, wholesale, retail, and police work. This is because the generation born during the baby boom is now at, or approaching, retirement.

As well, a university education in the following areas could lead you to fields in high demand: architecture; chemistry; geology; law; and civil, electrical, or mechanical engineering.

Low-demand areas in the near future include office workers and food industry workers. Note that these high- and low-demand fields will, of course, change over time. This is why it's important to check the HRSDC website (www.hrsdc.gc.ca) and other sources for current information.

Tip: The term "job futures" is used frequently in Canada and Australia only. As a result, if you type this term into any Internet search engine you'll get results for both Canada and Australia.

2.12 Social Assistance for the Unemployed

Situation

Looking for a job can take longer than you expect, so it's possible you could run out of money before you find work. Should this happen to you, you would qualify for social assistance. There are, of course, other possible **scenarios** in which you would also qualify for assistance.

It's important that you find out who qualifies for assistance (and why it is offered), what kind of assistance you can obtain, and how you should apply for it.

Information

There are income support programs (the old name for this was "welfare") in every province or territory of Canada. In British Columbia (BC) and Nova Scotia, the term "income assistance" is used. These programs are intended for people who do not have the financial resources to meet their basic needs, including food, clothing, and shelter.

If you have been unable to find a job due to language barriers, or if you need academic upgrading or training, you may be eligible to apply for income support. In BC, for example, the organization that administers the program is the Ministry of Employment and Income Assistance while in Alberta, it is Alberta Works. Do an Internet search to find details about the province that applies to you.

Why Does Canada Offer Social Assistance?

You may wonder why the Canadian government supports people who are able to work but do not. The unemployment rate in Canada is usually about 6 or 7 percent. This means that approximately 15 working people support 1 unemployed person. If this did not happen, a person who was unable to support themselves or their family could turn to crime. Efficient social assistance programs are probably one of the major reasons for the low crime rate in Canada.

How Social Assistance Works

Once you apply for social assistance, several steps are taken, no matter what province or territory you live in. As an example, let's say that you live in Thunder Bay, Ontario. This is what will happen:

- After you apply, you will be visited by an Ontario Works employee. This person will check your documents and help you fill out a questionnaire. Your answers will tell the government whether or not you require (and qualify for) assistance.
- The Ontario Works employee may ask you to prove where you have spent the money you brought to Canada. (You are permitted to use the help of a translator or interpreter when talking with an Ontario Works official.)
- If you do receive assistance, Ontario Works employees have the right to visit your **residence** at any time, without warning, to examine your home. During this visit, they will decide if you are living at a level of luxury that is not permitted while on social assistance. Note, though, that a television or inexpensive car is not considered a luxury.

When you're on income support, your records are examined on a regular basis, and you are not allowed to leave Canada. If the Government of Canada asks you to work through their system of public works, you are not allowed to refuse.

In addition to social assistance, you may be able to receive money for education or training if this will help you find a job.

Living on Social Assistance

It is possible, but difficult, to live on income support. You may have to rent a low-priced, one-bedroom or bachelor apartment, purchase cheap food, and buy used clothes in second-hand shops. You also have to report continually to government officials. It will be a relief to find a job.

Tip: When you arrive in Canada, spend your money carefully and keep detailed records. Then, if your application for social assistance is refused, immediately ask for a written explanation, provide new information proving that you need the support, and ask for a new decision. This follow-up request is called an "appeal." You may submit an appeal within 30 days of the refusal. Before you do this, though, it is a good idea to seek advice from a local legal clinic. To find a legal clinic, look in the phone book or on the Internet using the keywords "legal aid" or "legal clinics."

2.13 Gain Canadian Experience

Problem

Many Canadian employers refuse to hire people if they do not have Canadian experience—but how can you gain experience if no one will give you a job? All newcomers seeking work face this problem.

Solution

Many newcomers gain Canadian experience through volunteer work, **co-op programs**, **bridging programs**, or Canadian Practice Firms.

Volunteer Work

Finding a volunteer job in Canada is not difficult because many volunteer centres and not-for-profit organizations depend upon volunteers. To find and contact these organizations, look in business directories, phone books, and on the Internet.

Of course, it may be difficult to find volunteer work in your chosen field. But any type of volunteering will give you experience in a Canadian environment. The people you work for may act as references in your job search, and may also become part of your job-searching network.

Co-op and Bridging Programs

Co-op programs are offered by educational institutions and service centres across Canada. Through these programs, students are given jobs as part of their studies. This is called a "work placement." To find out about these placements, contact ESL schools, community colleges, Service Canada Centres, employment assessment centres, and employment resource centres.

Bridging programs are designed for foreign-trained tradespeople and professionals. They provide language training for specific occupations, technical upgrading for Canadian requirements, and work placements. (See the website for the Association of Canadian Community Colleges for more information.)

Taking It Online

Website Name	Website Address
Association of Canadian Community Colleges	www.accc.ca
Canadian Practice Firms Network	www.rcee-cpfn.ca

Immigrant Experience

In his home country of Iran, Bouzar was a successful civil engineer who worked for a company he loved. By the time his daughter graduated from high school, however, he and his wife had decided that they wanted her to obtain a university degree in North America. They chose to immigrate to Canada.

When Bouzar's daughter began taking the courses needed to qualify for post-secondary studies, he realized that he, too, needed to upgrade his education if he wished to work as an engineer. While he was highly qualified in Iran, he found that his credentials were not so easily recognized in the Canadian engineering field.

At first the challenges of adjusting to life in Canada and pursuing further education seemed so daunting that Bouzar and his wife considered moving back to Iran. However, his daughter was so successful and happy in her new environment that they decided to remain in their new country for one more year. After struggling to adapt to a new culture, and upgrade his credentials, Bouzar is now much happier and well on his way to finding success in his chosen career.

Canadian Practice Firms

Canadian Practice Firms are not real companies (or firms). They are set up to give you practice working in an environment similar to a real company. For instance, a practice firm at Douglas College in British Columbia provides a practice business office, with input from a real local company. Participants learn about Canadian business skills by playing the roles of workers in a realistic office environment.

Tip: Look for volunteer jobs in the Classified section of your local newspaper. Or, at the library, find names of not-for-profit organizations that might need volunteers. Look for voluntary work placement opportunities at community colleges and adult learning centres.

2.14 Volunteering in Canada

Problem

Volunteering means working without pay to help an organization. Some people may wonder why anyone would do this. However, in Canada, this type of job is both common and respected. And while you're looking for a job, volunteering can bring you many benefits. It can also be rewarding even after you are employed. How can you become a volunteer?

Solution

Many different kinds of people volunteer, and they do so for different reasons.

- Retired people who have saved money and wish to remain active will often volunteer. Volunteering allows them to do work they enjoy.
- Canadian secondary school students are often required to spend a specific number of hours volunteering before they are allowed to graduate.

Why Many Newcomers Do Volunteer Work:

- As a volunteer, you can obtain Canadian experience in a field that interests you. It gives you a chance to find out whether or not a job fits your interests, personality, and strengths.
- Volunteers have the opportunity to see how an organization works from the inside.
- A volunteer position can make you feel good if you are doing well. This can increase your feelings of self-worth and self-confidence.
- Volunteer jobs increase your network of contacts; they give you new and useful acquaintances.
- Most volunteer positions require you to speak and work with other people, usually in English. Your English speaking, writing, and comprehension skills will certainly improve.
- Volunteering can provide you with Canadian workplace references.
- If you can add a volunteer job to your resume, it will show that you have Canadian experience. It will also gain you respect.
- After proving yourself as a competent and helpful volunteer, you may receive a paid job offer for that work, or for a similar job.

Immigrant Experience

Judith is from the Congo, where volunteering is not common. Since she immigrated to Canada in 2001, she has discovered the joys and benefits of volunteering for important causes.

To gain Canadian experience when she first arrived, she began to do volunteer work at a senior citizens' residence close to her home. Her job was to assist the staff with social activities and help the residents with their daily routines. Over time, she developed close relationships with some of the senior citizens she helped, and her English also improved as she spoke with them.

Judith considers herself fortunate to have volunteered at the seniors' centre. She gained valuable Canadian experience and made lasting friends.

Newcomers can, and should, do volunteer work in order to gain experience and make new contacts while they are looking for work.

If you find a volunteer job in your field, it could lead to a paid job; just make sure that your employer knows you are looking for a paid job. Do not let anyone take advantage of you by asking you to continually work for free or for payment that is well below Canada's minimum wage.

Finding a Volunteer Job

All Canadian cities have volunteer centres that advertise volunteer work. For example, the Volunteer Centre of Toronto finds jobs for 30,000 volunteers in 1,300 public organizations every year. Volunteers may work with children, with elderly people in nursing homes and hospitals, or at food banks, schools, museums, or cultural centres.

If you cannot find volunteer work related to your occupation, you may be able to enroll in a co-op program that will help you find volunteer positions. Such opportunities are provided free of charge by many educational institutions.

You may even be able to find a volunteer job simply by approaching an organization that interests you.

Tip: For some volunteer positions, the organization you are working for may pay for your transportation to the workplace, meals on the job, or special clothing required by the job.

2.15 Create Your Portfolio

Problem

In occupations such as architecture or graphic design, potential employers will want to see samples of your work. These samples, as well as reference letters and other such documents, should be carefully selected and neatly arranged in a folder called a **portfolio**. How should you create your portfolio, and how can you use it to get a job?

Solution

Included in your portfolio should be documents outlining your work experience, your expertise, and any past **achievements**.

Work Experience	References and Letters of Reference
Education	Certificates, diplomas, and other documents which prove that you passed certain courses and seminars
Expertise	Articles, reports, or presentations you have written
Achievements	**Patents**, certificates of authorship, awards and prizes, sales reports

If you are a designer or architect, you should also include drawings and specifications of projects you have worked on. If you are a graphic designer, include printed samples of your artwork and graphics you have created.

Think about what your potential employer will expect of you in your new role, then choose samples that show your experience and expertise in that area.

Organize Your Portfolio

- Choose your sample work carefully (include only your best work).
- Check all materials for errors and have them translated into the language of the marketplace.
- If some samples were created as part of a previous job, you may need to obtain permission from your previous employer to include them in your portfolio.
- Put the most basic and important material near the front.

- Make a list of all the materials in your portfolio so you can find a particular item easily. (During an interview, you won't have time to search through your entire portfolio, and you should not make your interviewer wait.)
- Some items in your portfolio may not interest a particular employer. In that case, remove that item before showing them the portfolio. Add only items that will interest the potential employer.

Advertise Your Portfolio

It's a good idea to have your own website and to put your portfolio on it. This can be helpful for both you and your potential employers. It gives you an opportunity to show them your talent before the interview—and maybe even before you arrive in Canada. Posting your portfolio on the Internet allows employers to become familiar with your work before you meet. You may even get an interview because of the quality of your online portfolio.

Let employers know about your online portfolio by mentioning it and by including the website in your cover letter. Incorporate any brief explanations or comments you feel are necessary.

You may also want to send your portfolio to potential employers on a CD. Consider creating a professional-quality CD cover to make it more attractive.

Update Your Portfolio

Update your portfolio regularly, even after you get a job. It will be helpful for future career advancement within the company you're working for, or if you are searching for a new job.

Tip: Take your portfolio to every interview. Not everyone has a portfolio, so if you have one, you will have an immediate advantage over your competitors.

2.16 How to Fill Out Job Application Forms

Situation

Some organizations will ask you to fill out a job application form when you apply for a position. What is the purpose of an application, and how should you fill one out?

Information

Some employers say that application forms create equality between candidates. This is because the application form asks every candidate the same questions. And in an application form, you give information the employer wants to know about you, whereas in your resume you give information you want the employer to know.

You can work on a resume for days with a dictionary and then have someone proofread it, but you will usually be asked to fill out an application form while you are at the employer's office. This form is generally a one-to-four-page questionnaire. And, to avoid being unprepared, it's a good idea to always carry a notebook containing the information you may be asked to supply. Or photocopy the application in the Creating Your Canadian Experience at the end of this unit and bring it with you.

The Three Parts of an Application Form

Part One

The first part of the application asks for personal information (name, address, e-mail address, and phone number). You might also be asked for your Social Insurance Number (SIN) and date of birth. You can legally refuse to provide this information. However, in this situation, it may be best to show that you are cooperative by fulfilling both requests (as long as revealing your age doesn't hurt your chances of getting the job).

Other common questions in this section include whether or not you are willing to relocate if it's asked of you, when you can start work, and what salary you expect. For the last question, it is best to say, "Salary is negotiable."

Part Two

The next part of the application will likely ask you to outline your job experience. You will be asked to provide your current or most recent job title, start and end dates, reason for leaving, and a brief description of your duties. When explaining why you left your last job, always use a positive tone. For example, instead of saying you left because you were bored, you can truthfully explain that you left to pursue new challenges. You will not lose respect if you admit that you were laid off because your position was eliminated after reorganization or downsizing.

Many applications will ask directly, or indirectly, if you have a criminal record. The indirect way an employer will approach this is through asking whether or not you are "bondable." A person who has a criminal record cannot be bonded. (Being bonded means being insured against financial losses due to this person's actions.) These types of questions must be answered.

The application may also ask about your health; these may be inappropriate and do not have to be answered. However, if your future job involves lifting or strenuous activity, you could lose the job immediately if health problems mean you cannot do this work. In a case like this, you should answer health-related questions that relate to being able to do the job.

Part Three

Most application forms ask for the names and phone numbers of your references. Do not rely on your memory for this information! If the information is inaccurate, you will not make a good impression on your potential employer. Even if your references' contact information is included in your resume, take the time to write the information on the application form. Having everything in one place is convenient for your potential employer.

Double-Check Your Information

Avoid giving negative information on the application form and be sure to proofread what you have written before you hand it in. Also, take time to read the last part of the form where penalties for false answers are listed, and then sign and date the application form.

Tip: On an application form, do not leave any question unanswered. If a question does not apply to your situation, put N/A (Not Applicable) in the blank space.

2.17 Unit Summary

Key Words

achievements: things that are done successfully, especially through hard work or skill

assessor: a person who judges and forms an opinion about something

bridging program: a program that helps immigrants find and settle into their new jobs

certification: (the act of receiving) an official document showing that you have successfully completed a course of training for a particular profession

clicking: pressing one of the buttons on a mouse to choose a particular function or item on a computer screen

co-op program: a program in which students usually combine classroom studies with periods of time spent working

database: a large amount of data that is stored in a computer and can easily be used, added to, etc.

discipline: a subject of study

employment professional: a person who looks for someone for a certain job

fee-based: requiring money for an item, a service, etc.

follow-up: something that is done to continue something that has already started (a follow-up phone call, interview, etc.)

form letter: a very general letter that is intended for a wide audience

fundamental: important or basic; from which everything else develops

patent: an official licence from the government that gives one person or company the right to make or sell a certain product and prevent others from copying it

portfolio: a collection of pieces of work by an artist, a student, etc.

professional ethics: beliefs and principles about what is morally right and wrong behaviour in a particular job

region: a part of the country or the world; a large area of land

residence: the place where somebody lives

scenarios: ways in which things may happen in the future

tradesperson: a person who has a job for which he/she needs a special skill, especially with his/her hands

trends: general movements or changes in society or in a situation

Note: Entries taken or adapted from the Oxford ESL Dictionary.

Creating Your Canadian Experience

1. Search the Internet for the Service Canada Centre nearest to your house.

    Address: _____

    _____

    Hours of Operation: _____

2. In a notebook or on your computer, create a table similar to the one below. Use the table to make a daily job-hunting schedule and check off the tasks as you complete them. At the end of the week, look back at your accomplishments.

Task	Monday	Tuesday	Wednesday	Thursday	Friday

3. In the chart below, assess your employability skills and give an example of an experience that highlights those skills.
Tip: It is a good idea to break down your answers into three parts: the situation, what you did, and the results.

Fundamental Skills	Examples
Communicate	
Manage Information	
Use Numbers	
Think and Solve Problems	

Personal Management Skills	Examples
Demonstrate Positive Attitudes and Behaviours	
Be Responsible	
Be Adaptable	
Work Safely	

Teamwork Skills	Examples
Work with Others	
Participate in Projects and Tasks	

4. Look on the Job Futures website and answer the following questions.

a. What is the average salary for your occupation?

_____

b. What is the average unemployment rate for your occupation?

_____

c. In which province is your occupation in the highest demand?

_____

5. On the Internet, research the volunteer centre nearest to your home. Tip: Try searching using keywords "[your city]" + "volunteering."

Address: _____

_____

Hours: _____

6. List three courses you could take to raise your qualifications. Once you have chosen three, do some Internet research to find out where you could take these courses.

Courses that Will Raise Your Qualifications	Where the Courses Are Offered

7. On the Internet, research the language centre nearest to your home. Tip: Try searching using keywords "[your city]" + "language classes for newcomers."

Address: _____

_____

8. Think about the skills that you have that might be useful in different types of jobs (these are called "transferable skills").

a. _____

b. _____

c. _____

9. Looking at your transferable skills, make a list of three occupations and research their job futures to see which are fast-growing and in what region.

Occupation	Demand in Your Region	Region of Highest Demand

10. Fill out the form below with your information. Take a copy of it with you for when you need to fill out applications.

Application Form

The Applicant

Name: _____ Phone number: _____

Address: _____

SIN: _____ _____ _____ Date of birth (D.O.B.) ____ /____ /____

When can you start? _____ Are you willing to relocate? Y ____ N ____

Expected salary: _____

Job Experience

Job title: _____ Start date: ____ / ____ / ____ End date: ____ / ____ / ____

Reason for leaving: _____

_____

Description of duties: _____

_____

Job title: _____ Start date: ____ / ____ / ____ End date: ____ / ____ / ____

Reason for leaving: _____

_____

Description of duties: _____

_____

Job title: _____ Start date: ____ / ____ / ____ End date: ____ / ____ / ____

Reason for leaving: _____

_____

Description of duties: _____

_____

References

Name: _____ Phone number: _____

Relationship: _____

Name: _____ Phone number: _____

Relationship: _____

Name: _____ Phone number: _____

Relationship: _____

Studying in Canada

In This Unit

- Choosing a College or University
- Applying for College or University
- Canadian Apprenticeships
- Free Adult Education

3.1 Study for Success

Problem

The better your education is, the better your job will be. In Canada, it is not unusual for people to study for much of their lives. Some people take courses to find a fulfilling career, while others pursue education to find new uses for their skills and abilities. What opportunities for study are available in Canada, and how can you find them?

Solution

Most immigrants come to Canada with certificates, diplomas, or degrees they have received abroad. Those may be enough to start to work in Canada, but more study is usually required.

Twenty percent of Canadian occupations are regulated and therefore require Canadian licences. If you want to work in one of these areas, you will likely need to raise your qualifications. To find out if your occupation is regulated, look at the Canadian Information Centre for International Credentials (CICIC) and Foreign Credentials Referrals Office (FCRO) websites.

Before you rush into taking courses, however, note that your foreign credentials (licences, certificates, etc.) can be evaluated (see 1.6). An evaluation will tell you whether or not you need to take more courses and if so, which ones.

Where Should You Study?

The best place to study depends on the education you already have.

- **Secondary-school** equivalency programs allow you to take courses that move you to the level of a secondary-school diploma.
- Colleges and universities are a good place to further your education if you already have a secondary school diploma.

Taking It Online

Website Name	Website Address
CICIC	www.cicic.ca/en/index.aspx
FCRO	www.credentials.gc.ca

How Can You Afford It?

Newcomers are sometimes worried about the high cost of study in Canada. But the government offers substantial financial support. Interest-free student loans are available for a period of study, but you must begin paying back the loan as soon as you complete your courses. As well, grants, bursaries, and scholarships are also available. You do not need to pay these back.

What Are Your Options?

Distance Education

Many colleges and universities offer distance education through the Internet. These courses are helpful for people who live far away from a college or university and for those who need flexible hours.

Faster Upgrading

Academies, business schools, and colleges offer one- and two-year courses that will qualify you for a career. (University degrees, and some college diplomas, take much longer to complete.) Be sure that the diploma awarded by an academy, business school, or college is considered valid by potential employers.

Apprenticeships

To become a qualified and highly-paid tradesperson, you must enroll in an **apprenticeship** program administered by your provincial government. This means that you will become a paid apprentice while you learn your trade.

Which Courses Are Right for You?

If you're unsure whether or not to enroll in a particular course or program, you can often take a short introductory course or perhaps even audit a course. (When you audit a course, you go to classes but you do not have to write tests, exams, or essays.) This will help you decide if you like a course or program before you commit to it.

Tip: High-quality educational institutions are likely to be members of a provincial or federal association. The longer an institution has been operating and the fewer the complaints against it, the better chance it has of becoming a member. For example, membership in the Association of Canadian Community Colleges (ACCC) is an indication of a high-quality, recognized Canadian school or program.

3.2 What to Choose— College or University?

Problem

To pursue your career goals in Canada, it is important to have either a college diploma or a university degree. But how do you know which choice is right for you?

Information

College courses provide knowledge and practical application. University courses place more emphasis on theory and a broad perspective. Universities usually offer a wider range of subjects as well.

> **Tip:** If your priority is finding a job quickly, then go to college. A university degree, however, puts you in a better position to change your **career path** in the future, and can be required for certain occupations.

There are 141 member colleges in the Association of Canadian Community Colleges (ACCC), ranging from one college each in the Yukon Territory, the Northwest Territories, and Nunavut, to 49 in Quebec.

Over 90 universities have membership in the Association of Universities and Colleges of Canada (AUCC).

Taking It Online

Website Name	Website Address
ACCC	www.accc.ca
AUCC	www.aucc.ca

Colleges and Universities: How Do They Compare?		
	College	**University**
Duration of Study	Diploma—three years Certificates for some occupations—one or two years	Bachelor's degree—four years Master's degree—five or seven years Doctorate (Ph.D.)—up to ten years
Types of Subjects	There are usually four main streams: Applied Arts, Business, Technology, and Health Science.	Universities generally have nine or more main areas of study, including some or all of the following: Agriculture, Education, Engineering and Applied Science, Applied Arts, General Arts, Medical Science, Languages and Literature, Law, Math and Physical Science, and Social Sciences (which includes Business, Commerce, Economics, History, Political Studies, Psychology, and Sociology).
Educational Direction	Students train for a specific occupation, learning applied knowledge and skills. Up to 50 percent of training time is given to practice.	Most attention is paid to fundamental disciplines and **theoretical** knowledge. Up to 15 percent of training time is given to practice. The rest is dedicated to research and theory.
Requirements for Entrance	Secondary school graduation or its equivalent, with an emphasis on practical courses, including language, mathematics, and business courses.	Secondary school graduation or its equivalent, but with higher academic standing in a list of prerequisite courses.
Organization of Studies	The structure of courses is similar to high school, where classes and work are scheduled.	Students have to be ready for independent work.
Cost of Education	The cost of a three-year course, including **tuition**, textbooks, board, food, and spending money, is about $30,000 Canadian.	The cost of a four-year course, including textbooks, residence, food, entertainment, and other expenses, is approximately $50,000 Canadian.

3.3 Applying for College

Problem
Canadian colleges provide a high standard of applied knowledge for most occupations. How should you choose a college, and then apply to enroll?

Solution
To find the best college for you, look at directories of colleges on the Internet. Many colleges also have open houses. At these events, you can visit classrooms and labs and speak to the teachers and lecturers.

Requirements for College
- A secondary school certificate (or its equivalent) is usually required to enter a community college. (For some private colleges, or if you are over 21 years of age, you may not need this certificate.)
- Foreign college students must obtain a study permit. As soon as you have been accepted at a college, apply to your Canadian consulate, embassy, or other office for this permit.
- All your documents must be translated into English by an authorized translator. (Don't forget to make copies before sending them away!)
- The Association of Canadian Community Colleges (ACCC) offers assessment and credential recognition services for placement into English as a Second Language (ESL), English for Academic Purposes (EAP), French as a Second Language (FSL), and French for Academic Purposes (FAP) programs. This is also true for placement into career, technical, university preparation, and applied degree programs. In some cases, you may have to pay for, take, and pass entrance exams.
- If English is not your native language, your application should include the results of a language test, such as the Canadian Language Benchmarks (CLB) assessment or the Test of English as a Foreign Language (TOEFL). If you do not send either of these, you must take and pass an English test at the college.

Taking It Online

Website Name	Website Address
ACCC	www.accc.ca
OCAS	www.ontariocolleges.ca/portal/page/portal/ONTCOL/Home
PASBC	gateway.cotr.bc.ca/BritishColumbia/PASBC.asp

Peter's Personal Experience

When I came to Canada, I didn't know what type of work to look for. I had many years of experience in the IT field, where I worked primarily as a consultant and team leader. In my former job, I was responsible for selling managerial software to company managers and advising them on how to use it. My most common tasks included giving presentations, writing plans, creating blueprints, facilitating discussions, and formal company negotiations.

I knew that I couldn't do the same job in Canada because of my limited English. At first, I focused on looking for a job working with the Oracle database. I had considerable experience using it and thought this could lead to a good career. I sent out many resumes over several months but received no responses. I didn't know why until I spoke with a database administrator. I learned that the reason was simple: I didn't have a DBA (Database Administrator) certificate issued by Oracle. In Canada, people trust certificates. It's different in China, where they're not so important. Here, the best way to start a career in a field is to get a certificate in that field.

How to Apply

- For most colleges, you must apply half a year before courses begin. (But check the **deadline** for the college you are interested in!) The earlier you send your documents, the better your chance of acceptance.
- In some provinces, you do not apply directly to the college. Instead, you apply through an organization like Ontario College Application Service (OCAS) or the Post Secondary Application Service of British Columbia (PASBC).
- In Canada, you are allowed to apply to five colleges at the same time. If you are accepted into all five, you may choose the one you wish to attend. If you are not accepted into your first choice, you can be placed on a waiting list for that college or you will be able to choose another college from your list that did accept you.

Tip: Do not apply only to local colleges. Choose the best program for you, even if you have to consider moving to a different city. You may even be able to enroll in distance education at your preferred college.

3.4 Applying for University

Problem

Many potential employers greatly value university degrees. A university education allows you to change occupations more easily than a college education does, and the rate of unemployment among university graduates in Canada is currently no higher than 3 percent. (This is in contrast to an unemployment rate of 6 or 7 percent for Canadians in general.) If university is the right choice for you, how should you select, and apply to, the institution best for you?

Solution

Who Governs Canadian Universities?

Like colleges, Canadian universities are governed by the provinces and territories in which they are located. But all Canadian universities recognize university credentials from other provinces.

Requirements for University

- To enter an American university, you must pass entrance exams, but Canadian universities usually just look at secondary school transcripts.
- In most cases, you must have graduated from secondary school with a 60 to 80 percent average. Students with higher marks have priority.
- Immigrants with a first language other than English who have studied in Canada for less than four years usually have to pass the Test of English as a Foreign Language (TOEFL). Scores must be between 550 and 600 on the handwritten examination or 220 and 250 on the computer-based test. If you take the International English Language Testing System (IELTS) exam, you must pass with a mark of no less than 7. If you did not take either of these examinations, the university will tell you where to take them.

Taking It Online	
Website Name	**Website Address**
OUAC	www.ouac.on.ca
TOEFL	www.toeflgoanywhere.org

- If you began studying at a university outside of Canada, an evaluation service will translate your credentials into Canadian university equivalents. For example, Dalhousie University in Halifax, Nova Scotia, has an online chart called Admissions Requirements by Country. This chart tells you whether or not your international credentials will allow you to be admitted to the university.

How to Apply

- In some provinces, you may apply directly to the university.
- In some provinces, you must send your application to a central body. For example, all applications to universities in Ontario must be sent through the Ontario Universities' Application Centre (OUAC). The OUAC collects applications and sends them on to the universities. But each university makes the final decision about admission. After paying a registration fee, you will be able to apply to three universities at the same time on the Internet through OUAC.
- For most universities, you must apply about nine months before courses begin. (But check the deadlines for the universities you are interested in!) Include your secondary school transcript and any information about your achievements in subjects relating to the courses for which you are applying.
- For some programs, the university may ask you questions about your application and you may be invited for an interview. You may also be asked to show samples of your work or to write an essay on a certain topic. These essays are usually about why you chose to apply to that university or specific program.

Tip: To complete a four-year study term at a Canadian university, you will need to do a lot of reading, writing, and communicating with fellow students and professors. This will help you expand your Canadian network considerably. But be sure that your English language skills are high enough to manage all the hard work you will be doing—at least a CLB 8!

3.5 Applying for a Student Loan

Problem

Education (especially **post-secondary** education) is very important in Canada—but it's also expensive. How can you find the money to attend college or university?

Solution

Canada provides a lot of financial support for students who need help paying for their college or university education. Student loans help to cover the cost of tuition, residence, food, textbooks, manuals, and other school materials. If a student has to support a family, funds may be provided to help with that, too.

Loans can be received from either the federal or provincial government, depending on the type of educational institution you wish to attend.

Every year in the province of Ontario, more than 200,000 students obtain loans for their studies. Government loans in Canada total more than $1.6 billion per year.

Who Qualifies?

- Any college or university student in Canada may apply for a loan.
- As long as a student is enrolled at a college or university, he or she does not have to make payments on the loan. In fact, students may not have to begin paying back their loans until half a year or more after they graduate. From that point on, however, the loan must be repaid. Monthly payments are about 1 percent of the sum of the loan, and can range from $50 to $250 a month. With increasing interest rates, the cost of the loan can more than double if you take the maximum amount of time (eight years) to pay it back.

Taking It Online

Website Name	Website Address
OSAP	osap.gov.on.ca/eng/eng_osap_main.html

- To qualify for a loan, you must not already have a student loan that needs to be paid back. The schools and programs you plan to attend must also fit with the requirements of the financial assistance program. The Ontario Student Loan Assistance Program (OSAP) website, for example, has a handy School Search function that can help you determine which schools qualify.

How to Apply

- To obtain a student loan, you must fill out an application and enclose the necessary documents. In these documents, you must note your yearly income and expenses.
- Loans may be obtained by landed immigrants or citizens of Canada, but not by foreign students. To receive a loan, a student must also have the legal right to work in Canada and must provide a Social Insurance Number (SIN).
- It's also necessary for a student to have lived in the province for no fewer than 12 months before attending the college or university. However, an immigrant who has never lived in any Canadian province for 12 **consecutive** months may be allowed to apply for a loan if they can provide written documentation that they are a resident in Canada.

To obtain more complete information about how loans work in Canada, research your home province's requirements. Using an Internet search engine, enter "student loan" and the name of the province where you wish to take courses.

Tip: There is a concept in Canada called civil marriage (also known as a common-law relationship). For the purpose of student loans, if a student has been living with someone for at least three years or has children from such a relationship, they are considered to be a family.

3.6 Scholarships in Canada

Situation

As a post-secondary student in Canada, you may be eligible to receive awards, such as scholarships and bursaries, and other types of financial assistance that do not have to be paid back. How can you apply for this type of support?

Advice and Action Plan

Scholarships and Bursaries

Thousands of scholarships and bursaries are awarded in Canada each year. Scholarships are the largest source of student funding and are usually awarded because of a student's success in study, sports, public life, or volunteer work. Bursaries are usually awarded to students with limited funds. (Academic achievement is often considered, however, by the people who grant bursaries.)

Most scholarships and bursaries are administered by educational institutions themselves or by university and college associations. The Association of Universities and Colleges of Canada (AUCC) manages over $11 million and 175 scholarships each year. Many of these scholarships are awarded on behalf of leading corporations.

In 2006, at Carleton University in Ottawa, over 7,500 new and returning students were awarded more than $11.8 million in scholarships and bursaries. Every year at University of Alberta in Edmonton, over 300 awards ranging in value from $500 to $25,000 are made available to undergraduates, through the Office of the Registrar and Student Awards.

What Funds Might Be Available for You?

To find out what scholarships and bursaries are available,

- Look on the websites of universities, associations, student loan institutions, and corporations.

Taking It Online	
Website Name	**Website Address**
AUCC	www.aucc.ca/programs/index_e.html
CanLearn	www.canlearn.ca

- Check out websites like CanLearn. It has a free online scholarship and award matching service based on scholarships from major banks and other corporations.
- Go to a public library.
- Visit the financial aid office of any educational institution. The staff will speak with you, allow you to look at their scholarship or bursary list, and suggest grants that might be suitable for you.

Many scholarships and bursaries are available only to certain people. For example, some awards are available only to men, others only to women. Some—like the RBC Royal Bank Scholarship for New Canadians—are available only to Canadian citizens or permanent residents who were born outside of Canada.

How to Apply

- After you find a suitable scholarship or bursary (or several), send in your applications.
- With each application, include documents confirming that you are a good candidate. List your achievements in academics or sports, your volunteer activities, and your involvement in any public work such as a student committee.
- To prove your financial position, you may need to present information about your income and expenses or the income of your husband, wife, or parents (for students who are not married or in a common-law relationship).

Special committees make the decisions about scholarships or bursaries. If you are fortunate enough to receive one of these awards, you may still submit a new application for the same or different awards the following semester. Find out details about each specific scholarship, though. Some renew automatically each year!

Tip: Visit financial aid offices often and collect the documents you need to apply for as many awards as you can. It's important to work hard to keep your marks high and to get involved in public life, volunteer activity, and sports. This will only improve your chances of winning an award.

3.7 Canadian Apprenticeships

Situation

Skilled tradespeople are highly valued in the Canadian labour market. They can find jobs quite easily, especially if they have completed a Canadian apprenticeship program. What is an apprenticeship, and how do you know if it's the right choice for you?

Information

Apprenticeship is a form of training for people who want to do skilled work with their hands. Tradespeople include bakers, bricklayers, welders, carpenters, plumbers, electricians, hoist operators, and hundreds of other high-paying, in-demand occupations.

Every year in the province of Ontario, about 50,000 workers hired by 25,000 employers pass through apprenticeship programs. And Ontario has half a million skilled workers with apprenticeship certificates.

One of the best aspects of the apprenticeship program is that, in most provinces, about 85 percent of the training is performed in the workplace. The rest of the time is used for theoretical studies, which are conducted at a college, business school, or other training institution.

Benefits of Apprenticeship

For the Employer

In order to enter the apprenticeship program in any province, you need to find an employer who is willing to train you in their workplace. The government gives employers incentives to do this. For example, employers can train personnel according to the company's specific needs. In Quebec, employers participating in the Workplace Apprenticeship Programme Qualification Plan may be able to get a tax credit to fund part of the training expenses. The **journeyman** tradesperson who supervises an apprentice for a year can also receive a professional qualification certificate.

Taking It Online	
Website Name	**Website Address**
Red Seal	www.red-seal.ca/Site/index_e.htm

For the Apprentice

The apprentice benefits from the guidance of an experienced tradesperson; they also receive a professional qualification certificate and are paid for the workplace-training part of the program.

Find Apprenticeship Opportunities

To find apprenticeship opportunities, you can search the web using the keywords "apprenticeship" and the name of your province.

It's also a good idea to get in touch with the provincial ministry in charge of apprenticeships. They can probably help you to find apprenticeship opportunities and guide you through the process of signing up for the program once you have found an employer.

How Apprenticeships Work

Theoretical studies for apprenticeships are free, but you may have some expenses for application submissions and purchasing tools.

Training lasts between two and five years, depending on the occupation. During this time, you will work 4,000 to 8,000 hours. At that point, you will be expected to have mastered the techniques of your profession in accordance with Canadian standards.

Finally, you will take a professional examination. If your marks are high enough, you will obtain a Certificate of Apprenticeship and a Certificate of Qualification.

Tradespeople in 44 different occupations may also become certified through a program called Red Seal. This program allows them to practise their trade in any province or territory in Canada.

Tip: If you are a skilled tradesperson with international experience, you may be able to obtain a Canadian certificate more quickly if you can get credit for hours you worked at your trade in your homeland.

3.8 Free Adult Education

Situation

Education for adults in Canada is not always expensive! Across the country, adult learners can usually take courses free of charge at Adult Learning Centres (ALCs) or through adult education programs at secondary schools and colleges. How can you benefit from programs like this?

Information

If you do not have the equivalent of a secondary school diploma, adult education programs will be a great help to you. Before you enroll, find out how much credit you can receive for the education you already have.

Prior Learning Assessment and Recognition

The education you already have can be evaluated.

- In some provinces, such as Newfoundland and Labrador, the educational institutions themselves decide how much credit to give you for the education you already have. This is called Prior Learning Assessment and Recognition (PLAR). PLAR can be researched using the Canadian Information Centre for International Credentials (CICIC) website.
- In Ontario, and some other provinces, various government ministries administer PLAR.
- Manitoba created a PLAR project that resulted in more accessible assessment and recognition services within the community.

Adult Learning Centres

ALCs can be different depending on the province, territory, and region.

- Many ALCs across the country teach English for the Canadian workplace. They may offer grade 9, 10, 11, 12, and transition courses or help adults improve employability skills. They may offer courses in computer training, job skills, and ESL for the workplace, as well as credit courses to help students complete a secondary school diploma.
- Most ALC programs offer courses for new Canadians, including English as a Second Language (ESL) classes.
- A number of ALCs are run by school boards. Canadian citizens and landed immigrants may take these courses.
- Adult Graduation Diploma courses are offered free by most school boards and many colleges. Emphasis is on secondary school graduation. After graduation, a tuition fee may be charged for additional courses.

Peter's Personal Experience

When I first came to Canada, some friends told me that LINC classes were not so useful to Chinese learners. They said they focused too much on grammar and vocabulary and not enough on listening and speaking, which are weaker areas for Chinese speakers.

However, the only language class I knew of was a LINC class, so I went there for an assessment. As I had predicted, I scored a level 8 in reading and writing but only level 4 in listening and speaking. I wanted to improve my English, so I registered for a LINC class.

I soon found that the program was even better than I had expected. It was very interesting and practical for me; it focused on conversation, which was what I really needed then. I went to evening classes three times a week, even in heavy snowstorms, until I moved to another part of the city.

I think LINC classes can be extremely useful for newcomers, but you have to find the one that's right for you. And if you really want to learn English, I recommend that you speak it as often as possible—even with fellow students from your homeland.

How They Work

- To register at an ALC, you'll need your immigration documents and you will pay a small entrance fee. You may have to pass an English-language examination. These examinations often require a basic knowledge of grammar and the ability to write a one-page essay.
- Once accepted, you may take up to three courses at once for nine weeks.

Computer Literacy Courses at ALCs

To get a job in Canada, you must have excellent computer skills. Some ALCs offer computer courses, for which you can earn a diploma or certificate.

Tip: Phone your local school board or provincial Ministry of Education to find out who operates ALCs in your community.

3.9 Continuing Education

Problem

Many Canadians who already have diplomas or degrees pursue more education in order to improve their skills and knowledge. They do this by enrolling in continuing education programs. Newcomers also enroll in these programs to improve their professional skills or learn new skills required for a new occupation. Many continuing education courses take only one or two years to complete. How can you choose, and enroll, in a continuing education course that will work for you?

Solution

Continuing education programs are offered by many colleges, universities, and private training institutions.

Advantages of Continuing Education

- You can enroll in continuing education at any age.
- Requirements for previous education may be less strict than for other programs.
- Courses are generally available in evenings and on weekends.
- A two-year course usually costs less than $5,000.

> **These are some of the fields in which you can upgrade your qualifications through continuing education:**
>
> - Office work (secretary, computer operator, programmer, clerk, telephone operator)
> - Medical professions (nurse, dental technician, receptionist, chiropractic)
> - Factory work (technician, electrician, mechanic, assembler, machine operator)
> - Government jobs (law enforcement, firefighter, postal worker, military)
> - Service work (cook, travel agent, jeweller, auto mechanic, insurance agent, bartender)

Finding the Right Program

Colleges and Universities

If you take a continuing education course at a well-known college or university, you will benefit from their good reputation.

Career Colleges

Career colleges offer relatively short programs for different occupations, such as the Fine Art Bartending School in Calgary, Alberta; the Academy of Applied Pharmaceutical Sciences in Toronto, Ontario; Cape Breton Business College in Sydney, Nova Scotia; and the Northwest Law Enforcement Academy in Winnipeg, Manitoba.

Private Institutions

Many private institutions offer professional programs. However, they do not all have qualified instructors. The diplomas or certificates you receive from them may also not be recognized in the Canadian job market.

If you are considering going to a private educational institution, you should do the following:

- Ask someone at the workplaces you are interested in whether or not they will accept a certificate or diploma from this institution.
- Find out whether the institution has a licence in the province you're living and working in.
- Learn how long the institution has existed, how many graduates they have, and what percentage of graduates are employed in their fields.
- Find out if they have an employment placement service and what companies they work with.
- Consider what academic requirements you must have, including knowledge of English.
- Visit the institution (during an open house if possible) to find out whether it has adequate facilities.
- Find out if you can repeat courses free of charge if that becomes necessary.

Tip: To find out if a particular educational institution gives recognized certificates or diplomas, contact the appropriate government ministry, such as the Ministry of Education in Newfoundland or the Ministry of Advanced Education in BC.

3.10 Unit Summary

Key Words

apprenticeship: the state or time of being an apprentice

career path: the stages that you go through to get to a certain position in your working life

consecutive: coming or happening one after the other

deadline: a time or date before which something must be done

journeyman: a person who has completed his/her training and is now qualified to work with a more experienced individual

post-secondary: relating to college or university

secondary school: high school

theoretical: based on ideas and principles, not on practical experience

tuition: the money that a student must pay in order to take classes at a college, university, or private school

Note: Entries taken or adapted from the Oxford ESL Dictionary.

Creating Your Canadian Experience

1. Different types of schooling have advantages (pros) and disadvantages (cons). Create a list with pros and cons for some of the different types of schooling you learned about in Unit 3.

College		University	
Pros	Cons	Pros	Cons

Correspondence Courses		Career Colleges	
Pros	Cons	Pros	Cons

2. Search the Internet to find out which schools offer programs or courses that you are interested in taking.
   Tip: Search using keywords "[your program]" + "[your city]."

   School: _____ Program or Course: _____

   School: _____ Program or Course: _____

   School: _____ Program or Course: _____

   School: _____ Program or Course: _____

3. Contact a school (if one is near your home, see if you can attend an information night) and find out more information about the programs and courses.
   Tip: Ask about starting dates.

School	Further Information

4. One effective way of paying for additional schooling is through student loans. Using the Internet, research the loan requirements in your province.
Tip: Search using keywords "student loans" + "[your province]."

a. _____

b. _____

c. _____

d. _____

5. Find the contact information for the financial aid office at your school.
Tip: Start by looking on the school's website.

Address: _____

_____

Hours: _____

6. Create a list of bursaries that you are allowed to receive, and the steps required for the application process.
Tip: Start on your school's website and then try your provincial government's website.

Bursary	Application Process

7. Search the Internet for apprenticeships in your province and find some details about them.
Tip: Search using keywords "[your province]" + "[your job]" + "apprenticeship."

Occupation	Required Number of Hours	Cost of Tools	Other Information

8. Find the Adult Learning Centre closest to your home.
Tip: Search the Internet using keywords "Adult Learning Centre" + "[your city]."

Address: _____

_____

Hours: _____

Phone Number: _____

Survival Jobs

In This Unit

- Understanding the Pros and Cons of Survival Jobs
- Temporary Job Agencies
- Seasonal Work

4.1 Survival Jobs

Situation

When you come to Canada, be sure to bring enough money to last for half a year or more. Many newcomers do this but still run out of funds before they find a job. There are at least two solutions to this problem.

One solution is to apply for financial assistance through the Government of Canada. This is called "social assistance" or "income support." The other solution is to find a temporary job to cover living expenses while you continue searching for a job in your field. This type of temporary job is called a "**survival job**."[1]

Information

You should not feel embarrassed about taking a survival job. Most newcomers, and Canadians, have to do this at some point.

To make sure you have enough time to study and/or conduct your job search, consider taking on a part-time survival job instead of a full-time position.

Here are some pros (advantages) and cons (disadvantages) of taking a survival job.

Taking a Survival Job		
	Pros	**Cons**
Money	• You will be able to start paying off **debts**. • You will be able to pay for everyday expenses such as rent, food, transportation, and study.	• Most survival jobs do not pay well.
Time	• Survival jobs can often be done during evenings and on weekends.	• You may have to work long hours. This will leave much less time for study and job searching.
Experience	• Survival jobs count as Canadian experience, and you can put this on your resume. • You'll make new friends. • You may be able to build a business network.	• While you are working in a survival job, you many not be getting good Canadian experience in your own field of work.

[1]Throughout the next several chapters, you will find the most popular job descriptions based on the National Occupational Classification (NOC) website (www.23.hrdc-drhc.gc.ca). Wages and salaries are taken from the Service Canada website (www.labourmarketinformation.ca). Occupational trends are based on the Job Futures Service Canada website (www.jobfutures.ca/en/home.shtml).

	Pros	Cons
Experience	• Your employer can act as a Canadian reference.	
Knowledge	• You will learn about Canadian workplace culture and etiquette. • Your language skills will improve. • Many survival jobs do not demand special qualifications or strong English skills.	• The work will not likely be in your field, so you will not be using the knowledge and experience you already have. • Starting over at a low level can be frustrating.
Prospects	• Your confidence will improve. • You will feel a sense of accomplishment because you will be able to support yourself and your family.	• It can be hard to give up the money you make at a survival job when it is time to put more energy into searching for a career.

What to Look for in a Good Survival Job

• Try to find a job in an English-speaking environment and practise your English.
• Try to find a temporary job similar to one in your field to help build Canadian experience and a network of contacts.
• Look for seasonal work, such as summer jobs in park zones, resorts, and summer camps.

Create Your Own Job (Self-Employment)

Do you have any talents that could become a source of income? If so, you could make a living working for yourself!

Here are some possible jobs you could do on your own: be a math tutor, open a chess school for children, play or teach a musical instrument, paint, conduct tours, prepare delicious food, or do electrical or plumbing repairs. Get a licence if you need one, collect evidence of your qualifications, and place ads in your local newspaper.

Tip: The longer you stay in a survival job, the harder it may be to leave. Make sure that you do not stay in a survival job too long. If you do, you will not benefit from your many years of hard-earned education and experience in your field!

4.2 Temporary Job Agencies

Situation

Temporary jobs can be found quickly through temporary employment agencies. What can you expect from temporary (temp) jobs in Canada?

Information

If you use the services of a temporary employment agency (temp agency), you will find a job sooner than if you look on your own. However, you will have two bosses: the manager of the temp agency and the supervisor at your place of work (the client company). The temp agency is responsible for issuing your paycheque and taking care of deductions (workers' compensation, Canada Pension Plan, Employment Insurance, and income tax).

Pros and Cons of Using a Temp Agency

Pros

- Some temp agencies do not require Canadian education or experience.
- Some temp agencies employ people with lower-level language skills.
- Jobs will be found more quickly through a temp agency than on your own.

Cons

- Jobs offered by temp agencies are often low-paying, with no employee benefits, and often involve hard labour.
- Agencies seldom give proper instructions about safety **precautions**. (Accidents at temporary workplaces happen five times more frequently than at permanent jobs.)
- An agency may place obstacles in the way of you getting a permanent job with a client company.

Tip: If you have an accident, report it immediately to your workplace supervisor and your temp agency. Get medical help right away. Workers' compensation will cover medical costs and any wages you lost as a result of your injury. If you feel that your rights are being ignored by the temp agency or workplace, use an Internet search engine to find a local workers' rights organization.

Nina's Personal Experience

Because of our limited English skills and lack of Canadian experience, many of us find we have to take temporary "survival jobs" when we first come to Canada. While these jobs are often unrelated to our profession in our homeland, they offer certain advantages: you usually don't need to present a resume or cover letter to get one and they are plentiful and easy to find—as long as you really want to work.

Some people I know have been working at factories or restaurants for many years and are quite content with their current employment. My present job is a survival job: I'm working as a customer service agent for an outbound call centre doing telemarketing for a local telephone company. The work is challenging and nerve racking but also exciting. I never thought I could do telemarketing—in English, in Canada! The good news is that I made some sales on my very first day at work, and I have been their top salesperson ever since!

Getting a Job Through a Temp Agency

Look in your local phone book or in the Classified section of newspapers for addresses and phone numbers of temp agencies in your area. Call them to find out what types of jobs they offer. Let them know what jobs you'd be interested in and what hours you'd like to work. Remember, you will have to show your SIN card before you can start work.

After you agree with an agency about salary and working conditions, you will be sent to the workplace. If, at the workplace, you are asked to do work that is different than what you were hired for, or you do not feel safety regulations are properly observed, you should immediately contact the representative of the temp agency to make sure that the problem is solved.

Although the agency keeps track of your work, you should also keep track by using the Temp Workers' Calendar form, such as the one on the Settlement.org website.

Finally, in some cases, a temp agency will try to hire you as an "independent contractor" (a self-employed worker). They do this so they will not have to deduct Employment Insurance (EI) or income tax from your paycheque. This means that you are responsible for declaring your income to the government and making the necessary payments yourself.

4.3 Caregivers

Situation

Caregivers are so badly needed in Canada that Citizenship and Immigration Canada (CIC) has developed a special Live-In Caregiver Program. Under this program, people from foreign countries can come to Canada for temporary work. What does being a caregiver involve, is it the right job for you, and how does the Live-In Caregiver Program work?

Information

The support workers' field, which includes job titles such as babysitters, adult caregivers, and **live-in** caregivers, is expected to grow substantially in the next 20 years (but may suffer a temporary decline in the next year or so). See the chart below for a summary of the qualifications needed to be a caregiver in Canada, what to expect, and how to seek a job in the field.

Caregivers		
	Child Caregivers (NOC code 6474)	**Adult Caregivers (NOC code 6471)**
Description	If you enjoy working with children, this job may be for you. Under its National Occupational Classification (NOC) you'll find that the most common titles for this job are "babysitter," "child caregiver," or "nanny." Caregivers help care for children when parents are not present. Live-in caregivers live in the houses in which they work.	Many Canadian families employ people to care for an elderly, sick, or disabled family member on a part-time or full-time basis. The National Occupational Classification job title is Personal Support Worker. Also called "companion" or "personal aide," these people may be employed by a hospital, government organization, or social services firm. When working in a private home, you may either come into work on a schedule or live with your employers.
Possible Duties	• Feed, bathe, and dress children and babies while parents are absent. • Perform light housekeeping duties such as cooking and laundry. • Take the children to school or to appointments.	• Aid in walking, exercising, bathing, and personal hygiene. • Prepare meals, often according to special diets, and feed people who can't feed themselves. • Administer medications, change bandages, and collect specimens. • Shop for groceries and perform light housekeeping duties.

	Child Caregivers (NOC code 6474)	Adult Caregivers (NOC code 6471)
Qualifications	To get this job, you should have some training in childcare. Many local babysitter's training courses are available. Look for a course that will give a recognized certificate.	Some secondary school and home-management experience is usually required. You may need to have college or other courses in home-support, as well as first-aid certification.
Find a Job as a Caregiver	Babysitters are always in demand in Canada. A good way to find babysitting jobs is through relatives or friends. Babysitters often advertise on posters or in newspapers. Use an Internet search engine and type in "childcare worker" and the name of your city. Also, look into the Live-In Caregiver Program.	An aging population will increase the demand for adult caregivers, but demand may also increase as the government encourages patients to be moved out of institutions and cared for in the community instead. Look in Classified sections of local and city newspapers for job postings. Search on the Internet as well by entering "personal support worker" and your city. Also, look into the Live-In Caregiver Program.
Wages, Hours, and Working Conditions	Babysitting wages are often about $10 per hour. Before you are hired, you may be asked for a police document showing that you have no criminal record.	The average wage is about $12 per hour. Some caregivers work all day for one family or person. Others visit a number of homes each day.

The Live-In Caregiver Program

The Live-In Caregiver Program is intended to attract workers who can live in the home of an employer. The caregiver must be provided with a private bedroom and free time that can be spent as desired. After two years in Canada, workers with a temporary Live-In Caregiver visa are allowed to submit documents to obtain permanent resident status for themselves and their families.

There are four main requirements for an individual to enter Canada using this program:

- They must have the equivalent of a Canadian secondary school education.
- Their language skills must be high enough to read labels and instructions and communicate with employers and others.
- They must have spent either six months of full-time classroom training or a year of paid work experience in a similar field.
- A written and signed contract describing duties, hours, and salary must be obtained.

Adapted from: National Occupational Classification, CIC. Working Temporarily in Canada: The Live-In Caregiver Program, CIC (www.cic.gc.ca/english/work/caregiver/index.asp).

4.4 Cleaners

Situation

There is always demand for cleaners in homes, office buildings, and other establishments. The high demand for cleaners is why newcomers sometimes take this kind of survival job during their first year in Canada. What does being a cleaner involve, and how can you get this type of job?

Information

The code for cleaners in the National Occupational Classification (NOC) is 6661, and they are usually called "light duty cleaners." Light duty cleaners clean the lobbies, hallways, and rooms of hotels, motels, resorts, hospitals, schools, company offices, and private residences. They are employed by government establishments, cleaning service companies, and private companies and individuals. When talking to cleaning service companies about a position, you may be asked to invest money as an employee, subcontractor, or franchisee—be very careful about this. Many of these firms have made the news in recent years for dishonest hiring and subcontracting practices.

Possible Duties

- You may be asked to wash floors, walls, windows, and other surfaces.
- It can involve vacuuming carpets and dusting furnishings.
- You may be required to make beds, change bedding and towels, restock toiletries.
- You might have to keep kitchens and bathrooms clean by washing and disinfecting sinks, baths/showers, countertops, and toilets.

Taking It Online

Website Name	Website Address
NOC	www5.hrsdc.gc.ca/NOC-CNP/app/index.aspx?lc=E

- The position could require you to gather and dispose of trash.
- If working in a public institution, you may have to answer inquiries and handle complaints.

Qualifications

There are no educational requirements, but employers prefer to hire people with experience. Many employment agencies offer workplace training to teach employees how to use cleaning equipment and chemicals.

Physical health, precision, honesty, and a sense of responsibility are all crucial qualities for a light duty cleaner. Cleaners should be people who can be trusted as they work near material assets, since the job is usually without supervision. For this reason, references are sometimes required.

Find a Job as a Cleaner

Job ads for cleaners are published in newspapers and on the Internet. Some employers will invite you to visit their office in person for negotiation. Others will simply ask you to send in your resume.

Wages, Hours, and Working Conditions

Wages for cleaning private houses are about $9 to $10 per hour. Wages for cleaning public offices or buildings, restaurants, kitchens, and public washrooms are between $8 and $12 per hour.

Work hours may be full- or part-time on weekdays or weekends. You may also be asked to be "on call." (This means you can be called in to work at any time.) Cleaners often work early in the morning or late at night.

Adapted from: National Occupational Classification, CIC.

Tip: In some job ads for cleaners, employers will offer training. They may charge you a fee for this training, but you are not guaranteed a job afterwards. Before you pay, make sure that you will likely be hired.

4.5 Security Guards

Situation

To be a security guard, you do not need a high language level, special education, or Canadian licence (unless you are a security guard who must carry **firearms**). Although the majority of security guards in Canada are men, women may also seek employment in the field. What are the duties and responsibilities of security guards, and is it the right job for you?

Information

Security guards are listed under Security Guards and Related Occupations in the National Occupational Classification (NOC code 6651). Different types of security guards include airport security guards, armoured car guards, bodyguards, bouncers, commissionaires, crossing guards, gate attendant/security guards, and night watchpeople. Employers include private security agencies, retail stores, transportation facilities, residential complexes, industrial establishments, cultural establishments, government organizations, and educational, financial, and health institutions.

Possible Duties

- You may have to supervise and regulate entrances to buildings and other facilities—either in person or through remote monitoring and surveillance equipment.
- The position could require you to help people with special needs.
- It can involve patrolling construction sites, warehouses, and other assigned areas, and checking for trespassers or signs of illegal entry.
- It might include making sure motorists yield the right of way to children and other pedestrians at public crosswalks.
- You could be required to enforce rules at nightclubs and other entertainment facilities to preserve order and prevent or resolve conflicts.
- The job might require you to perform security inspections of passengers and baggage at airports.

Taking It Online

Website Name	Website Address
NOC	www5.hrsdc.gc.ca/NOC-CNP/app/index.aspx?lc=E

- You may have to guard and transport money and other valuables for financial institutions and retail establishments.
- Your employer might ask you to ensure that establishment safety and emergency procedures are followed; respond to fire alarms, bomb threats, and other emergencies.

Qualifications

A minimum of secondary school education is preferred, and a driver's licence may be required. You may need to be **bonded**, which requires a police background check to prove that you have no criminal record. You may also need a licence to carry firearms. For some occupations, training is provided.

Find a Job as a Security Guard

Demand for this occupation is increasing, as many security guards are expected to retire soon. Industry growth, the high rate of worker turnover, and increased business investments in expensive equipment and machinery will also increase demand.

Job ads for security guards can be found in newspapers and on the Internet.

Wages, Hours, and Working Conditions

The average annual income for security guards who work full-time throughout the year is about $30,000.

Many security guards work alone and/or at night patrolling buildings, parking lots, and industrial sites. This means that no one may be there to help if you were injured. Shifts usually last eight hours and may take place at any time of night or day and on weekends and holidays. If you are working alone, you will be constantly on-duty and unable to take lunch or other breaks, so you will have to eat on the job.

Adapted from: National Occupational Classification, CIC.

Tip: Security jobs can be dangerous, so you should be physically fit and emotionally well-grounded before you consider becoming a security guard.

4.6 Drivers

Situation

Do you have a car and a valid Canadian driver's licence with a clean driving record? Do you enjoy spending time at the wheel of a car or truck? If so, maybe you should look for a job as a driver. What are the duties and responsibilities for this type of job?

Information

Drivers		
	Delivery and Courier Service Drivers (NOC code 7414)	**Taxi and Limousine Drivers and Chauffeurs (NOC code 7413)**
Description	Service drivers drive bicycles, cars, vans, and light trucks to pick up and deliver various products. They are employed by dairies, drug stores, newspaper distributors, take-out food restaurants, mobile caterers, and courier companies. You may also be self-employed.	Taxi drivers drive passengers to local destinations in small passenger vehicles. Some work for taxi companies and others are self-employed. **Chauffeurs** work for businesses, governments, families, or individuals.
Possible Duties	• Drive established routes to pick up, deliver, and occasionally sell a wide range of products. • Inspect vehicles for safety and road-worthiness. • Keep records of pick-ups, deliveries, mileage, and problems encountered.	• Transport passengers between destinations. • Help passengers put luggage in the vehicle. • Collect fares. • Interact with dispatchers. • Pick up clients and their guests on a pre-arranged schedule. • Perform errands like picking up mail or delivering business documents. • Clean and maintain the vehicle and take it for servicing.

Tip: If you enjoy interacting with people, you could be a good taxi driver. If not, you may be more comfortable as a delivery driver.

	Delivery and Courier Service Drivers (NOC code 7414)	Taxi and Limousine Drivers and Chauffeurs (NOC code 7413)
Qualifications	Qualifications include a secondary school diploma, a driver's licence appropriate to the class of vehicle, and one year of safe driving experience and on-the-job training. Eligibility for bonding and transportation of dangerous goods (TDG) certification may be required. Good physical health is required, because you may have to load and unload goods. Some English is needed for conversation with customers and clients. Ability to work on a computer may also be required. (Data may need to be entered into a computer database for pick-up and delivery of goods.)	Taxi drivers and chauffeurs in most Canadian provinces and territories require a special driver's licence. To obtain this licence, you may need to do a written test and an on-the-road test. A Class G driver's licence is required in other provinces and territories. You must have extensive knowledge of the area where you work. You may also need a municipal taxi permit. To otain a taxi driver's licence, you'll need fairly strong English skills (Canadian Language Benchmark 7). You also need a medical report from a physician showing that you are physically capable of performing the duties.
Find a Job as a Driver	Employment prospects for delivery drivers and couriers are fair. As many older drivers retire or take leave in the next few years, demand will increase for qualified younger drivers.	Employment prospects for chauffeurs and taxi drivers are good until approximately 2010.
Wages, Hours, and Working Conditions	Wages begin at $8 to $10 per hour. If you have excellent knowledge of your city's streets and are able to work independently, your wage may be increased to $15 or $20 per hour. Delivery drivers often work night shifts, weekends, and on call. ("On call" means you could be called in at any time to work.)	A full-time taxi or limousine driver can make up to $45,000 per year. Chauffeurs often have to wear uniforms and usually receive an hourly wage or monthly salary. Some taxi drivers own, lease, or rent their vehicles and are essentially self-employed. Most work for taxi companies and drive company vehicles. To do this job, you may need to work nights, weekends, or holidays.

Adapted from: National Occupational Classification, CIC. Human Resources and Social Development Canada.

4.7 Labourers

Situation

Working as a construction trades helper, labourer, or material handler requires physical strength, good health, and enough English to understand supervisors' instructions. Finding this sort of job in Canada is not difficult. What duties do labourers perform, and is this field right for you?

Information

Working as a labourer or material handler is good for tradespeople who are awaiting certification or journeyman status. Working as a labourer in Canada, you will become familiar with the jobs, materials, and tools—and you may gain valuable industry contacts.

Labourers		
	Construction Trades Helpers and Labourers (NOC code 7611)	**Material Handlers (NOC code 7452)**
Description	Job titles related to Construction Trades Helpers and Labourers include asphalt spreader, demolition worker, and helpers for bricklayers, carpenters, concrete mixers, plumbers, glaziers, drillers, and roofers. Labourers perform **manual work** at construction sites and are employed by construction companies and contractors.	Material handlers include freight handlers (except air transport), furniture movers, storage workers, and warehouse men/women. Material handlers are employed by transportation, storage, moving, manufacturing, and processing companies, as well as warehouses.
Possible Duties	• Move materials to work areas and help heavy equipment operators load and move equipment. • Construct and take down scaffolding, catwalks, concrete forms, and barricades. • Mix and spread concrete, asphalt, and other materials; dig, fill, and level earth with rake and shovel. • Demolish with pry bars, hammers, and other tools; salvage materials; clean up construction sites. • Operate pneumatic and power tools.	• Load and unload materials by hand or using forklifts, winches, and other equipment. • Set up showroom and event displays. • Weigh, sort, pack, or unpack items and boxes as instructed; fill warehouse orders, take inventory, and check materials and packaging. • Transfer liquid products into or out of tank cars or storage tanks. • Dump, pour, or operate conveyors to transfer loose or aggregate materials such as grains or gravel to transport vehicles, containers, or other storage areas.

	Construction Trades Helpers and Labourers (NOC code 7611)	Material Handlers (NOC code 7452)
Qualifications	Some experience as a general construction labourer may be required. If you want to be a flagman/woman, you may need to obtain a traffic control certificate.	Material handlers should be physically strong and possess at least some secondary school education. To operate equipment, such as winches or forklifts, you must take a brief training course and pass an exam to obtain a certificate.
Find a Job as a Labourer	The best way to find a job as a general labourer is to visit the nearest construction site or to look in the Classified section of your local newspaper.	Job ads for material handlers can usually be found in newspapers and on the Internet. Conduct Internet searches by typing "material handler," "warehouse jobs," or "forklift operator," along with the name of your city or province into a search engine.
Wages, Hours, and Working Conditions	The normal workweek of a construction labourer is 35 to 40 hours. Since labourers are usually paid by the hour, overtime can bring in lots of extra money. But low seniority means that labourers are among the first in a company to be laid off when less work is available. If you are working only part-time or for part of the year, you can probably expect to make only about $20,000 per year as a construction helper or labourer. If you're employed full-time throughout the year, however, you can expect to make $35,000 or more.	The average material handler earns about $30,000 per year. However, new equipment has made it easier to handle materials. This will mean fewer jobs for material handlers. More jobs will be available for equipment operators.

Adapted from: National Occupational Classification, CIC.

Tip: If you want job security as a material handler, take a course to learn how to operate handling equipment.

4.8 The Food Industry

Situation

Jobs for food service workers are among the easiest to find. (These jobs are sometimes advertised on "help wanted" signs in the windows of restaurants and cafes.) Grocery clerk, shelf stocker, and retail clerk jobs are also relatively easy to find. No special education or certificate is needed, and there are many job opportunities in every city in Canada. What are these jobs like, and would this field be right for you?

Information

Food Service Workers		
	Food Counter Attendants, Kitchen Helpers, and Related Occupations (NOC code 6641)	**Grocery Clerks and Store Shelf Stockers (NOC code 6622)**
Description	This occupation includes job titles like bus boy/girl, cook's helper, counter attendant, dishwasher, food preparer, kitchen helper, and sandwich maker. Jobs are found in restaurants, cafes, delicatessens, hotels, fast food outlets, cafeterias, hospitals, and other establishments.	This occupation includes job titles like grocery clerk, supermarket clerk, retail clerk, and shelf stocker. Jobs are found in retail establishments such as grocery, hardware, and department stores, and in warehouses.
Possible Duties	• Serve customers and take food orders. • Prepare food for cooking or serving using common kitchen tools or appliances. • Keep refrigerators and salad bars stocked and keep track of inventory. • Take payments for food purchases. • Clear trash and empty garbage containers in kitchen. • Keep work areas, appliances, and cupboards clean and disinfected. • Clear and wipe tables and trays. Take dirty dishes to kitchen and clean dishes to serving areas. • Set tables. Refill condiments and restock supplies at serving stations and tables.	• Put customer purchases in bags or boxes for pick-up, shipment, or delivery. • Take products received by the store out of boxes. Price items. Update computerized stock inventory using barcode scanning equipment. • Keep shelves stocked and keep display areas clean and orderly. • Order stock. • Help customers find the products they're looking for. • Operate cash register.

	Food Counter Attendants, Kitchen Helpers, and Related Occupations (NOC code 6641)	Grocery Clerks and Store Shelf Stockers (NOC code 6622)
Possible Duties	• Wash cooking pots, cups, glassware, cutlery, and plates by dishwasher or by hand.	
Qualifications	More and more complex, automated equipment is being used in kitchens so some special training may be required. Cafe and restaurant owners are usually looking for young employees. However, some fast food companies recruit mature people, including retired people, who can do part-time work.	Some secondary school education is usually required.
Wages, Hours, and Working Conditions	The average starting wage for workers with no experience is $7 to $8 per hour. Annual average employment income (full-time and full year) is $16,000. Full-time food service workers who work all year earn about $20,000 per year.	The average starting wage for workers with no experience is $7 to $8 per hour. Annual average employment income (full-time and full year) is $16,000. After some training to operate cash registers, optical price scanners, computers, or other equipment, you may work as a cashier. Full-time cashiers who work all year earn about $20,000 per year.

Adapted from: National Occupational Classification, CIC. Human Resources and Social Development Canada.

Tip: Jobs in the food service industry can be hard and the income is relatively low. So, you would not likely want to do this type of work for a long time. However, they can be excellent short-term survival jobs.

4.9 Seasonal Work

Situation

Seasonal work is a popular means of temporary income in Canada. This type of work is often the best source of income for newcomers studying at colleges or universities (but is certainly not limited to students). Where and how can you find seasonal jobs, and is this type of work suitable for you?

Information

When most people think of seasonal work, they think of summer jobs. And it's true that there are more temporary jobs during the summer than at any other time of year.

During the winter, however, many people find work plowing snowy streets, maintaining ice surfaces at skating rinks, working at ski resorts, and working in the retail industry during the extremely busy pre-Christmas season. (These retail positions usually become available in late autumn.)

Every spring, many people with bookkeeping and accounting backgrounds find temporary work helping to prepare income tax returns.

Municipal Jobs

All Canadian cities and towns offer temporary summer jobs. These jobs are usually in places of entertainment.

To find information about these types of jobs, call or visit your city hall or municipal offices, or do an Internet search using the name of your city, or another municipality, as keywords. This will lead you to your municipality's

---

Here are some places newcomers can apply for seasonal work:

- Amusement parks, annual fairs, and exhibitions;
- Tourist attractions such as zoos and water parks;
- Student gardening/lawn services; painting, landscaping, roofing, and similar businesses;
- Golf, tennis, and lawn tennis clubs;
- Museums, archives, libraries, and historic sites;
- Canadian Forces Reserves (military); and
- Gardener, grass cutter, golf course worker, grounds maintenance worker, maintenance worker, gardening helper, landscape labourer, and facility maintenance staff.

---

website. On that site, enter keywords like "summer jobs" or "parks and recreation."

Farming

One source of many summer jobs in British Columbia, Ontario, and Quebec is fruit and vegetable farming. Because the Canadian summer is so short, most of the outdoor work happens during four or five months.

Wages for harvest workers (pickers) range widely, depending on the skill of the picker and what kind of produce they are harvesting. You won't get rich doing this, but you can expect to earn between $50 and $185 per day. Fruit and vegetable picking is extremely hot, hard work, and it is nearly always paid as **piecework**. This means that the more you pick, the more you earn. (You are not paid by the hour.)

To find harvesting work, contact local agricultural labour organizations such as the Agricultural Labour Pool in Abbotsford, British Columbia.

Tree Planting

Tree planting begins in April and, in British Columbia, employers pay up to 50 cents per tree planted. In Alberta and Ontario the wages are a bit lower. Income can reach $100 a day—it's even possible to earn up to $200 a day. Charges for food and shelter are about $150 a week.

For this work, you will need waterproof clothes and comfortable, durable footwear. You will also need to be very physically fit.

Fishing

In the Atlantic provinces, seasonal work is available in fishing and fish processing. Most of these jobs go to local residents, though. Fishing vessel deckhands have to be physically active and skilled at commercial fishing. They also need to be familiar with personal survival techniques (the job can be dangerous). Jobs for labourers in fish processing include cannery labourer, fish briner, fish salter, fish weigher, and shellfish packer.

Adapted from: National Occupational Classification, CIC. Work Your Way Around the World. (Oxford, 2005).

Tip: The application deadline for summer positions is often in February or even earlier. It's never too soon to start making inquiries to make sure that you're first in line!

Key Words

bonded: legally guaranteed

chauffeurs: people whose job is to drive a car for somebody else

debt: a sum of money that you owe somebody

firearm: a gun that you can carry

live-in: (about a person) who lives with you

manual work: work that requires you to use your hands

piecework: work that is paid for by the amount done and not by the hours worked

precaution: something that you do in order to avoid danger or problems

survival job: a temporary position that people accept while they work towards gaining more experience for better positions

Note: Entries taken or adapted from the Oxford ESL Dictionary.

Creating Your Canadian Experience

1. You may be most qualified for survival jobs that are in your field, and these jobs may help you to network and can even lead to a permanent job. List three survival jobs that you could apply for.

   a. _____

   b. _____

   c. _____

2. Many people find that self-employment can be a good way to earn some extra income. List three talents or skills you have that you may be able to use to earn additional income.

a. _____

b. _____

c. _____

3. Look in your local phone book, or search the Internet, for three temp agencies that you could contact about temporary work.

Agency	Contact Information	Type of Work They Offer

4. List three friends you could contact about finding work as a babysitter (child caregiver). Be sure to ask if they have any friends that might need help.

a. _____

b. _____

c. _____

5. With your spouse or a friend, discuss the pros and cons of being a delivery driver or a taxi driver.

6. Write down three construction sites that you have recently seen in your area that you could visit to ask about work as a labourer. (If you haven't seen any sites yet, walk or drive around your neighbourhood to find them.)

a. _____

b. _____

c. _____

7. Search the Internet to find out about seasonal jobs in your area and when they are in demand.
   Tip: Search using keywords "[your city]" + "seasonal work"

Seasonal Job	Season

8. If you decide to take a survival job, you'll need to remember that it is supposed to be a temporary solution (often, to financial problems). Write down a realistic date by which you will return to a career in your chosen field.

_____

Section 2

Your Job Search

If opportunity doesn't knock, build a door.
—Milton Berle

The Visible Job Market

In This Unit

- Understanding the Visible Job Market
- Newspaper Classified Ads
- Job Banks
- Responding to Job Ads

5.1 The Visible Job Market

Problem

The visible job market refers to advertised job openings. Where are the best places to find those job advertisements (ads), and how can you use them to your advantage?

Solution

The visible job market in Canada contains no more than 20 percent of all job **vacancies**. The other 80 percent are not published anywhere and make up the hidden job market.

Job opportunities in the visible job market are the easiest to find and apply for. But, of course, hundreds of your competitors will be applying for the same positions. So it's best to spend no more than 20 percent of your job-searching time looking in the visible job market. Leave 80 percent of your time to explore the hidden job market (see Unit 6).

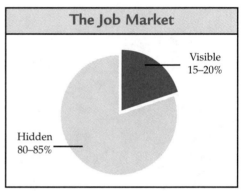

Know Where to Look

Newspapers, Magazines, and Journals

Most job ads are published in city and regional newspapers, in special sections called Classified or Career. But you don't need to buy newspapers every day just to look for job **postings**. You can find free newspapers at libraries and employment resource centres, and in some newspaper boxes on street corners. Some specialized newspapers print only job ads. These can be found at local libraries or they can be delivered to your home if you subscribe to them.

Magazines and scholarly journals also print job ads.

Internet Job Banks and Recruiters' Websites

Great opportunities for searching job ads are available on the Internet. There, you can find websites devoted only to jobs, called "job search engines" or "**job banks**." These sites contain job postings and other information connected with employment.

If you are interested in employment opportunities across Canada, you can find provincial job bank sites with job ads related to any province or territory. You can also look up industry job banks, which collect job ads from specific industries and post them in one place.

The best source of job ads across Canada is a job bank website provided by Human Resources and Social Development Canada (HRSDC). To find it, just do a web search by typing "HRSDC" and "job bank."

Recruiters (also known as "headhunters") work for employers to seek suitable employees. They have websites with job ads, too. You cannot contact the employers directly using these ads because the recruiters are paid to find employees for the employer. Therefore, they do not publish the names and addresses of employers. You must contact the recruiter instead.

Many job-search websites will ask you to sign up for a service called Job Alert. After your registration, a Job Alert agent will send you free job ads related to your field by e-mail. Do not overlook this service! It can often lead to success.

Help Wanted Signs

Stores, restaurants, cafés, and offices sometimes post "help wanted" signs in their windows. You may apply for these jobs simply by walking into the place of business with your resume and cover letter. Ask to speak to the manager. Be prepared to answer some questions or even to fill out an application or to have an interview right away.

After finding a job ad that interests you, look carefully at all the available information and contact the employer. Do this by phone, mail, or e-mail. If you make contact by mail or e-mail, be sure to include your resume and cover letter.

Tip: Be careful when answering job ads, especially if you use Internet sites offering paid job-searching services. In Canada, official job-searching services are free!

5.2 Newspaper Classified Ads

Problem

The best way to enter the visible job market in Canada is to look at job (or "help wanted") advertisements. Many job ads are published in the Classified or Careers section of newspapers. How, and where, can you find the newspapers that print these ads?

Solution

National and Local Newspapers

Canada's leading national daily newspaper, the *Globe and Mail*, is aimed at university- and college-educated professionals. Many job ads for supervisory or management positions are placed in their Careers and Classified sections, particularly in the Monday, Wednesday, and Friday issues. These jobs ads can also be found on the *Globe and Mail* website. On this site, you may register your name and submit ten copies of your resume (free of charge) to their CareerAlert! service. This service selects job ads in your field from the *Globe and Mail* database and sends them to your e-mail address on a regular basis.

CanWest Global Communications Corporation publishes 10 major newspapers and 23 smaller dailies across most of Canada, from Victoria to Montreal. On their website, you can check out any of the individual newspapers and most of the major daily newspapers, including the *National Post*. You will also find the following newspapers:

- Western Canada: Victoria's *Times Colonist*, *The Vancouver Sun*, Vancouver's *The Province*, the *Calgary Herald*, the *Edmonton Journal*, Saskatoon's *The StarPhoenix*, and Regina's *Leader-Post*
- Eastern Canada: the *Ottawa Citizen*, the *Windsor Star*, and Montreal's *The Gazette*

For newcomers living in Toronto, the most popular daily newspaper is the *Toronto Star*. It has two sections of job ads—Careers and Classifieds. The Careers section has separate segments for general help wanted, office help, skilled engineers, and technical postings, including mechanics and electricians.

Employer Experience

Employers use different ways to find employees. Each one has a different cost. Placing an ad in the newspaper is quite inexpensive in comparison to using an executive headhunter. The amount of money employers spend is based on the level of the position they are trying to fill.

Candidates should keep this in mind when they are searching for work. If you are looking for a high-level job, you are much more likely to find it in magazines or journals whose readers are high-level employees or on recruiters' (headhunters') websites. If you are looking for an entry-level position, search in places that would not charge high fees for ads, such as newspapers or websites.

Career Newspapers

Career (or job-search) newspapers contain only job ads.

- Mediacorp Canada Inc. publishes a weekly job-search newspaper called *Canada Employment Weekly*. You can buy a three-month subscription to have this newspaper delivered to your home. For a smaller fee, you can buy a password that allows you to read it online for three months.
- *Canada Employment Weekly* contains more than 1,000 job ads. The publisher states that their newspaper brings readers thousands of new career-level positions in over 80 occupations. All the positions in each issue are new every week.

Tip: Many excellent local and national newspapers, as well as career newspapers, can be used free of charge in the periodicals section of your public library.

5.3 Magazine Job Ads

Problem

Canadian **trade magazines** and newsletters for different professions are good sources for job ads. By subscribing to one that relates to your field, you may find a job. You will also remain updated on the latest news in your occupation. You'll learn about important events and discover the names of contacts who may be able to help you in your job search. What trade magazines are published in Canada, and how can they be found?

Solution

Libraries

Trade magazines published by professional associations, public organizations, and business companies can be found at the library. Many of them have Career and Classified sections with job ads for your profession. Generally speaking, the larger the library, the more magazines you will find. Ask a librarian for help if you cannot find a magazine directed to your occupation.

On the Internet

Many magazines have their own websites on the Internet, and these sites typically include numerous job ads. Below are some of the magazines that have websites, along with the types of ads posted there.

- *Marketing Magazine* (www.marketingmag.ca). Click Career Central and then Classifieds. On the left, you will find ten groups of trades in the column entitled Available Positions. After clicking on any of these positions, you will see the most current job ads.
- *CA Magazine* (www.camagazine.com/index.cfm?ci_id=13941&la_id=1). Includes job ads for bookkeepers, accountants, and those in the financial sector.
- *Canadian Apparel*, the fashion industry magazine (cam.apparel.ca/eng/index.cfm). Offers career opportunities for fashion designers, cutters, and tailors.

- *University Affairs* (www.universityaffairs.ca). Shows vacancies in Canada's institutions of higher learning.
- *Bakers Journal* (www.bakersjournal.com). Posts job ads from across Canada for bakers.
- *Canadian Medical Association Journal* (www.cmaj.ca). Caters specifically to medical workers.
- *Canadian Insurance Magazine* (www.cdnins.com). Caters specifically to insurance agents.
- *Materials Management and Distribution* (www.bizlink.com/materialsmanagementdistribution.htm). Posts jobs available in logistics.
- *Northern Miner* (www.northernminer.com/products/northernminer/nm.asp). Posts mining industry jobs.
- *Pharmacy Gateway* (www.pharmacygateway.ca). Caters specifically to pharmacists.

More Magazines in Print

Despite the increasing number of magazines now on the Internet, many magazines and newsletters are still available only in printed format (although a few have online supplements). Here are some such magazines, where you will find useful job ads: *Computing Canada, Canadian Footwear Journal, Medical Post, Canadian Nurse, Canadian Gardening, Canadian Jeweller, The Lawyers Weekly, Canadian Machinery and Manufacturing, Pharmacy Post,* and *Canadian Textile Journal.*

Tip: First read the latest news in your field in a professional magazine. At some point, you may decide to write and send in your own article, or even your own ad, to the magazine. Professional exposure improves your credibility, and this increases your chances of finding a job in your field.

5.4 Job-Scam Ads

Situation

Some ads are intended to deceive and cheat you. These are called "job-scam" ads. How can you distinguish these ads from real, legitimate ads, and which job-scam ads are the most common?

Information

A legitimate employer would never ask you to pay for equipment, training, or anything else as a condition of employment. They are supposed to be paying you. You may want to ask more questions about the position and do more research on the company before going any further. Also, be cautious of ads that do not contain an employer's name, address, or phone number; instead, you will see only a mailbox or fax number. These are referred to as "blind ads." Advertisers have different reasons for hiding their name and address. For example, they might not want competitors to find out what they are doing.

Be cautious of blind ads. It's possible that your current firm is advertising and that you could send your resume to your own boss! It's also a way for people that are trying to scam not to be tracked. One newspaper published a blind ad that appeared to be from a modelling school asking pretty girls to send in their photos. It turned out that a young man had decided to wallpaper his bedroom with photos of young beauties.

Typical Job Scams

"Work-at-Home" Scams

Newcomer Elena was interested in an ad that read, "Work at Home. Assembly of Christmas tree decorations. Easy work, earn $1,000 a week." She paid $35 and received materials with a sample and assembly instructions. She assembled one decoration and sent it to the employer for quality testing.

After a couple of days, she received congratulations. The decoration had been approved and she was hired. All she needed to do was send in $150 for materials and she would be on her way to riches. But something bothered Elena. The quality of the decoration was estimated in percentages, and hers was ranked at 82 percent. She was told that if the quality ever fell below 80 percent, the decoration would not be bought. It would be returned to her to be fixed.

She was only 3 percent away from failure! She also read that the quality of the decoration was based on about 100 different factors. Therefore, it would be all too easy to drop from 82 percent to 79 percent. Elena then estimated the time spent for assembly and realized she would earn between $1 and $2 per hour.

She stopped work immediately, but hundreds of others went on to waste their time and their $150.

"Help Wanted" Scams

Newcomer Anna responded to a help wanted sign she saw in a bakery. The employer told her that she would have to work as a volunteer for the first week. During this time, she would have to become skilled at her duties, learn the names of the bakery products, and become an expert at working with customers. The employer would then decide whether or not she was good enough to be hired full-time.

Anna agreed. During that first week, she worked very hard to impress her employer. She carried boxes of bread, cleaned the bakery, and put baked goods in the show windows.

Then, after all her hard work, the employer told Anna that she did not fit the job description. She was told to leave.

"Experience Not Required" Scams

Some job ads will say that experience is not required and that the employer will provide training. Be warned! This may mean you will have to pay for the training.

Newcomer Peter answered an ad like this. He took training to work as a croupier at a casino. There was a promise of huge earnings. After paying $400 for training, Peter was allowed to work with clients at a card table. During his first day at work, the manager watched and told him he was working too slowly. Peter tried to work faster, but then he made mistakes in his calculations and was scolded. After his third mistake, he was asked to leave. He would be allowed to come back only if he paid for training again. Peter did not return.

5.5 Provincial Job Banks

Situation

Every province in the country now has one or more job banks specifically for jobs in that province. These sources of information will help you to focus on regions that need workers in your field. What are the addresses of some reliable job banks, and what can you find from these sources?

Information

This chart will tell you more about the job banks listed on the websites of Canada's provinces and territories.

Canada's Job Banks	
Province	**Where to Look**
British Columbia	**www.BCJobs.com** By clicking on View All Jobs, you will find all of the site's available job listings in British Columbia (BC). You can also post your resume on this site so potential employers might see it. On the BC Government website, you'll find job openings in different cities and areas. You can register to use the large job database at **www.britishcolumbiajobs.com**.
Alberta	**www.pao.gov.ab.ca/jobs** On this website, you can focus on an industry you are interested in or look at all job ads on the site. Register your e-mail address to receive monthly job ads in your field from their job alert service.
Saskatchewan	**www.gov.sk.ca/careers** Here, you can find detailed information about this province and useful tips for employment.
Manitoba	**www.gov.mb.ca/csc** This website offers information about various employment programs in Manitoba. Jobs in Winnipeg, Manitoba's capital city, are presented on **www.allwinnipegjobs.com**.
Ontario	**www.jobsontario.net** This site includes ads for jobs in Ontario, and **www.torontojobs.ca** allows you to post your resume and to order job alert services.
Quebec	**www.quebecjobs.com** Although this site is written in English, you must be fluent in French to work in Quebec.

Province	Where to Look
Nova Scotia	**www.gov.ns.ca/psc** **www.careerbeacon.com/corpprof/govns/govns.html** These sites allow you to send out your resume and become acquainted with employment programs in the province. Additional opportunities for those in search of work in Nova Scotia are available at **www.theworkplace.ca/page.asp?sect=19**.
New Brunswick	**www.find-a-job-canada.com/nb.html** This site features jobs in many areas of the province, including the capital city of Fredericton, the cities of Saint John and Moncton, and the northern region of the province. You may also subscribe to regular job alert services. Note that in parts of New Brunswick, knowing French is an asset.
Newfoundland and Labrador	**regionalhelpwanted.com/home/177.htm?SN=177&** This site contains names and phone numbers where you can find additional information.
Prince Edward Island	**www.peijobs.ca** **www.gov.pe.ca/jobs** These sites give detailed information about PEI and allow you to order job alert services.
Yukon Territory, Northwest Territories, and Nunavut	**www.jobsnorth.ca** **employment.gov.yk.ca**

Tip: Before searching for jobs in any part of Canada, learn more about the region by doing research on provincial or territorial government websites (see Unit 14).

5.6 Industrial Job Banks

Situation

Some Canadian Internet job banks collect job ads related only to specific industries. What are some of these job banks, and how can you find and use them?

Information

You can find industrial job banks using Internet search engines and keywords like "job(s)," the name of your industry, and the name of your province or city.

The Job Bus Canada website is an excellent Canadian website for job-searching by industry. It provides an alphabetical listing of more than 20 industries, from advertising, marketing, and public relations, to transportation. Click on any industry to receive a list of organizations working in this field. Click on any of these organizations to be linked immediately to a site with job ads for that industry.

Tip: When looking for job ads, pay attention to the website's home location. Some may be located in the US or other English-speaking countries around the world—not necessarily Canada.

Specialized Job Banks Devoted to Specific Occupations	
Industry	**Specialized Sites**
Bookkeepers and Financial Workers	**www.payroll.ca** This site includes job ads from across Canada and information about bookkeepers' certification. **www.cma-canada.org** Members of the Society of Certified Management Accountants association can search for job openings in the financial field.
Builders and Construction Workers	**www.frontline.nf.net**
Teachers	**teachingjobs.com** The site provides job ads and allows you to post your resume. **jobsearch.educationcanada.com** This gives information about job openings across Canada.
Engineers and Technicians	**www.frontline.nf.net** The site is a national online index.
Medical Nurses	**www.canadianrn.com** Canada's Nursing website has helpful information, including addresses of medical schools, rules, and advice on how to write a medical resume.
Therapists	**www.cmps.ca** The website has job ads, along with information about licensing doctors in Canada and the US.
Oil and Gas Industry	**www.psac.ca**
Miners	**www.infomine.com/careers**
Tradespeople	**www.canjobs.com** The jobs in retail and sales careers are in sections of the CanJobs website.
Information Technology Professionals (IT)	**www.aboutus.org/PositionWatch.com** **www.computerwork.com** (part of a network called Jobserve) Here, you'll find job ads for IT professionals in Canada's larger cities, including Calgary, Edmonton, Ottawa, Toronto, and Vancouver.
Mechanics and Millwrights	**www.jobs.com** Look for the **Journeyman Mechanics** section.
Hospitality Workers	**www.hcareers.com** You'll find thousands of hospitality jobs on this website.

5.7 Responding to Job Ads

Problem

It's always encouraging to find a job ad that seems to fit your education and experience. But most ads will not be a perfect fit for your experience and skills. How much should your qualifications fit the employer's requirements? How should you respond? And, when you do, what are your chances of success?

Advice and Action Plan

Should You Apply for the Job?

Many people wonder if they should respond to job ads when their skills, education, and/or experience do not fit all the requirements listed. The truth is that you will likely be a good fit if your qualifications match about 50 percent of the requirements. Carefully study the terminology and description of duties in the announcement, and try to use these words in your resume. Also, mention useful qualifications the employer did not ask for—such as fluency in another language or knowledge of international markets.

Pay Attention to Detail

One job ad will usually attract hundreds of resumes. Though only an approximated 5 percent of people find a job using classified job ads, why should you not be among them? It's certainly worth a try. In order to improve your chances you must pay attention to the details.

- Note the name, address, and phone number of the potential employer.
- Make a note of names of executives if these are shown.
- Take notes on the requirements. (Even if you don't get the job, these requirements will give you an understanding of industry standards and expectations.)
- Notice the number of job ads published in your field. (This will give you some sense of the demand for employees in your field.)

Respond to Job Ads

Respond Quickly

Respond to ads quickly—the same day the ad appears, if possible. Pay attention to the deadline for applications (also called the "closing date"). If no date is given, it probably means that resumes will be accepted at any time, or as soon as possible.

Your Cover Letter

- Address your cover letter to the person in the company who is doing the hiring. If their name is not shown in the ad, phone or e-mail the company to find out who this person is. But, do not speak to the person directly and do not give your name. Individuals who are hiring often do not want to get calls or e-mails from candidates.
- At the beginning of the letter, mention where you found the job ad and include the ad number and the name of the position you are applying for.
- Emphasize the skills that most closely fit the requirements of the employer.
- Some ads ask for your salary expectations. Say, "Salary is negotiable," so you do not eliminate yourself right away. This question will be asked again during, or soon after, the interview.

Sending in Your Application

Job ads usually say how to send in your application. These instructions should be followed. However, if there are no instructions, deliver your application in person if possible. Otherwise, send it by mail or courier.

Follow-Up

If you receive no response within about a week of the deadline or closing date, phone or e-mail the potential employer to check that they actually received your application.

Is It Worth It?

Some people think that the chances of getting a job through classified ads are the same as winning a million-dollar lottery. It's true that the chances are not great. But people do win lotteries, and people do find jobs through classified ads, so it's worthwhile to answer these ads. If nothing else, it's great job-searching practice!

> **Tip:** Keep your job applications in a special folder, along with the job ads. Also, keep a log of when you sent in applications and when you followed up. This will create a good job-search database. It will also be useful if you ever need to apply for government social assistance (income support) or Employment Insurance (EI) payments.

5.8 Unit Summary

Key Words

job bank: lists or organizations that show what jobs are available

post: to put a sign, notice, etc. on a wall or in a public place such as an Internet site so that everyone can see it

recruiter: a person who finds new people to join something, such as a company or an organization

trade magazine: a magazine that is written for people in a particular business or job

vacancy: a job opening that has not be filled

Note: Entries taken or adapted from the Oxford ESL Dictionary.

Creating Your Canadian Experience

1. List two publications in each category below that have career sections where you can search for job ads.
   Tip: Try searching the Internet using keywords "[your city]" + "[type of publication]"

Category	Publication	Leads Week 1	Leads Week 2	Leads Week 3	Leads Week 4
Newspaper					
Newspaper					
Career Newspaper					
Career Newspaper					
Trade Magazine					
Trade Magazine					
Provincial Job Bank					
Provincial Job Bank					
Industrial Job Bank					
Industrial Job Bank					

2. In order to find out which publication is the most useful for your occupation and location, keep track of the number of good leads each publication returns on a weekly basis.

3. Ask a friend about job scams that they have heard of and compare stories. Discuss what could have been done to prevent the scam.

4. Do some research to find out which day of the week the newspapers you are looking through have the most number of ads.
   Tip: Try calling the newspapers to ask them, or ask friends or classmates.

5. On your computer or in a notebook, create a sheet with the headings in the table below. Keep track of the resumes you send out and the responses you receive from your search in the visible job market.

Date	Company	Position	Publication	Action Taken	Response

The Hidden Job Market

In This Unit

- Understanding the Hidden Job Market
- Finding Potential Employers
- The Art of Networking
- Employment Agencies

6.1 The Hidden Job Market

Situation

Many jobs in Canada are advertised, but most are not. These non-advertised jobs are part of the hidden job market. How can you find jobs in this market?

Information

Of all the jobs available in Canada, 80 percent are in the hidden job market. That's why it's so important to look for these non-advertised jobs.

Why Would Employers Hide Jobs?

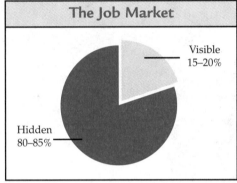

- Some corporations don't want their competitors to know they're looking for applicants. If they advertised, competitors might learn that they were increasing production or opening new places of operation (new branches).
- Some companies might want to replace existing employees (by firing them or through layoffs), but they don't want these employees to know, so they don't advertise.
- Some places prefer to hire people they already know or people recommended by colleagues.
- Some companies are too small to have a **human resources** (HR) department or manager. So they may ask employees, relatives, and friends for suggestions. They may also apply to recruiters, employment agencies, and search firms.
- Some companies simply want to avoid having to respond to large numbers of inappropriate applicants.

Know How to Find the Hidden Jobs

- Ask relatives, friends, acquaintances, neighbours, and colleagues for help or advice. Tell them that you are searching for a job and give them your resume. Talk about your job search with teachers and classmates from your English courses. Tell other people you know who are looking for work.
- Contact recruiters, employment agencies, or search firms.
- **Distribute** your resume to firms and companies in the industries where you would like to work. Ask for the name of someone you can contact to check that they have received your resume. At the same time, ask for an informational interview. If yours is the right resume at the right time, you may even get the job.
- Visit job fairs. These are regularly organized by government, public, and private organizations. At these job fairs, it is possible to meet personally with employers without scheduling an interview. You can usually give them your resume and they might even interview you at that time.
- Contact professional associations in your field. These associations will have lists of companies, as well as addresses, phone numbers, and e-mail addresses.
- Send your resume to resume banks (see 6.9) on the Internet. Many employers visit these resume banks to search for skilled workers.

Job hunting in the hidden job market is not easy. You will need patience, creativity, courage, and persistence. But since this market has 80 percent of the jobs, the effort will be worth it!

Tip: If you conquer the hidden job market, you will beat your competitors. Most of them are fighting for the smaller number of positions in the visible job market

6.2 Find Employers Locally, Provincially, and Nationally

Situation

To enter the hidden job market, you will need to hunt for businesses that operate in your field. To help you in your search, take a look at Canadian business directories. What information can you find in directories, and where are these business directories found?

Information

The Information You'll Find

Business directories will provide you with the following kinds of information:

- Names, addresses, phone numbers, fax numbers, e-mails, and websites of businesses
- Names of people on administrative boards
- Manufacturing processes and services
- Standard Industrial Classification (SIC) or North American Industry Classification System (NAICS) codes
- The number and location of branch offices or franchises (if any)
- The location of the head office and the company's budget

Take into consideration how long a company has been in business—are they growing or becoming smaller? Does the company have a good future?

Business Directories

Business directories can be found in public libraries and employment resource centres.

Taking It Online	
Website Name	**Website Address**
Dun & Bradstreet Database	www.dnb.ca/about/ourdatabase/default.html
NAICS	www.naics.com
SIC	www.osha.gov/pls/imis/sic_manual.html

There are two types of directories: geographical and industrial. Geographical directories contain information about firms and companies located in particular provinces, cities, or even on certain streets. Industrial directories, however, list businesses by industry. Be sure to do a complete search. Look in local, provincial, and national business directories.

Local Directories

- If you want to find work in a city—for example, in Vancouver, Montreal, or Halifax—ask for the business directory for that city at your local public library.
- A popular directory in Metro Toronto is the two-volume *Scott's Greater Toronto Business Directory*.
  - The first volume covers Metro Toronto, and the second volume, the Toronto Boundary edition, covers outlying areas.
  - Each volume contains both alphabetic and industry indexes.

Some directories are based on the SIC, while others are based on the NAICS.

Industrial Classification Systems

Whichever directory you use, it helps to know the special industry code for the type of business you're looking for. There are two code systems used in business directories: the old one—SIC, and the new one—NAICS.

Canada adopted the NAICS in 2000 because it is used and understood by the US, Canada, and Mexico. The six-digit NAICS codes identify specific industries and types of operations, and they also contain a country code.

Provincial Directories

Whatever province you live in, you will find one or more directories that focus specifically on providing information about businesses in your province. Most provincial directories sort businesses by both city and industry. They often include lists of the largest firms and companies (with 100 workers or more).

National Directories

To find more than 1.5 million businesses throughout Canada, look for the directory called *Dun & Bradstreet Canada*. It can be found in public libraries.

Tip: Directories are a great place to start when you are searching for a company where you might want to work. Keep in mind, though, that there are thousands of businesses that do not appear in any directories.

6.3 Find Employers by Industry

Problem

Industry directories can help you focus on companies in your own field. What information do they contain, and where can you find industry directories?

Solution

The Information You'll Find

Industry directories present information about companies in certain fields, such as the automotive, pharmaceutical, or service industries. They contain the following kinds of information:

- Names, addresses, phone numbers, fax numbers, e-mails, and websites of businesses
- The names of people on administrative boards

Reliable directories usually contain detailed information. For example, the *Canadian Directory of Shopping Centres* lists stores and shops located at each shopping centre, as well as ownership, management, and administrative contact information.

On a larger scale, *The Blue Book of Canadian Business* contains two full pages of information approximately 2,500 large Canadian firms with an annual financial turnover of not less than $10 million.

Canada's Top 100 Employers directory contains detailed descriptions of the one hundred companies that the authors claim have the best conditions for employees.

Taking It Online

Website Name	Website Address
Canada's Top 100 Employers	www.canadastop100.com

Find Business Directories

You can find directories either on the Internet or in public libraries. Don't hesitate to ask a librarian for help in locating them.

Examples of Industry Directories

Some of the following industry directories might be helpful to you. But it's also a good idea to do your own Internet search for a directory that is especially useful for you!

- *Aerospace Industries Association of Canada (AIAC) Guide to Canada's Aerospace Industry*
- *Canadian Chemical Directory*
- *Canadian Directory of Shopping Centres*
- *Canadian Medical Directory*
- *Canadian Oil Register*
- *Plastic: UHMW*
- *Directory of Restaurant and Fast Food Chains in Canada*
- *Financial Services Canada*
- *Food in Canada Buyers' Guide*
- *National Graphic Design Services*
- *Pulp and Paper Canada*
- *Pharmacy Sourcebook: Your Complete Guide to the Canadian Pharmacy Market*
- *TCA Annual Construction Industry Membership Directory & Buyers' Guide*

Tip: *The Blue Book of Canadian Business* and the *Directory of Canadian Manufacturers* (nicknamed the "BOSS") both feature companies that want to cooperate with foreign partners. These will be useful resources if you are interested in establishing links between Canadian companies and an industry in your home country.

6.4 The Art of Networking

Situation

The best way to enter the hidden job market is through networking. What does networking mean? How can you create your own **network** in Canada, and how can you use it to find a job?

Advice and Action Plan

Almost every day, we communicate with a certain number of people. These people make up our networks. They may include relatives and friends, neighbours and colleagues, or teachers and schoolmates. The average adult's network includes hundreds, or even thousands, of people.

The people in your network can become good contacts in your job search. It's important to keep records of their names, addresses, phone and fax numbers, and e-mail addresses in a notebook. Make sure your network includes people in your field of work, potential employers, and employment agencies. There are three ways to network: in person, by phone, and in writing (by e-mail, fax, or letter).

In-Person Contacts

When you are meeting face-to-face with friends, colleagues, or other contacts, tell them you are searching for a job. Explain the type of job you are looking for and give them a "calling card." A calling card is printed, like a business card. Also include a brief description of your skills, education, experience, and the type of position you are looking for.

To set up an in-person meeting, e-mail or phone the person you want to meet with. Ask if you can arrange an appointment with this contact person.

It is sometimes possible to go to a place of business without an appointment. However, you may not get an interview. If this happens, simply thank the person you are speaking with for their time. It is generally better to make an appointment before going to a place of business.

Telephone Contacts

There are two sorts of telephone contacts—warm calls and cold calls.

Warm calls are made to people who already know you or who are expecting your call. Do not hesitate to say that you are searching for a job and ask for advice or help. Appropriate questions include: Can you give me any advice about how to contact potential employers? Does your company currently have vacancies? Would you be able to recommend me for an

Immigrant Experience

Before she immigrated, Sylvia came to visit her brother and sister who had moved to Canada several years earlier. She asked them many questions about their new country, including one about how to meet potential employers when looking for work. They had been in Canada for some time, so they told her of the importance of networking. They stressed the value of meeting new people who might one day introduce her to a potential employer.

During her first few months in Canada, Sylvia was overwhelmed by culture shock and forgot her brother and sister's advice. One day, however, she went out for dinner with her sister and some friends. During the meal, her sister's friend mentioned a job opening for an administrator at her workplace. The job required the very skills that Sylvia had. With some encouragement from her sister, Sylvia applied for the job and was called in for an interview. Based on this experience, Sylvia now reminds friends that networking is very important!

interview? May I use your name as a reference? Could you call me back if you hear of an opening? (An "opening" is an available job.)

Cold calls are made to people who do not know you, or who do know you but are not expecting your call. Before you make a cold call, write down what you plan to say. This type of communication is an art that takes practice to master. By making cold calls, however, you may discover information you wouldn't have learned in another way. For example, you might happen to call on a day when an employer has posted a job ad (see 6.5 and 6.6).

Written Contacts

Writing is a simple and pleasant way to contact a person. You can take as much time as you need to write a letter and get it right before sending it by fax, regular mail, or e-mail. There is a drawback to writing letters, though. Out of one hundred letters sent to strangers, you would be lucky to receive five replies. And most of those will just thank the sender for their interest.

Tip: Are you shy or reserved? Don't worry. You can improve your communication skills with practice. Consider taking a course on communication skills.

6.5 Cold Calls

Problem

To find opportunities in the hidden job market, one of the most powerful tools is the cold call. How can you best use a cold call to your advantage?

Solution

A cold call is a phone call to someone you've never met, or someone you have met but who is not expecting your call. You have likely received many cold calls from people trying to sell you something. These sales people are called "telemarketers." Telemarketers (and often regular salespeople) are sometimes required to do up to 50 cold calls per day. If done properly, no other sales tool is nearly as effective.

From now on, treat telemarketing calls as a learning experience. When you get one, do not hang up. Pay close attention to the caller's methods. Figure out what the caller is doing poorly and what he is doing well to win your attention. How much time does he spend introducing himself? How does he describe the purpose of his call? Does he sound as if he believes in the product or service he is selling? Does talking to him make you want to hear more or does it make you want to hang up? Use what you have learned to improve your own cold calls.

How to Make Effective Cold Calls

Pronounce Names Correctly

Before you call any potential employers, call the receptionist of the company first to get a correct pronunciation of the employer's name.

Call the Right Person

To find the names of potential employers, look in business directories in libraries or on the Internet (see 6.2 and 6.3). Avoid calls to human resource departments. They will often just tell you that there are no vacancies. But if you contact the head of a department, they may become interested in your skills, education, and experience.

Prepare in Advance

- Work hard to learn the proper pronunciation of words that you are likely to use in the conversation. Find a course or program that offers telephone training with an English teacher.
- Try to learn as much as possible about the company you are calling, its production or services, and any of its problems.
- Write down convincing reasons why the employer should hire you. Define what you can offer him and practise saying these things out loud ahead of time.

Start Calling!

As soon as you are confident in your knowledge of the English language and how it can be used in cold calling, start making cold calls on a regular basis. Don't be discouraged if you see no immediate results. At least you will be making your name known in the hidden job market.

Ask for Advice

When you do connect with a potential employer, ask them for advice or about how they became involved in the industry. People love to give advice and to talk about themselves when they have time. It's also a good idea to ask for names of other people who might give you advice.

How to Handle "No"

Be prepared for people who refuse to speak with you, who hang up on you, or employers who say that there are no vacancies at present. Do not take it personally. If the conversation doesn't seem to be going as you had hoped, thank the employer for his time and end the conversation politely. Then try again in a couple of weeks or call someone else at that office.

If a secretary or assistant does not let you talk to the employer, ask when you might be able to call back. Never leave a voice mail message. If you do, your call will likely get lost among others.

Tip: To make sure your call goes as well as possible, create a plan, script, or point-form notes before you pick up the phone. Before the call, set these notes in front of you, along with your resume, information about the company you're calling, a calendar, and a pen and paper. Standing or sitting up straight may help you speak more clearly and confidently (see 6.6).

6.6 Cold-Calling Script

Problem
Now that you understand cold calls and their purpose, you must learn the most effective way of approaching a cold call. What should you say to leave a good impression and get the most information?

Solution
Having a prepared cold-calling script will help to ensure success. Below is a sample cold-calling script. The dialogue is shown in italics. Write your own script to make sure that you are comfortable with the wording. Your script should give you a chance to talk about everything you want to talk about. Read it over many times, both silently and out loud. Practise it with friends, family members, and fellow job hunters. And don't hesitate to change it a bit as you go along.

1. Speaking to the secretary or assistant
   Hello, may I speak with _____?

   > Make sure to ask for the person by their full name. Do not use Mr. or Ms. If you mispronounce the person's surname, the secretary will likely correct you. This is valuable information.

2. Speaking to the potential employer
   Hello, my name is _____.
   I've worked for _____ years as a _____ in _____,
   and _____ recommended that I call you.

   > When you get through to the person you are calling, begin by introducing yourself.

   Or, if no one referred you, introduce yourself in this way:

   > Be sure to give the name of the person who referred you.

   <u>Your company</u> came to my attention while I was researching the leading firms in my field. I was wondering if there were any unadvertised employment opportunities at your company or in your department.

   [Wait for a response.]

   > If you have the right person, carry on with the conversation. If not, get the appropriate contact information. If they try to direct you to human resources, take the names, but carry on with the current conversation.

3. *Are you the person I should be speaking with or should I talk to someone else?*

Immigrant Experience

Soon after coming to Canada, Judith learned that to find a job she would have to call people she had never met to discuss job openings and qualifications. That is, she'd have to make cold calls. Although her English was a bit weak, she felt optimistic that she would be given interviews based on her friendly and outgoing personality. What she did not expect, however, was how strongly her language level would affect potential employers' first impressions of her ability to perform a job in Canada.

Judith soon realized that to make her cold calls effective, she would have to improve her English. So she took additional language courses. Now her English skills help her make a good impression!

4. If the person is willing to talk to you, be polite and be brief. The conversation should last **no more than ten minutes**. Begin by describing your workplace skills—both hard skills (specific knowledge and training related to the occupation) and soft skills (people and social skills). Describe why you think you would be a good fit for the company.

5. *I would appreciate the chance to speak with you in person. I would like to*

   _____.

6. *Thank you for taking the time to talk to me. I look forward to meeting you at the interview/in the future.*

> Give them a reason why the meeting would be a good idea both for yourself and for the company (for example, it would give you a chance to show them your portfolio, give them your resume, and give them a chance to evaluate you face-to-face).

Tip: When you practise your script with friends, be sure to go through many different possible answers so that you are prepared for any situation.

6.7 Job Fairs

Situation

One way to uncover the hidden job market in Canada is through job fairs. What are job fairs, who attends them, and how do they work?

Information

Job fairs are conducted on a regular basis in many cities throughout Canada. They are large gatherings of businesses and people looking for work. They are places to gather information about your industry or specific employers. They are also good places to hand out your resume.

How Do Job Fairs Work and Who Attends Them?

- Admission to job fairs is usually free, but be prepared to pay a small fee.
- Each potential employer at a job fair has a display (a booth or a table) with flyers or booklets. **Representatives** will tell you about the advantages of the firm and accept resumes.
- Some job fairs feature large companies. Others are devoted to special groups such as newcomers, women, or youth.
- Organizations such as Human Resources and Social Development Canada (HRSDC) are usually represented by agencies they fund, including employment resource centres and job-finding clubs.
- Representatives from colleges, business schools, and training centres may also attend to promote their programs of study.
- Employment agencies and recruiters ("headhunters") may also attend. Recruiters are hired by potential employers to find good candidates.

Different fairs are organized by government, public, and private organizations. Advertisements for these fairs usually include a list of potential employers who will attend. Even if you are not sure what company interests you, it is worthwhile to attend some fairs. You never know what opportunities you might find.

There are several benefits of attending a job fair.
- You can become acquainted with potential employers and organizations who attend the fair.
- You can learn about job vacancies and job requirements.
- You can distribute your resume, cover letter, and references.
- You might be given a short interview by a potential employer.
- You will meet many more contacts at a job fair than you would over several weeks or months of searching on your own.

Peter's Personal Experience

In my opinion, there are advantages and disadvantages to job fairs. It is really hard to find work at a job fair. I don't know if there are statistics about how many people are hired through these fairs, but I know only a few people who have found work this way.

I have attended some job fairs myself; the potential employers take your resume, ask you some basic questions, and give you some written information about their organization. If you're lucky, you'll get a call from them. Usually, you don't hear back.

I don't think companies really want to hire people at job fairs. Instead, they collect resumes and save them for future use. That's why people go to job fairs—to distribute their resumes. The company might call you when there is a job opening or, if you call the company, you can mention that you met their representatives at the fair.

How Should You Prepare?

- Before you go to a job fair, assemble your resume, calling cards, references, portfolio, and Social Insurance Number (SIN).
- Dress professionally.
- If you are nervous about going alone, you could attend the fair with a friend who is also looking for employment. But if you go with a friend, make sure you talk to people separately, as well as together.

Find a Job Fair near You

Look for announcements about job fairs in newspapers, in flyers, and in and pamphlets at employment resource centres, job-finding clubs, and libraries. Also look for announcements on the websites of agencies like employment resource centres and conference centres.

Tip: If a company is participating in a job fair, they may likely be looking for new employees. Consider visiting their human resources department before the fair in order to get more background on the company.

6.8 Employment Agencies

Situation

Many newcomers find work in the hidden job market using employment agencies. How can these agencies help you find a job?

Information

There are thousands of employment agencies, recruiters, search firms, headhunters, or temporary employment agencies (temp agencies) in Canada. Their representatives bring potential employers and potential employees together. Before you use an employment agency, however, do some research to find out if it will really help you.

Which Agency Will be Best for You?

When you look up various agencies, ask yourself these questions:

- Does the agency specialize in your profession or trade? (Many agencies search for professionals, but there are firms who look for tradespeople as well.)
- What geographical area do they serve?
- Does the agency find jobs for supervisory personnel, or for intermediate positions?
- Can you find a permanent job through this agency, or a temporary or contract job?
- Does the agency do all the hiring for any companies? (Some companies use a particular agency as an **off-site** human resources department. They do nearly all their hiring through this agency.)

Tip: Never pay employment agencies to help you find a job. Potential employers are already paying them to find workers. For you, an agency's service should always be free.

Immigrant Experience

Before Mostafa immigrated to Canada, he did some research into the Canadian job market. He soon realized that the Internet provided a wonderful tool for looking for work. So he spent many months job hunting online. From time to time he came across websites that offered to post his resume in exchange for a fee. Confused by this, Mostafa followed his instincts and avoided these sites. He couldn't imagine that Canadian employers would request that applicants pay a fee to submit their resumes.

It turns out that Mostafa's instincts were right. The Internet sites he avoided were created by job scam agencies that unethically ask for money in exchange for services that should be free. Luckily, Mostafa posted his resume only on government and other well-known websites that don't charge for this service. As a result, he has been called for several interviews and is hoping to find a job in his field soon.

How to Work with an Agency

- Go to an agency's website and become familiar with it.
- Send your resume to the agency by fax or e-mail.
- If you haven't heard from them after about ten days, follow up by calling to confirm that they've received your resume. Before you call, see if you can get the name of the agent from a directory or from the receptionist and be prepared for a conversation. Address the agent using Mr. or Ms. and their surname.
- If an agent thinks you may be appropriate for a potential employer's needs, she will invite you to an interview at the employment agency.
- At the interview, the agent will determine if you fit the potential employer's needs. At the same time, you can get a better idea of whether or not you would like to work for that company.
- If you meet the potential employer's needs, the agent can arrange an interview for you with the employer.
- After this interview, the employer will tell your agent if they want to hire you, and the agent will give you their decision.
- To increase your chances of success, keep in touch with several employment agencies and contact them once a week.
- If an employment agency wants you to sign a contract, read it carefully.

6.9 Resume Banks

Problem

The Internet is used effectively for all types of promotion and marketing by different companies and organizations. You can also use it to promote yourself on the job market. How should you advertise yourself using the Internet?

Solution

You could create your own website and post your resume, portfolio, and other credentials on that site. Another effective method of advertising yourself on the Internet is to send your resume to an Internet resume bank (or job bank).

How Resume Banks Work

- Many employers prefer to look for resumes on job banks rather than to advertise. This is because they can focus on resumes that meet their needs. If they advertise, they might receive hundreds of unsuitable responses.
- Your resume must be submitted to a job bank through e-mail. This means it should be prepared in a format that can be accepted by the bank's e-mail.
- Your resume should also be prepared in a format that an employer can read quickly. Use keywords that reflect your skills, education, and experience, and that reflect the needs of your field of work.

Distinguish the Good from the Bad

- Use only the best-known resume banks (such as those run by large newspapers).
- Make sure that the website is Canadian.

Taking It Online	
Website Name	**Website Address**
SkillsInternational.ca	www.skillsinternational.ca/index-en.php

- If possible, find one or more resume banks directed to your own occupation (such as engineering or medicine).
- Find out about fees. Some resume banks will charge you to post your resume but will give employers free access to the bank. Others will charge employers to browse through the resumes.
- Banks that charge job applicants like yourself will charge an average of $20 to $50 for a term of three months or up to one year. If you are being charged, find out what the fee covers. For example, will the resume bank help you transfer your resume to the electronic, scannable format? Will you be allowed to change or revise your resume free of charge if, after some time, you do not receive many responses?

Posting Advice

- If you are currently working and don't want your employer to know that you are searching for a new job, you can ask the resume bank to post your resume without personal data (personal data includes your name, address, phone number, and e-mail address). If an employer becomes interested in your information, the resume bank will contact you asking for permission to forward a resume that includes your personal information. There is usually a fee for this service.
- Before sending your resume to a particular bank, look over the resumes in your field that are already posted. Compare your skills, education, and experience with those of your competitors. Be sure to revise your resume, if necessary, to make it attractive and competitive.

Tip: SkillsInternational.ca, an Ontario-based resume bank, posts resumes from newcomers who have completed certain Canadian job placement programs. This agency also works with settlement and job placement agencies to convince major Canadian corporations to select new employees from the resume bank. No fees are charged for any participants. (See 8.9.)

6.10 Unit Summary

Key Words

distribute: to give things to a number of people

human resources: the department in a company that is in charge of employing new workers and taking care of all the workers in the company

network: a group of people or companies, etc. that work together closely

off-site: away from a particular place, especially the place where somebody works

representative: a person who has been chosen to act or speak for somebody else or for a group

Note: Entries taken or adapted from the Oxford ESL Dictionary.

Creating Your Canadian Experience

1. Make a list of five people you know who you can talk to about your job search (try to find people that have experience in your industry). Schedule a time to talk to them and record their responses (ask about trends in the industry, the top companies, and other networking opportunities).

Person	Contact Date	Response

2. Using the information about directories in 6.2 and 6.3, make a list of five companies in your field. Contact them about current job vacancies and submitting your resume. Record their responses.

Company	Contact Date	Response

3. Search the Internet and your local career newspapers for job fairs in your area.
   Tip: Use the keywords "job fair" + "[your city]."

Job Fair	Date	Description

4. Search the Internet and your local career newspapers for job agencies that specialize in your occupation and that focus on your part of the country.
   Tip: Search for "[your city]" + "[your occupation]" + "job agency."

Agency Name	Contact Information	Description

5. Search the Internet for three resume banks where you can post your resume.
   Tip: The keywords "resume bank" + "[your city or province]" should give you the most results.

Resume Bank	Web Address	Date Posted	Number of Responses

6. Keep track of any responses in order to see which resume bank is the most effective and suitable for you.

Employment Services in Canada

In This Unit

- Employment Resource Centres
- Professional and Trade Associations in Canada
- Job Finding Clubs

7.1 Service Canada Centres

Situation

The Government of Canada offers a large number of programs and services for almost every part of Canadian society. If you need to find information or application forms for health, language, or employment programs, or if you urgently need financial help, start your search at Service Canada. What is Service Canada and what services do they offer?

Information

Service Canada was created in September of 2005 to provide easy access to a wide range of government services and benefits in one place. As Service Canada has grown and matured, it has become the best way to connect with the services offered by the Government of Canada. Anyone, including newcomers, can contact Service Canada by phone, e-mail, or in person (at a Service Canada Centre) to connect with specific government organizations that could help.

A Year in the Life of Service Canada

Each year, Service Canada …

- pays $65.7 billion in benefits ($180 million per day)
- receives 1.5 million requests for Social Insurance Numbers
- posts 80,000 job ads
- deals with more than 65 million phone calls to the Government of Canada
- posts more than 20 million letters
- provides electronic services to more than 2.5 million Canadians each week

---

Visit Service Canada on the Internet

On the Service Canada website (www.servicecanada.gc.ca), you'll see that this agency pays a lot of attention to newcomers.

- In the Housing section, you'll find information about funding for housing.

- In the Education and Training section, you'll find information about funding for education for families and children, youth and students, newcomers, and people with disabilities.
- In the Employment section, you'll find a job bank, information about Employment Insurance (EI), work permits, and programs for youth.
- In the Health section, you'll find information about health insurance, including temporary health insurance for refugees, refugee claimants, and protected persons.

You'll also find information about income assistance, managing debt, having your credentials recognized, legal assistance, starting a business, and how to become a Canadian citizen.

Visit Service Canada in Person

To find a Service Canada Centre, click on "Find a Service Canada Centre Near You" on the home page of the Service Canada website.

At a Service Canada Centre you can do several tasks:

- You can obtain a Social Insurance Number (SIN) in one visit.
- You are able to access printed copies of Government of Canada forms and publications.
- You can access Government of Canada websites and online forms and publications.
- You are able to obtain assistance in completing forms related to a variety of Government of Canada services, including Employment Insurance (EI) benefits.
- You can use on-site computers and printers.

Service Canada also provides a multi-language extension service program in the Greater Vancouver Area. This is a mobile service that provides Government of Canada information in Punjabi, Cantonese, and Mandarin.

Adapted from: Service Canada Annual Report (2005-06).

Tip: Service Canada centres across Canada now work with the Foreign Credentials Referral Office (FCRO) (see 8.8). Together they help you gain faster recognition of your employment and educational credentials—as well as answering your questions about immigration issues in general.

7.2 Employment Resource Centres

Situation

After you've contacted Service Canada, they will refer you to Employment Resource Centres (ERCs). What are ERCs, and how will they help you in your job search?

Advice and Action Plan

ERCs are self-help job-search centres. They provide free access to the resources you'll need to find a job. At these centres, newcomers have access to computers, the Internet, printers, phones, fax machines, and libraries filled with current newspapers, magazines, and books about employment. Many ERCs have **job boards** where potential employers post job ads.

The best way to use an ERC is to treat it as your workplace. Some ERCs even have rooms where your children can play while you are looking for work. Go there to work at finding a job!

Speak to a Consultant

ERCs have consultants (also called advisors) who can give you advice and assistance. These are some of the things they can do for you:

- They can give you their centre's schedule and tell you what kinds of services they offer.
- They can advise you on your employment problems or answer your employment-related questions—sometimes even in your first language.
- They can assess your background and skills.
- They can help you to create a personal career plan.

Attend a Workshop

- ERCs offer workshops that give you training in useful computer programs such as Microsoft Word, Excel, Access, and Power Point.
- You can learn how to use the Internet and e-mail for job searching, and you'll be given the names of good online job banks.
- At some workshops, you'll learn many of the following skills:
  - You will be taught how to create a resume and cover letter.
  - You will explore the art of networking.
  - You may go over the interview preparation.
- ERC workshops also cover topics such as evaluating international credentials, volunteering as a way to get Canadian experience, and collecting information about potential employers.
- The hidden job market is a theme of many workshops. (See Unit 6.)

Immigrant Experience

Before Thomas came to Canada, he knew it would be difficult to find a job. But he felt confident because he had many friends in Canada who had managed to find a position in their field, so he decided to emigrate from his homeland.

Soon after his arrival, however, he realized that his search for employment would be more difficult than he'd expected. At first, he took a survival job to support himself. But after only a month, he quit so he could spend more time looking for a career in his field. He attended a job-search workshop at an Employment Resource Centre, where he learned about the effective job-search skills for the Canadian labour market. While there, he met a classmate who told him about a co-op program. He hadn't thought about this option before, but he joined the co-op program and was given a work placement.

Five months later the company where he was doing that work placement offered him a job!

Join an Employment Program

Many ERCs have, or can direct you to, 12- to 18-week employment programs. These programs include job-finding clubs and assisted job-search programs. At these programs, you will be trained in job searching, and you'll receive assistance in your job search. You may attend meetings with experts who will tell you about occupations that are in high demand, Canadian job market futures, professional associations, Canadian labour laws, workplace culture, and employability skills.

ERCs will also help you gain Canadian experience by guiding you to co-op programs, volunteer jobs, and subsidized jobs. (See 2.13.)

If you dream of being self-employed, you will find many useful ideas to help you prepare to open your own small business.

Tip: At ERCs, you can meet with other newcomers to practise your English and find new friends. In some ERCs, you can even have your English level evaluated and learn about appropriate language courses or schools.

7.3 Professional and Trade Associations in Canada

Situation

On the Internet and through an Employment Resource Centre (ERC) (see 7.2), you'll be able to find the professional or **trade association** that governs your occupation (see 2.5). These associations protect the public by maintaining high standards of professional training and ethics. They also help people of the same occupation network with each other. How can a professional or trade association help you in your job search?

Information

There are more than 20,000 professional associations and societies in Canada. Some of them are for companies or professions and trades across the country. Others restrict membership to professionals or tradespeople in a particular province or city.

After your arrival in Canada, look for an appropriate professional association in the city or province where you've settled.

There are many benefits you'll receive as a member of a professional association:

- Newsletters, **seminars**, conferences, and exhibitions
- Useful business contacts with specialists
- Information about programs for newcomers
- Rules for obtaining a licence if your profession or trade is regulated in Canada, and assistance in preparation for the licensing exam
- Addresses of members of the association
- The possibility of obtaining a volunteer position in your field
- Information about job banks or an actual job bank on the association website
- The privilege of putting your resume on the association's website for potential employers to see

---

Taking It Online

Website Name	Website Address
CICIC	www.cicic.ca/en/profess.aspx?sortcode=2.19.21.21

Some Notes on Associations

If you want to start your own small business, your association can help you solve problems you might encounter in this process. You may become part of an association connected with your field, or you may become a member of an association of small business owners.

Some provinces have clubs and associations just for newcomers to Canada, such as the PEI Association for Newcomers to Canada.

All large associations have websites and issue newsletters, booklets, or magazines to inform members and customers about production, membership issues, or their services. Some organizations are growing rapidly and becoming global. You might even be able to join a Canadian chapter of an association you belonged to in your homeland.

Many potential employers look for new employees through their professional associations. If you let your association know that you are trying to find a job in Canada, they may recommend you to a potential employer.

Tip: After joining a professional association, ask about the possibility of having a mentor (an advisor) to consult about professional questions.

7.4 Job Finding Clubs

Situation

At Employment Resource Centres (ERCs) and some colleges across Canada, you'll often hear about Job Finding Clubs. These are not actually clubs. They're programs to help people find jobs. What do you do at these programs, and how can you benefit from them?

Information

Activities of a Job Finding Club

To find Job Finding Clubs in your area, enter the keywords "Job Finding Club" on an Internet search engine, along with the name of your city or province.

These are some of the activities you will be involved in at a job finding club.

- Job Finding Clubs are intensive employment programs often lasting about three weeks; in some cases, two or four weeks. (In this chapter, we focus on a three-week program.)
- They consist of workshops with trained leaders who will teach you how to find a job as soon as possible, and to prepare yourself with effective job-search techniques for the future.
- Usually, you will attend a number of all-day workshops where you learn to master effective job-searching methods.
- While you are taking the workshops, you are expected to practise what you are learning by applying for jobs.

Tip: Job Finding Clubs are in high demand, so priority is given to anyone who is receiving Employment Insurance (EI) now, or who has received it within the last five years. But as long as there's a vacancy, anyone can join—almost always free of charge!

Week by Week Activities

Week One

- Do a self-assessment to emphasize your strengths and set job-searching goals.
- Write a resume and cover letter with the help of a consultant.
- Create a calling card showing the kind of job you're looking for and your qualifications for this job.
- Learn how to distribute your card effectively.

Week Two

- Learn the basics of networking (people you know who might help you find a job—see 6.4).
- Learn how to call people you don't know (make cold calls) to obtain information and offer your services (see 6.5).
- Learn about the visible and hidden job markets. (See Units 5 and 6.)
- Learn how to use the Internet effectively.
- Learn how to prepare for an interview, including learning the best ways to answer questions and discuss salary. This stage usually involves practice interviews, where you can rehearse the interview, watch other people's interviews, and sometimes even watch your own videotaped interview.
- Learn how to assemble a portfolio (for creative professions, this will include samples of your best work).

Week Three

During this week, you'll receive one-on-one help from an instructor as you investigate the job market, focus on employers' requirements, and start your direct job search. You will be contacting employers, distributing resumes, and going to interviews.

You're Done! Now What?

After completing the Job Finding Club program, you generally meet the instructor within three months to discuss the results of your job-search activity. All Job Finding Clubs have excellent results, usually with a success rate of about 70 percent of participants finding a job. Some clubs, such as the Scarborough Job Finding Club in Ontario, claim that more than 80 percent of their participants are employed within 90 days.

7.5 Employment Resources for Young People

Problem

In some cases, Canadian employers prefer to hire young employees. But, in general, it can be difficult to enter the job market for the first time as a young person. What help is available for you if you're in this position?

Solution

The Canadian government has set up a nationwide network of youth centres to help young men and women in their job searches.

Many of these centres fall under the supervision of Human Resources and Social Development Canada (HRSDC). They supply listings of full-time, part-time, and summer vacancies for students, volunteer placements, and youth programs supervised by HRSDC.

Youth who want to operate their own small business can receive advice and even start-up loans through youth employment centres.

Youth centres offer the following services:

- Information about the job market is available so graduates of secondary schools can determine their skills and choose a career path.
- There are a variety of options, including apprenticeship information and workplace training for skilled tradespeople.
- Youth can inquire about summer jobs.
- You can find information regarding business schools, colleges, and universities.
- There are special workshops for post-secondary (college or university) graduates on preparing effective resumes and getting ready for the first interview with a potential employer.

Taking It Online

Website Name	Website Address
Career Edge	overview.careeredge.ca/index.asp?FirstTime= True&context=0&FromContext=1&language=1
Service Canada (Youth Employment Strategy Programs)	www1.servicecanada.gc.ca/en/epb/yi/yep/newprog/ /yesprograms.shtml

In addition to youth centres, HRSDC has developed youth programs in which young men and women can participate: SkillsLink, Career Focus, Federal Student Work Experience Program (FSWEP), and Summer Work Experience.

For financial assistance, young people can apply to HRSDC's Youth Awareness programs. To learn more about these programs browse the Service Canada website or visit an employment resource centre (ERC).

A number of organizations offer scholarships or three- to twelve-month internships to graduates of colleges and universities who cannot find a job. For example, the Career Edge organization gives a grant of $1,500 a month for work in a number of enterprises in the Vancouver, Toronto, and Hamilton areas.

Tip: Career counsellors at your secondary school, college, university, or other educational institution can give you good job-searching advice before you graduate. Don't hesitate to use their services! Another way to receive experience is through a co-op program or volunteer job.

7.6 Employment Resources for Women

Situation

Many organizations in Canada have special employment programs for women. In most cases, these programs are free of charge. If you are a woman—especially a woman who is new to Canada—what programs are available to help you in your job search?

Information

Here's a small, region-by-region, sampling of job-search programs for women.

Western Canada

- The Pacific Immigrant Resources Society in British Columbia (BC) offers settlement and integration support programs for newcomer women.
- The South Asian Women's Centre in Vancouver, BC, provides information sessions on a range of topics, including employment.
- The Calgary Immigrant Women's Association in Alberta features employment counselling, a credential assessment service, networking opportunities, and employment skills training.
- The Changing Together Centre for Immigrant Women, Edmonton, Alberta, offers pre-employment programs for women of different cultures. Help is available in over 40 languages (www.changingtogether.com).

Central Canada

Ontario

Outside Toronto

- Immigrant Women Services Ottawa provides individualized career counselling and job-search workshops (www.immigrantwomenservices.com).
- The Focus for Ethnic Women, in Waterloo, is a resource centre for immigrant women.
- Women Working with Immigrant Women, in Windsor, offers employment assistance service, including one-on-one counselling, resume writing, interview practice, labour market information, and mentoring.

In Toronto

- Immigrant Women on the Move, in Etobicoke and Scarborough, has job-skills workshops and skills training which are offered by the Toronto District School Board.
- Jewish Vocational Services (JVS) Women in New Roles is for unemployed Toronto women with grade 12 (or equivalent) and some previous

experience. The program provides work in groups and individual consultations, as well as access to computers, job banks, and other resources (www.jvstoronoto.org/index.php?page=womens_services).

- Microskills, in Etobicoke, features programs for women who would like to be self-employed or to run their own businesses. To qualify, you need business experience at a supervisory level in another country or just a good business idea.
  - Microskills is one of several agencies offering a Home-Based Childcare Training Program that includes 14 weeks of in-class studies and 6 weeks of practice.
- COSTI offers a four-week Home Childcare Training Program.
- Mothercraft offers a variety of academic child-care courses.
- On-Track Pre-Employment Program for Women is a three-week program operating from two Toronto locations (www.get-on-track.net).
- Newcomer Women's Services Toronto, in Toronto and Scarborough, provides a range of employment search preparation and assistance programs and resources, including volunteer work placements. Job counselling and one-on-one consultations may be available for up to six months after the completion of the program (www.newcomerwomen.org).
- YWCA Training and Development has workshops to help prepare women for the Canadian job market, including leadership and management training and career assessment and planning.
- Others include: Afghan Women's Organization; Association of Women of India in Canada (AWIC); Immigrant Women's Job Placement Centre; Elspeth Hayworth Centre for Women; Rexdale Women's Centre; Riverdale Immigrant Women's Centre; and Canadian Centre for Women's Education and Development.

Eastern Canada

- Women's Employment Outreach, in Halifax, offers employment services to all women, including newcomer women.
- The East Prince Women's Information Centre (EPWIC), in Prince Edward Island, has a resource library and focuses on job re-entry, new work skill development, and networking assistance.

Tip: Women have many opportunities in Canada that don't exist in some other countries. Use these resources to find out how to grow in your existing occupation or find a new career.

7.7 Employment Programs for Mature or Disabled Workers

Situation

Unfortunately, it is sometimes difficult for mature or disabled workers to find and keep a job in their field in Canada. For example, when businesses are closing, cutting back, or restructuring in Canada, mature workers may be laid off before younger workers. ("Mature" can sometimes mean over 45 years of age.) And according to official data, one in eight Canadians is disabled and may encounter extra obstacles in looking for a job. Where and how can you find a job in Canada if you are facing these kinds of challenges?

Information

Mature Workers: Barriers and How to Overcome Them

The age barrier can make it twice as hard for mature Canadians and newcomers to find jobs as their younger rivals. This is partly because employers do not usually want to invest a lot of money in training an employee who won't stay with them for many years.

But, there are always advantages of hiring a mature worker. Surveys reveal that many human resource people think mature workers are more reliable, more dedicated to their jobs, and have a stronger work ethic than the average worker. It's a good idea to use these arguments in cover letters and interviews.

Here are some tips for making sure you present yourself in a positive way:

- Avoid clinging to old ways of doing things.
- Be open-minded to changes in the workforce.
- In your resume and in interviews, emphasize your qualifications, skills, and knowledge of up-to-date technologies—not just your past experience.
- Don't hide your experience and the skills you've developed over the years—they can be great assets to an employer.
- Limit your career description to the last ten years and omit your date of graduation from college or university.
- Make sure your interview clothes don't look too old-fashioned or too "young."

Programs for Mature Workers

Many programs and resources are available for mature workers. You can access them on the Internet by entering the keywords, "employment," "mature worker," and your province or city. Below are two examples of such programs:

- The Career Resource Centre, Amherst, Nova Scotia, provides the Age Advantage Program for Older Workers.
- The Centre for Experienced Workers (operated by Humber College), Toronto, deals with job hunters over 45. Their three-week program called New Tools—New Rules is designed for mature Canadians and newcomers.

Taking It Online	
Website Name	**Website Address**
Ability Edge	www.abilityedge.ca
March of Dimes	www.marchofdimes.ca/dimes

Programs for People with Disabilities

Wherever you live in Canada, you can find useful information on employment opportunities for people with disabilities by searching the web using the keywords "employment," "disabilities," and the name of your province or city.

Here are two examples of programs for people with disabilities:

- Ability Edge, for college and university graduates with disabilites, gives six-, nine-, and twelve-month internships in such fields as bookkeeping, marketing, and computer technologies to people without experience who have the right to work in Canada.
- The March of Dimes (an Ontario charitable organization) offers a range of programs and services, including rehabilitation, recreation, training, and employment programs. Those who visit their employment centres have a 70 percent success rate in finding jobs, and March of Dimes now has a number of national programs.

Tip: Different programs are connected with different types of disabilities. So, before you sign up for a particular program, phone the organization to find out if it's suitable for you.

Key Words

job board: a place on a wall or on a website that shows lists of jobs that are available

seminar: a short course, class, or meeting in which certain topics are taught and discussed

trade association: a group of people or organizations that govern or regulate particular industries or professions

Note: Entries taken or adapted from the Oxford ESL Dictionary.

Creating Your Canadian Experience

1. On the Service Canada website, find the location of the Service Canada Centre closest to your home.

   Address: _____

   Hours: _____

2. On the immigration section of the Service Canada website, use their quick calculator to find out if you have lived in Canada long enough to become a citizen.

   Date you entered Canada: _____

   Date you became (or are eligible to become) a permanent resident of Canada: _____

3. Search the Internet for the employment resource centre (ERC) nearest your home. What workshops are offered?

Address: _____

Hours: _____

Workshops Offered: _____

_____

_____

4. Conduct research on the Internet or by going to an ERC to find a Job Finding Club that is suitable for you.
Tip: Try searching using keywords "Job Finding Club" + "[your city]" + "[your profession]."

Address: _____

Contact Information: _____

5. Search the Internet for different associations in your area. Contact them to find out more about how to become a member and what services they offer.
Tip: Use the keywords "[your city]" + "association" + any of the following: "newcomers," "[your profession]," or "[your native country]."

Association	Membership	Member Service

Career Assistance for New Canadians

In This Unit

- Newcomer Employment Services in Canada
- Mentoring Programs
- Immigrant Employment Loan Program
- Foreign Credentials Referral Office

8.1 Newcomer Employment Services

Problem

Beyond the employment services for all Canadians described in Unit 7, Canada provides extra services for newcomers. Where can you find these services?

Solution

In this unit you'll find descriptions of programs and resources provided by public agencies with federal and provincial government funding. Most of these agencies fall into three categories: information and employment centres; colleges, universities, and other educational institutions; and local associations.

Information and Employment Resource Centres

Most employment resource centres (ERCs) offer seminars and workshops about topics such as obtaining licences for regulated occupations, workplace ethics and behaviour, multinational culture in Canada, effective job-search methods, the hidden job market, and the visible job market.

They have computers and libraries, and have printed materials in many languages. Some offer special programs for internationally educated professionals (IEPs) and tradespeople. Employment information is also available at most general information centres that help newcomers adjust to Canada.

Colleges, Universities, and Other Educational Institutions

Many educational institutions in Canada make special efforts to help newcomers. For instance, colleges and universities have developed systems of weighing foreign educational credits against their Canadian equivalents. This means that newcomers wishing to continue their education in Canada do not have to repeat courses they have already completed. (But check the website of the institution you wish to attend to be sure.)

Tip: As soon as you arrive in Canada, visit an ERC or newcomer information centre near you. Take a list of your questions, your resume, and basic documents proving your education and experience.

Local Associations

Many Canadian cities have associations that offer specialized job searching for newcomers. The following table outlines the programs that can provide help in finding employment.

Types of Programs	Description
Job-Search Workshops	Generally half-day or full-day seminars to teach newcomers the basics about looking for employment in Canada.
Employment Resource Centres (ERCs)	Free, self-service job-search centres that provide computers, phones, fax machines, libraries, job postings and staff to answer your questions and offer advice.
Skills Training	Coaching and classroom study for specific fields, such as hospitality or accounting.
Mentoring	One-on-one meetings where newcomers can get advice from a person who has lived in Canada for a long time, has has worked in their field or a related field, and is willing to share their knowledge and insights.
Sector-Specific Enhanced Language Training (ELT)	Newcomers learn workplace language and jargon used in their industry.
Job Connect or Job Bridging	Provide work placements for newcomers to obtain Canadian experience.
Job Finding Clubs	A group of newcomers works together with an advisor to actively search for jobs. Resumes, cold calls, and interviews are monitored and critiqued.

In Toronto, for example, the Toronto Region Immigrant Employment Council (TRIEC) helps newcomers use their skills, education, and experience. They have created several programs such as the following:

- One program provides subsidized work experience opportunities (internships) for immigrants in occupations important in Canada.
- Communication with potential employers helps explain the value of new technologies and knowledge brought from abroad.
- Loans for immigrants help to give them time to study for licensing examinations.

Canadian government and public organizations have developed numerous online sites that can give you tips on how to use the Internet efficiently for job hunting. They can also provide the names of special projects and employment programs for immigrants, and places where you can find answers to your employment questions.

8.2 ERCs for Newcomers

Situation

According to the Canadian government, lack of information is the single worst problem for newcomers looking for work. As a result, Canada provides funding for employment resource centres (ERCs) and information centres across the country. How can you find these centres and how can they help you?

Information

Information centres and ERCs for Newcomers can be found across Canada. An Internet search using the keywords "employment resource centre," "employment centre," or "information centre" will help you find these agencies. To focus on agencies in your area, add the name of your city or region. If you still cannot find one of these agencies, contact your nearest Service Canada Centre (www1.servicecanada.gac.ca/en/gateways/where_you_live/menu.shtml).

Here are descriptions of a number of employment resource centres and information centres from across Canada.

Western Canada

- Surrey BC's Multilingual ERC offers employment-search assistance for immigrants. Their services include employment counselling, information about language and skills training, and resume and referral services in clients' own languages.
- Saskatchewan has several employment centres, including at least 20 Career and Employment Services Centres.
- Manitoba has many ERCs, including Notre-Dame-de-Lourdes Bilingual ERC.

Central Canada

- In Quebec, most employment information and services are offered in French on the Internet and in person. A good place to start is the website of Immigration et Communautés culturelles (www.micc.gouv.qc.ca).
- Job Search Workshop (JSW) in Ontario includes free three- to four-day seminars for training in effective job-search techniques, writing of resumes and cover letters, and interview preparation.
- Woodgreen Employment Services, East York (within Toronto) offers seminars, lectures, and meetings on a number of employment topics.

Nina's Personal Experience

Before coming to Canada, I didn't know anything about employment opportunities here, nor did I know where to look for information. I had heard that immigrants often find it very difficult to get work in their field and sometimes choose to pursue an entirely new career.

In my country, I worked in various areas, including sales, marketing, human resources, and training, and in a number of different fields. Once in Canada, I didn't know what type of work to look for. One evening, while exercising at my local YMCA, a friend told me about an Employment Resource Centre in the neighbourhood. I met with a counsellor who helped me identify possible paths to follow in Canada. She recommended I take some job-search workshops and computer training. At last, I was on my way!

Ontario's New Initiative

- Ontario receives about half the immigrants who arrive in Canada. As a result, this province places special importance on centres for immigrants through its Newcomer Information Centres (NICs). Here is some of the information you will find at an NIC, free of charge:
  - Addresses of not-for-profit organizations that serve immigrants.
  - Assistance in finding accommodation and learning tenants' rights.
  - Names of ESL schools where immigrants can study English or improve their qualifications.
  - Access to a large library as well as computers with Internet access, printers, fax machines, and photocopiers. You do not need to set up an appointment to use these facilities.
  - Information about employment and regular seminars.

Eastern Canada

- Nova Scotia has full-service ERCs in Halifax, Sydney, and New Waterford.
- In St. John's, Newfoundland, the Association for New Canadians operates a program called AXIS Career Services. This service includes a Career Information Resource Centre.
- Throughout the Atlantic provinces, the Association for New Canadians offers the Strategic Transitions and Employment Partnerships (STEP) program. This program includes five- to ten-week career placements, connecting local businesses with job-ready international clients.

8.3 Assisted Job-Search Programs

Situation

Newcomers often need extra support in improving language skills and adjusting to the Canadian job market. This is why assisted job-search programs and specialized Job Finding Clubs have been set up. What are these services, and where can you find them?

Advice and Action Plan

Service Canada (see 7.1) is helping to create and support the growth of these service centres in the Greater Vancouver Area. Meanwhile, the Toronto District School Board's Assisted Job Search Program (AJSP) helps newcomers improve their language skills. Please note the following points about the AJSP:

- Most job programs require English skills at Canadian Language Benchmark Level 6, but newcomers with Level 3 can be accepted into the AJSP program.
- Your English level, your status in Canada, your level of education, and your job experience are determined first.
- After you are interviewed, the instructors will decide who will be in the class (made up of 12 to 15 people).

Similar Programs near You

Programs similar to Toronto's AJSP are carried out across the country at organizations called Job Finding Clubs (see 7.4). Some, like the VPI Specialized Scarborough Job Finding Club, are especially for newcomers. Others accept both newcomers and longtime Canadian residents.

Below is some information about job finding clubs.

Taking It Online	
Website Name	**Website Address**
CRE Association	www.cre.qc.ca
Employment Manitoba Online	www.gov.mb.ca/employment/eas/eas_wpg.html
Saskatchewan Abilities Council	www.abilitiescouncil.sk.ca/regina/html/services/ supported_empl/new_opp_work.shtml

Immigrant Experience

When Sylvia first arrived in Canada, she didn't like it very much. She found that looking for work in her new country was very different from looking for work in her homeland. She experienced more culture shock than she expected. She had been an executive secretary, but after a few months, she gave up looking for a similar job here.

Sylvia was volunteering at her children's school when someone suggested that she join a Job Finding Club that offered skills assessment and training for newcomers. She followed this advice, and after some career counselling and training she received a certificate in secretarial skills.

Her efforts paid off. Sylvia currently has an administrative job that she enjoys. In the future, she is going to do more training so she can try out a new field of work.

To locate a Job Finding Club (club de recherche d'emploi) in Quebec, visit the Centres de recherche d'emploi du Québec (CRE) website. In Manitoba, check out Employment Manitoba Online's website. In Saskatchewan, visit the Abilities Council website.

Theoretical and Practical Training

Once accepted into the program, you must attend classes every day. In class, both theoretical and **practical** training are conducted. There are many activities you'll be involved in:

- The instructor will teach you how to determine job-search goals.
- You will learn about different sources of job ads.
- You'll likely go on a trip to a library, where you'll learn how to collect information about employers and job possibilities.
- You'll learn how to carry on phone negotiations with potential employers.
- Practice interviews are videotaped so your performance can be evaluated and corrected.
- After finding an interesting job ad, you will call the potential employer while the instructor listens on another line. The instructor will then give you advice about how to correct your mistakes.
- After lectures, instructors will hold individual consultations with you and your fellow students. Group work contributes to a feeling of teamwork.

8.4 Support for Tradespeople

Problem

Tradespeople such as electricians, millwrights, mechanics, and steamfitters are in high demand in Canada. But if you are a tradesperson, you may have to add Canadian qualifications to your international ones. How can you do this, and what support is available to help you?

Solution

First, contact the workplace support service office (or apprenticeship office) in your province or territory. To find these, go to the Red Seal website and search under Apprenticeship Offices and Contact List. (For more about the Red Seal program, see 1.5.)

Proof of Experience, Provincial Examinations, and Certificates of Qualification

To be employed in regulated skilled trades, you must have a Certificate of Qualification. To obtain such a certificate, you must pass a provincial examination. And before you can write that exam, you need to prove that you are experienced in the trade. To do this, you may need to show documentation or other evidence indicating that your training time meets the minimum industry standards of the region where you are applying for work. Note that before you write a provincial examination, you will need to make sure your English skills are strong enough.

Obtaining a Canadian certificate usually takes hard work. Even if you taught your trade in your homeland, you'll have a lot to learn. Canadian

Taking It Online

Website Name	Website Address
Ontario Ministry of Training, Colleges and Universities	www.edu.gov.on.ca/eng/training/foreign.html
Red Seal	www.red-seal.ca
Skills for Change	www.skillsforchange.org/trades
Canada Trade Jobs	www.canadatradejobs.com
Settlement.Org	www.settlement.org/sys/faqs_detail.asp?passed_lang= EN&faq_id=4000252

building codes and industry standards may be very different from those in your home country.

The following are some trades for which a certificate is likely needed in most provinces or territories: autobody repairer, electrician, plumber, refrigeration mechanic, sheet metal worker, and steamfitter/pipefitter.

Ironworkers require certification in Alberta, but not in Ontario or BC. Hairstylists require certification in Alberta and Ontario, but not in BC. Bricklayers must be certified in Nova Scotia, but not in BC, Alberta, or Ontario. Roofers and sprinkler installers need certification in BC and Nova Scotia, but not in Alberta or Ontario.

And, for some trades, a certificate is not always needed—for example, bakers, carpenters, cooks, and millwrights don't require certificates to practise.

Go to an Apprenticeship Office for Help

Training consultants at apprenticeship offices can advise you about the documents that you need to prove you have the skills necessary to write the exam. These documents include a Social Insurance Number (SIN) proving your right to work in Canada; references from employers for whom you have worked; a letter from your trade union in your country of origin; international diplomas, certificates, or licences; and documents about training in your field. All of these must be translated into English and confirmed by signature and stamp of a licensed translator.

Entering an Apprenticeship Program

Before you can enter an apprenticeship program in any province, you must have a potential employer. After that, the apprenticeship office will decide whether or not your employer is qualified to have you take an apprenticeship with them.

Preparing for the Exam

Some agencies, such as Skills for Change in Toronto, offer courses to prepare people in various trades for their qualification exams. These courses can greatly improve your chance of passing the exam.

For more about regulated occupations in Canada, see 1.5.

Tip: To find apprenticeship rules and certification requirements in your area, search the Internet using keywords such as "skilled trades," "apprenticeship," and "journeyman certification," along with the name of your province or territory.

8.5 Mentoring Programs

Problem

Even if you are skilled in your field, you'll face challenges as you look for a job in Canada because you're working in a new environment with a different language. To help you overcome obstacles and avoid mistakes, it's a good idea to have a mentor—someone who has lived in Canada for a long time, who works in your field, and who wants to help you. How can you find a mentor who will be suitable for you?

Solution

Your Professional Association

One possible source of mentors is your own professional association. To contact the association for your profession, do an Internet search using the keyword "association," along with the name of your profession, and your province. Or, find the association at a library or employment resource centre (ERC).

The Mentoring Partnership

Ontario

If you are in the Toronto area, investigate the Toronto Region Immigrant Employment Council (TRIEC) general mentoring program. It's called The Mentoring Partnership (an alliance of community agencies in the City of Toronto and the Regions of Halton, Peel, and York). A person already established in the workplace (a "mentor") is matched with a newcomer (a "mentee") who is looking for employment in their field. The member helps the mentee with everything from resumes to networking.

Newcomers who want to become a mentee must register with one of the partner agencies listed on the Mentoring Partnership website. They must also be immigrants to Canada, be educated abroad, have a Bachelor's degree, and have at least three years of work experience in their field with no prior Canadian work experience in that field. They must also have a "job-ready" resume, be eligible and available for work full-time, and be fluent in English (LINC Level 5 or Canadian Language Benchmark Level 5 or 6).

Taking It Online

Website Name	Website Address
Metropolitan Immigrant Settlement Association	www.misa.ns.ca/wins.php
Progressive Intercultural Community Services	www.pics.bc.ca/programs_sho_job_mentoring.php
The Mentoring Partnership	www.thementoringpartnership.com

Mentors must understand Canadian workplace culture, professional terminology, and the demands of the marketplace. They should be able to give advice on accreditation and guide the mentee in mastering self-marketing techniques, selecting skills upgrading programs, locating resource materials, and establishing professional networks.

Mentors and newcomers work together for a total of 24 hours over a four-month period. They agree about when and where they will meet and how they will communicate (in person, through e-mail, etc.).

Mentoring Programs across Canada

British Columbia

Job Mentoring Service (through Progressive Intercultural Community Services Society in Vancouver, British Columbia). For more information, see the Progressive Intercultural Community Services Society website.

Nova Scotia

The Professional Mentor Program, through the Work in Nova Scotia (WINS) Program, matches newcomers with professionals in their field for building skills and networking and to better understand their occupations in Canada. For more information, see the Metropolitan Immigrant Settlement Association.

Tip: Mentoring programs will help you learn more about the Canadian job market and meet Canadians who practise your occupation. It's a great way to learn things that only a long-time resident of Canada and an expert in your field would know.

8.6 Immigrant Employment Loan Program

Problem

It takes money to upgrade your qualifications, and many newcomers already face financial challenges during their first years in Canada. For example, recently arrived immigrants cannot usually receive regular bank loans. This is because most Canadian banks, and other financial institutions, require either a long-term credit history or some other guarantee of repayment. Fortunately, funding programs are available to help you upgrade through studies and examinations. What are some of these programs, and how can you access them?

Solution

Here's an example of one loan program for newcomers—The Maytree Foundation–Alterna Savings Immigrant Employment Loan Program.

The Maytree Foundation–Alterna Savings Immigrant Employment Loan Program (Toronto)

- The program assists unemployed internationally trained professionals and tradespeople with loans of up to $5,000 to pay for short-term study (up to one year) to help them find work in their occupation, or to obtain an evaluation of a diploma or pay an examination/entrance fee to a professional association.
- Recent loans have been used for studying such occupations as midwifery, pharmacy, engineering technology, truck driving, and welding.
- Participants must report to the loan program on a regular basis about the success of their studies.

Taking It Online

Website Name	Website Address
The Maytree Foundation	www.maytree.com

Requirements for Receiving a Loan

- Applicants must be immigrants or have convention refugee status, and be a permanent resident of Toronto.
- They must have sufficient vocational training abroad.
- They need to have good English skills.
- Applicants shouldn't have Canadian credit history (that is, unable to obtain a loan elsewhere).
- The training should be for a position that is in demand in the Canadian job market.
- The salary of the job being sought must allow for repayment of the loan and its interest.

Participants must find an appropriate loan program and educational institution. That educational institution must meet several requirements.

- It must be recognized in Ontario and have a good reputation.
- After a participant's graduation, they must supply a certificate that will allow the participant to apply for a job immediately.
- The program should last one year or less.
- Training must improve a participant's skills and knowledge based on employers' requirements.

Payment of Loans to Participants

During the course of the loan program, funds will be sent directly to the participant's educational institution.

Paying Back Loans

During her course of studies, the participant needs to pay only interest and insurance. She must start repaying the loan either 90 days after completing her course of studies or once she has found a job—whichever comes first. Typically, the entire loan should be paid back within three years.

Finding Loans in Your Area

For programs in your area, search the Internet for "immigrant employment loan program" or "immigrant loan" and "[your city or province]."

Tip: Student loans are usually easier to get than other types of loans. Talk to your educational institution about student loans, grants, and bursaries. (See 3.5.)

8.7 Bridge-Training Programs

Situation
If you are in a regulated occupation, it can take a long time to obtain a Canadian licence. This means more time will pass before you can apply for a job. Fortunately, bridge-training programs help to speed up the process. What are these programs, and how can you apply to one?

Information
Bridge-training programs are in high demand because tens of thousands of specialists arrive annually in Canada.

How It Works
Qualifications Check
- An educational institution and regulatory body will evaluate your international credentials together (they look for college or university, as well as two or three years' experience in your field).
- You must achieve at least Canadian Language Benchmark Level 6 (ESL intermediate level) on an English test, but the level may vary slightly between programs.
- You must have legal status and the right to work in Canada.

Your Individual Bridge-Training Plan
- You will usually receive an individual plan, including the theoretical studies and practice required to improve your qualifications.
- You'll start the training you need to pass the licensing exam. (You do not need to repeat relevant courses you've completed abroad. You only need to take the additional subjects required to work in Canada.)
- Training often includes professional language preparation.
- You'll then enroll in a college or university course. (You have to pay the regular fee for these studies.)
- After graduating, you must take and pass the regulatory examination for your occupation in order to obtain your licence.

Locate a Bridge-Training Program
The Alberta International Medical Graduate Program
Canada's first bridging program for medical professionals has been set up in Alberta—the Alberta International Medical Graduate Program (AIMG) (www.aimg.ca). The following steps outline how the AIMG works:

- International graduates from medical schools outside of Canada or the US are invited to compete for post-graduate residency training positions.
- The applicant must be an Alberta resident.
- The applicant must pass the Objective Structured Clinical Examination (OSCE).

Bridge-Training Programs in Ontario

The Government of Ontario has created 24 new bridge-training programs to help more than 3,000 internationally trained professionals obtain licences and find jobs. Here is a sampling of these programs:

- Architecture
  - Ontario Association of Architects (www.oaa.on.ca)
- Construction
  - George Brown College, Toronto (www.georgebrown.ca)
  - La Cité collégiale, Ottawa (www3.lacitec.on.ca)
- Early Childhood Educators
  - Association of Early Childhood Educators Ontario (AECEO) (www.aeceo.ca)
- Engineers
  - ACCES Employment Services Ltd. (www.accessemployment.ca)
- Environmental Planners and Geoscientists
  - Toronto and Region Conservation Authority (www.trca.on.ca)
- Health Care and Hospital Administrative Positions
  - Algonquin College, Ottawa (www.algonquincollege.com)
- Midwifery
  - Ryerson University, Toronto (www.ryerson.ca/continuing)
- Nursing
  - School of Nursing, York University, Toronto (www.atkinson.yorku.ca/NURS)
- Teaching
  - George Brown College, Toronto (www.georgebrown.ca)
  - Teach in Ontario (www.teachinontario.ca)
- Tourism Sector
  - Ontario Tourism Education Corporation (OTEC)/Customer Service Excellence (CSE) (www.otec.org)

Bridge-Training Programs across Canada

A number of similar programs are currently under development in other parts of Canada. For example, the Prior Learning Educational Assessment Program (PLEA) allows qualified international midwives to become licensed in a number of provinces, including BC, Alberta, and Manitoba.

8.8 Foreign Credentials Referral Office

Situation
If your occupation is regulated in Canada, the Foreign Credentials Referral Office (FCRO) can help you become licensed to work in this country. What is the FCRO, and how can you benefit from their services?

Information
Established by Citizenship and Immigration Canada (CIC) in 2007, the FCRO helps internationally trained individuals find information about how to have their credentials assessed and recognized in Canada.

The FCRO also provides information about the Canadian labour market, and it helps make Canadian employers more aware of the benefits of hiring internationally trained professionals.

Contact the FCRO
On the Internet (www.credentials.gc.ca)
- The FCRO's website features a Working in Canada Tool, which helps newcomers looking for credential recognition:
  - The site identifies a newcomer's occupation in Canada by National Occupational Classification.
  - It lists the regulatory body relevant to their occupation.
  - It offers detailed job market information based on where the job seeker lives or plans to live.

By Telephone
- Available from within Canada only, newcomers can use their toll-free number (1-888-854-1805). An agent will answer questions and provide information about foreign credential recognition and the labour market.

In Person
- If you are a newcomer living in Canada or are here on a visit, the best option is to visit one of 320 Service Canada Centres. FCRO representatives are available to answer questions and provide information and advice on how to have your credentials recognized.

Tip: Before you phone or e-mail the FCRO, or have a meeting at a Service Canada Centre, prepare a list of questions. Don't forget to take notes when you receive your answers!

The FCRO Website

The FCRO website contains detailed descriptions of programs intended to help newcomers enter the Canadian job market quickly and easily. The website includes overseas orientation programs and links like What You Need to Know and Job Search Tips (for job seekers), and Hiring and Recruiting and Tools and Resources (for potential employers). You can also send e-mails to the FCRO through their site.

The Working in Canada Tool

When you use the Working in Canada Tool on the FCRO website, the following is the type of report you will receive about your occupation.

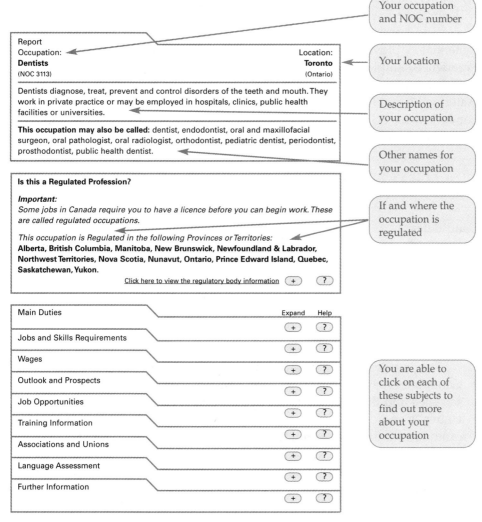

Source: Foreign Credentials Referral Office.

8.9 Skills International Service

Situation

Many internationally trained professionals encounter employers who question their credentials. This means that many skilled newcomers who could be contributing to Canadian society are left without work. Skills International was set up to help employers connect with qualified international employees. How does this tool work?

Advice and Action Plan

The Skills International website links internationally trained professionals with employers who need their skills (www.skillsinternational.ca). When employers search the Skills International site, they know candidates (potential employees) have been pre-screened and recommended by experienced employment advisors throughout Ontario.

This Internet service was set up as a collaborative project between the Waterloo Region District School Board, WIL Employment Connections in London, and COSTI Immigrant Services in Toronto. Their services should be available across the country soon.

How Does Skills International Work?

Candidates and employers both use the Skills International website.

Candidates

- Candidates are allowed to have their resumes posted on this site only if they meet the following requirements:
    - They are currently living in Canada.
    - They have the right to work in Canada.
    - They are ready to start work immediately.
    - Their English is at Canadian Language Benchmark 7 or better.
    - They are working with a community-based training agency to become prepared for employment in Canada.
- Candidates may not post their own profiles. The profiles must be screened and then posted by the agency they are working with.
- Under "Candidates" on the website, there is an Agency Locator that candidates can use to search for partnering agencies in their area.
- Candidate profiles include a resume. Each profile also has space for an audio/video clip, scanned documents such as certificates, and education equivalency assessments.

Immigrant Experience

Carol has a Bachelor's degree in Engineering from China, where she worked as a localization engineer translating software interface from English to Chinese. She admits now that when she first came to Canada, she had no idea how to find a job. When she began to look for work, people told her it would be difficult to find a position in her field. Discouraged, she didn't even try.

Now, however, Carol wishes that someone had told her not to give up! After eight years in Canada, she understands the system a lot better. While it would have been difficult, she knows that if she had asked the right people and collected the proper documentation, she could have gained the experience she needed to take the professional engineering test.

- Agency staff working with a candidate may add their own personal reference.
- Candidates can see the number of times their own profile has been matched to a potential employer.
- Candidates pay no fee for this service.

Potential Employers

Employers visit the Skills International website intending to hire a newcomer like you. They can do three different types of searches based on skills, experience, and education:

- The first is a basic search: a keyword search matched against keywords in candidates' profiles.
- This second is an advanced search: based on artificial intelligence that analyzes candidates' skills and experience in context.
- The third is a perpetual search: a type of advanced search that allows an employer to be notified by e-mail whenever a suitable new candidate profile is posted.

Tip: Since you create your own profile, you can do things to give yourself an advantage. For example, if you speak well and are personable, you can post a video clip, introducing yourself directly to employers.

8.10 Unit Summary

Key Words

practical: concerned with actually doing something rather than ideas or theory

Note: Entries taken or adapted from the Oxford ESL Dictionary.

Creating Your Canadian Experience

1. Search the Internet for a newcomer information centre in your area.
   Tip: Try searching using keywords "[your city or province]" + "newcomer information centre."

   Name: _____

   Address: _____

   Hours: _____

2. Now that you know where the newcomer information centre is and what its hours are, make a plan to go and visit it and ask some questions.

   Visit Date: _____

Question	Answer

3. Research colleges and universities near your home for newcomer assistance programs.
Tip: Using the Internet, find the schools near your home first by using keywords "[your city]" + "colleges or universities." Then search on the schools' websites for newcomer assistance programs.

School: _____ Program: _____

School: _____ Program: _____

4. Search the Internet for local associations in your area that assist newcomers.
Tip: Try using keywords "[your city]" + "newcomer assistance" + "association."

Association: _____

Contact Information: _____

Assistance Offered: _____

5. Search the Internet for the newcomer employment centre nearest your home.

Name: _____

Address: _____

Hours: _____

6. If you are a tradesperson, search the Internet to find out if you need a certificate of qualification, and what you need to do to get one.
Tip: Search using the keywords "[your trade]" + "qualifications" or "[your trade]" + "association."

Trade	Certificate (Y/N)	Certificate Details

7. If your occupation requires a licence or certificate, what must you do to get one?

Requirements: _____

_____

8. Do some research about mentoring programs in your field or geographical area.

Tip: Search the Internet using keywords "mentoring program" + "[your profession]" + "[your city]."

Program: _____

Requirements: _____

Contact Information: _____

9. Search the Internet for immigrant loan programs and their requirements.

Program	Requirements	Contact Information

10. Find out about your occupation on the FRCO website and fill in the boxes below.

NOC Number		Description	
Occupation Names		Regulated	
Main Duties		Requirements	
Wages		Opportunities	
Training Information		Associations and/or Unions	
Additional Information			

Note: If you are considering other occupations in your field, look them up on the FCRO website and fill in the information on a separate piece of paper.

Resume Writing

In This Unit

- What Is a Resume?
- Writing Different Formats of Resumes
- Sample Resumes
- Writing a Top-Quality Cover Letter

9.1 What Is a Resume?

Situation

A resume is an advertisement. It's a flyer advertising you—your skills, education, and experience. With this piece of paper, you'll make a good first impression on potential employers if it's top quality in form and content. How can you create an attention-grabbing resume that presents you in the best possible light?

Information

In the *Oxford Dictionary*, a resume is defined as "A brief account of one's education, experience, previous employment, and interests, usually submitted with a job application." Using only this piece of paper, you have to convince the employer that you, instead of all the other people that applied for the job, should be chosen to fill the vacant position.

Nina's Personal Experience

Resume writing is challenging and time consuming. Each time you apply for a new job, you have to research it and change your resume to fit its requirements.

At first, I created one standard resume and sent it to dozens of potential employers. I thought that the more resumes I sent out, the more responses I would get. But I was wrong—I got no responses at all.

So I tried a new approach. I visited a couple of employment agencies where I learned about the importance of carefully focusing my resume on each position I was applying for. I learned that I should include the particular work experience, skills, and education that fit the position I was seeking—and to omit information that did not relate to that job.

I've worked in sales, marketing, and office administration in different fields. Now, if I apply for a sales or marketing position, I focus on my experience in those two areas. I don't mention my work in office administration. If I apply for a position in office administration, I leave out information about my work in sales and marketing. Or I don't emphasize it. I recently sent out only three resumes, carefully focused on the positions advertised and, to my surprise, I got two interviews!

Here's a chart of sections you'll want to include and the information that should appear within them. Think of your suitability for a particular position as a thread that connects all the sections.

Section	Information to Include
Objective	Define the purpose of your resume by naming the position the employer wants to fill.
Highlights	Describe your degree, diploma, licences, knowledge, and skills that correspond to this position.
Experience	Describe past experiences that will allow you to have an immediate positive impact on productivity in your new workplace.
Education	Describe your education, proving your competency for the job. If you have a degree from another country, have your credentials evaluated to provide Canadian academic equivalents (see 1.6).
References	Indicate that references are available upon request.
Languages or Hobbies	Talk about other languages you know or things you like to do outside of work. This is especially important if they in some way relate to the job for which you're applying!

In the sections of the resume, do not include information that has no direct relation to the position for which you are applying. Keep your resume concise and clear. This will make you look as appealing as possible to your potential employer.

Tip: Keep a "master" resume on file. Then revise parts of it to suit each position you apply for. When you match your resume to the job description as closely as possible, you'll be giving yourself the best chance of getting an interview.

9.2 Preparing to Write Your Resume

Situation

When you apply for almost any job in Canada, you'll be asked for a resume. This document is the most important resource in your Canadian job-hunting toolkit. So you'll need to spend a great deal of time preparing to write it. As you do this, how can you make sure it's written and presented in a powerful and convincing way?

Information

Organize Your Employment History

- Go through any employment records you have. Use these to reconstruct a detailed account of your employment experience, noting exactly when and where you worked in the past.
- Write a brief description of each job and the duties that accompanied it.
- Mention all the achievements, awards, and promotions you've received.
- Describe how your efforts saved your employer money, increased efficiency, or made them more competitive in the marketplace. Be specific in your explanations, such as stating exactly how much money you saved a previous employer.

Organize Your Education History

- Go through the same process with your education that you did with your employment history. List where and when you studied, including all seminars, **self-improvement** courses, and certificate courses.

Organize Your Job Requirements

- Get acquainted with the National Occupational Classification (NOC). You'll find it on the Human Resources and Social Development Canada (HRSDC) website. Then go to Occupational Descriptions to find a description of your occupation, including education and experience requirements. The NOC will tell you whether or not you need to have a Canadian licence or certificate.
- Search newspapers and the Internet for career advertisements in your field. The requirements listed in these ads will tell you some of the items you should include in your resume.

Peter's Personal Experience

I had no idea how to write a resume when I came here because I'd never written one before. I didn't know where to start or what to include. Although I looked at some books and attended a workshop on resumes, the first one I wrote wasn't very good. I did some more research and learned that the problem was not with my writing skills, but with the content of my resume.

I realized from what I was reading and hearing that a resume is like a portfolio: it provides a picture of you over time. So I began to collect information for my resume, listing everything I could remember about my work experience: my qualifications and skills, my various positions and related responsibilities, my most important accomplishments, and the awards I'd received—all the highlights of my working life. (If I hadn't done this, I would never have known I'd achieved so much in my career!) I prepared two versions. One was in chronological format and the other was in functional format. Then I asked someone with fluent English to check them for me.

Now when I apply for a job, I simply select the appropriate document from my portfolio and make minor changes so that it suits the position. It's convenient, and my resume is always well done.

Organize Your Resume Resources
- Look for books, videos, and CDs in libraries, bookstores, and employment resource centres (ERCs) that describe resume writing.
- Do research on the Internet to find samples of resumes on resume banks, including some specifically for your occupation.
- Get acquainted with the resumes of Canadian or American colleagues in your trade. If you are searching online, use the name of your industry, possibly your job title, and the keyword "resume" or "sample resume." Pay attention to their structure and the professional terminology they use. Where appropriate, use the same structure and terminology in your own resume.
- Visit Canadian ERCs and join resume-writing workshops. There, you will receive information booklets and learn the basic rules of resume writing in Canada. If possible, set up a private meeting with your instructor, so he can read your resume and give you advice about changes you should make.

How to Write a Resume in Chronological Format

Situation

Before you start working on your resume, you should know that in the Canadian workplace, resumes are quite often written in chronological format. (Meaning, placed in the order things happened. Usually the most recent events are listed first.) Understanding a chronological resume, and learning how to apply your knowledge, is crucial to your job search.

Information

Most Canadian employers prefer chronological format for a resume because it's easy to read and understand. This format is especially suitable when your experience and education are in the same field. Before you prepare a resume like this, however, do some Internet research to find out if this format is often used in your field.

Sections of a Resume in Chronological Format

- Personal Information
  - First, second (middle), and last names appear at the top of the page, along with your full postal address (including postal code), phone number, fax number (if available), and e-mail address.
- Objective
  - Write the title of the position you're applying for. Use the same words that appeared in the job ad. For unadvertised positions, search for an appropriate job title on the National Occupational Classification (NOC) website.
- Highlights
  - This is a summary of your employment history. Mention any special knowledge, skills, or achievements related to the position you are applying for. State how long you have worked in the field and list

Taking It Online

Website Name	Website Address
NOC	www5.hrsdc.gc.ca/NOC-CNP/app/index.aspx?lc=e

any relevant diplomas, licences, and certificates. Include computer skills, customer service and communication skills, availability to work on evenings or weekends, possession of a driver's licence, and other data that might be important for the position. Usually, this section contains about ten sentences. It is *very* important to describe your Canadian education and experience in detail.

- Experience and Education
  - Chronological resumes are actually often arranged in "reverse chronological order." This means that your experience and education are listed starting from the most recent date and ending with the earliest date. (Note: both Experience and Education should have their own sections within your resume.) Begin with your most recent job, and list your employers and their locations (names of city and country are enough), along with starting and termination dates. For each workplace, name your position and describe your duties (about eight sentences). Begin each sentence with a verb in the past tense (conducted, assisted, inspected, prepared, etc.) and avoid using the first person narrative form (I conducted, I assisted—that is, leave out the "I").
- References
  - This section usually contains only one phrase: Available upon request.

If relevant, you can include such sections as Selected Projects, describing the most interesting projects in which you've taken part. Or you might create a section called Languages, where you specify languages you know.

Ideal resume length is between one and two pages, depending on your occupation, experience, and the level of the position for which you're applying.

Tip: You don't have to only use the names of sections shown above. In books or on the Internet, you'll likely find other section names with similar meanings. It's fine to use these instead.

9.4 A Sample Resume in Chronological Format

Your full legal name
Phone number
Mailing address
(including postal code)

Fax number
E-mail address

Objective: A Civil Engineer position.

Highlights:
- Five years' experience as Civil Engineer
- Bachelor of Science in Civil Engineering
- Skilled with coaxial, fibre optic, telephone, and electrical cables, and equipment installation
- Experienced in construction and testing underground and building conduits
- Skilled with computer systems and software: Windows NT, Microsoft Office, and AutoCAD 2007
- Self-motivated, rises to challenges, responds well to deadlines
- Developed reputation for accuracy and attention to detail; strong teamwork skills
- Able to work night shifts and weekends
- Own a vehicle and G driver's licence with clean record

Experience:

ABC Company
Underground Civil Engineer

City and country
2002–2007

- Supervised and coordinated activities of contractors engaged in construction of overhead and underground cable systems
- Tested cable systems and equipment wiring to detect broken circuits and incorrect connections
- Applied knowledge and engineering and mathematical skills to perform cost calculations and feasibility studies based on data collection and analysis
- Interpreted company policies to contractors and enforced safety regulations
- Analyzed and assisted contractors in solving work problems
- Consulted with municipalities to determine their needs and priorities and demonstrated communication and negotiation skills

EFG Company
Civil Engineering Technician

City and country
1998–2001

- Participated in planning and designing public, commercial, and residential projects
- Calculated strength of enforced concrete constructions
- Participated in preparing and modifying project studies reports, specifications, plans, and designs
- Visited construction sites with civil engineering staff to assess progress and confirm adherence to engineering plans, specifications, and standards

XYZ Company
Shift Supervisor

City and country
1995–1998

- Supervised and coordinated activities of workers engaged in tempering, sawing, and cleaning metal preparatory to production of aluminum-alloy structural forms
- Studied production schedules and estimated worker-hour requirements for completion of job assignments

- Interpreted specifications, blueprints, and job orders to workers and assigned duties
- Established and adjusted work procedures to meet production schedules using knowledge of capacities of machines and equipment
- Assisted workers in performance of tasks such as riveting, welding, bolting, and chipping, using portable power tools

Education:	Name of educational institution **AutoCAD 2007 Course Certificate**	City and country 2007
	Name of educational institution **Contractor Project Supervisor Certificate**	City and country 2000
	Name of educational institution **Bachelor of Science in Civil Engineering**	City and country 1991–1995
Languages:	List the languages in which you are fluent	
References:	Available upon request. (When you drop your resume off or are called in for an interview take your list of references, including contact information, in case you are asked to provide them.)	

Taking It Online

Website Name	Website Address
Jobpostings.ca— Canada's Student Job Site	www.jobpostings.ca/resource.cfm?id=23
Education Canada	resource.educationcanada.com/r_tips3.html
NextSteps.org	www.nextsteps.org/resume/resform.html
Jobhawk.com	www.jobhawk.com/resume_writing_tips_12.php
BCjobs.ca	www.bcjobs.ca/re/Career-advice/career-advice/ resume-advice/chronologicalresumes

9.5 How to Write a Resume in Functional Format

Situation

The functional format is used less often than the chronological format because employers find the chronological format easier to read and understand. But the functional format can be helpful when you have enough knowledge to do well in the position for which you are applying, but not enough experience.

Information

When You Might Use a Functional Resume

Imagine that you're competing for a position as an accounting clerk in a financial company. Although you have never actually worked in the accounting field, you may have worked for a construction company where you regularly carried out accounting clerk duties, so you know how to perform these duties well. The functional resume format will allow you to highlight your skills, even though you don't have "official" experience in that field.

Employer Experience

Many employers worry about job applicants who have no Canadian experience. This is because they have no way of evaluating job titles from other countries. The title "branch manager," for example, might refer to a person who has been with the same branch for twenty years. In another case, it might refer to a manager who does not work at the branch but has the final say on all decisions made at the branch.

To help employers understand the meanings of terms in their resumes, applicants should provide some extra description (context). Explain duties, where the position fit in the company's structure, and where the company fit in the market. This will go a long way to helping employers understand foreign experience. It will improve the chances of a candidate being called in for an interview—or called back for a second one.

As another example, imagine that you worked for a long time in the same field and that your duties were similar at every workplace. If you used chronological format, you'd have to repeat the same description (about six to eight sentences) for each workplace.

The functional resume is useful if you want to skip over periods in your job history. For example, you might have an engineering diploma and don't want to mention the three-year period when you worked as a kitchen helper. Undesirable, or simply unnecessary, facts like these are easier to hide in a functional resume than they would be in a chronological resume.

How a Functional Resume Is Organized

Section headings in a functional resume are different from the ones you'd use in a chronological resume. After the Highlights section, the format allows you to choose headings that better reflect your skills and experience.

- If you are an expert in the field of civil engineering, you could use headings like: Construction Management, Design Skills, Site Supervision, Road Construction, and Building Construction. Under each heading, you would write four to six sentences describing your experience in each area of expertise.
- For an accounting position, your headings might be: Cost Accounting, Accounting and Budgeting, Auditing, Management, and Administration.

Instead of the single Experience section you would use in a chronological resume, make two sections: Work Experience (where you'll describe your functions and skill sets) and Work History (where you'll name each workplace—including city and country, starting and termination dates, and your job titles).

You might actually choose to leave out this section entirely or to revise it to say how long you worked at a particular job without mentioning specific dates. But be aware that this approach might make employers wonder what you are trying to hide, and why.

Tip: Employers usually prefer resumes in chronological format, so be prepared at any time to give an explanation for choosing the functional format.

9.6 A Sample Resume in Functional Format

Your full legal name
Telephone numbers
Mailing address   Fax number
(including postal code)   E-mail address

Objective: A Civil Engineer/Technician position with [insert name of company here]

Highlights:
- 20 years' progressive experience in residential, commercial, industrial, and public construction
- Experienced in water, sewage, gas, ventilation, and heat supply systems
- Working knowledge of materials, machines, and equipment used in the construction industry
- Skilled with computer systems and software: Windows NT, Microsoft Office
- Able to work independently and with a team
- Able to adhere to high standards in all aspects of performance including scheduling, budgeting, and quality control
- Able to work night shifts and weekends
- Own vehicle and G driver licence with clean record

Selected Projects: Working as Civil Engineer, was in charge of, and provided engineering support for, construction of the following industrial projects developed by the company Building International:
- Canned fish industrial shop
- Poultry processing plant
- Fruit juice and tomato ketchup factory
- Metal cans manufacturer

Working as Civil Engineering Technologist/Technician, supported construction and inspected the following residential, commercial, and public projects:
- Holiday Inn and summer camp for sick children
- Nine-storey Public Health Centre and Shopping Mall
- Kindergartens, school, and nine-storey residential buildings

Working as Site Foreman/Supervisor, supervised and inspected the following construction of industrial buildings:
- Diesel engine assembling and boiler shops
- Industrial refrigerated cold rooms
- Chemical laboratory building

Work Experience:
- Examined drawings, blueprints, and reports; analyzed data including geology, topography, soil composition, and other information related to project design
- Prepared and modified projects, specifications, plans, schedules, designs, and environmental studies
- Prepared contracts with architects, clients, and subcontractors, and employed trade subcontractors to do specialized work such as plumbing, heating, and electrical work
- Worked out sketches of construction installations that deviated from blueprints and reported such changes for incorporation on master blueprints

- Prepared detailed estimates of time, materials, tools, equipment, and number of workers
- Established systems of quality control and provided on-site instructions on working procedures and processes
- Conducted inspections of construction sites to monitor progress, quality control, construction, and safety standards; ensured accordance with engineering plans and specifications
- Measured distances to verify accuracy of dimensions of structural installations and layouts and verified levels, alignment, and elevation of installations using surveyor's level and transit
- Prepared and received reports on progress, materials used, and costs; adjusted work schedules as indicated by reports
- Turned over completed projects to customers

Work History:	ABC Company Civil Engineering Technician	City and country 2007
	EFG Company Civil Engineer	City and country 2001–2006
	XYZ Company Construction Supervisor	City and country 1999–2000
Education:	Name of educational institution Regular Professional Courses	City and country 1991–1995
	Name of educational institution Hardware and Software Computer Courses	City and country 1992
	Name of educational institution Modern Construction Technology Course	City and country 1990
	Name of educational institution B. Sc. in Civil Engineering	City and country 1982–1986
References:	Available upon request	

Originally written by Efim Cheinis and reproduced on the Russian website: *www.russianexpress.net/details.asp?article=1887&category=71.*

Taking It Online

Website Name	Website Address
SaskNetWork	www.sasknetwork.gov.sk.ca/html/Home/ jobsearchhandbook/JSearch_Resume.htm
Career Centre— York University	www.yorku.ca/careers/jsm/resumes.htm

9.7 How to Write an Electronic Resume

Situation

Many employers prefer electronic resumes because then they don't have to read every resume they receive. Instead, they can use keyword searches to weed out inappropriate applicants. When you prepare a resume for electronic distribution, should it be different than a traditional resume?

Advice and Action Plan

One of two methods is most commonly used to send an electronic resume: either include the resume as an attachment or copy and paste the resume into the body of an e-mail.

Many employers and search firms prefer the copy/paste method because attachments can too easily contain viruses. But the copy/paste method has special challenges. Sentence and paragraph breaks can disappear, and words and lines can end up running together. Your carefully constructed resume can come out looking like a broken jigsaw puzzle.

To make sure your resume keeps its shape when you cut and paste it into an e-mail, create an ASCII (American Standard Code for Information Interchange) version and save it as a text file, following these rules:

- Replace bold fonts with capital letters. Do not use italics, underscores, or special fonts. Use the space bar key rather than the tab key to create indents and new paragraphs.
- Use dashes in place of bullets and keep line length to 60–65 characters (letters and spaces).

Taking It Online

Website Name	Website Address
NOC	www5.hrsdc.gc.ca/NOC-CNP/app/index.aspx?lc=E

- Save the resume as a Text Only document. In the "Save As" dialogue box, choose the extension .txt (text) or .rtf (Rich Text Format).
- Make sure the text of your resume contains at least 8 to 10 keywords related to the position you are applying for. Put the keywords that would be most important for the employer in job titles, as well as in the Highlights, Experience, and Education sections. You may find these words in the text of the ad to which you are responding, in similar ads you find at job banks, or in the National Occupational Classification (NOC).
- You could also include, right at the beginning of an electronic resume, a special section called Keywords Summary. In this section, you would list the keywords you think an employer might be looking for. This might just help make the employer select your resume over hundreds of others.
- It will be easier to read your resume **on-screen** if you use "**sans serif**" fonts like Arial or Verdana. Avoid symbols, images, and columns. The best font size is 12 point. Never use less than 10 point.

A resume made specifically for electronic distribution keeps its format much better, and has a much better chance of being read. You can advertise yourself further by posting a resume like this on Internet resume banks.

Tip: After you've prepared your resume for electronic distribution, check its suitability by sending it to yourself or to your friends. This way, you'll find out how it looks to the person receiving it.

Your Full Legal Name
Mailing address (including postal code)
Telephone numbers
Fax number
E-mail address

KEYWORD SUMMARY
- Civil Engineer
- Civil Engineering Technician
- Shift Supervisor
- Bachelor Degree
- AutoCAD 2007
- Coaxial, fibre optic, telephone, and electrical cables installation
- Underground and building conduit construction and testing

OBJECTIVE: A Civil Engineer position

HIGHLIGHTS:

- Five years' experience as Civil Engineer
- Bachelor of Science in Civil Engineering
- Skilled with coaxial, fibre optic, telephone, and electrical cables, and equipment installation
- Experienced in construction and testing underground and building conduits
- Skilled with computer systems and software: Windows NT, Microsoft Office, and AutoCAD 2007
- Self-motivated, rises to challenges, responds well to deadlines
- Developed reputation for accuracy and attention to detail; strong teamwork skills
- Able to work night shifts and weekends
- Own a vehicle and G driver's licence with clean record

EXPERIENCE:

ABC Company. City, country 2001 - 2007
UNDERGROUND CIVIL ENGINEER
- Supervised and coordinated activities of contractors engaged in construction of overhead and underground cable systems
- Tested cable systems and equipment wiring to detect broken circuits and incorrect connections
- Applied knowledge and engineering and mathematical skills to perform cost calculations and feasibility studies based on data collection and analysis
- Interpreted company policies to contractors and enforced safety regulations
- Analyzed and solved work problems and assisted contractors in solving work problems
- Consulted with municipalities to determine their needs and priorities and demonstrated communication and negotiation skills

- Analyzed and solved work problems and assisted contractors in solving work problems
- Consulted with municipalities to determine their needs and priorities and demonstrated communication and negotiation skills

EFG Company. City, country 1995 - 2000
CIVIL ENGINEERING TECHNICIAN
- Participated in planning and designing public, commercial, and residential projects
- Calculated strength of enforced concrete constructions
- Participated in preparation and modification of project studies reports,
specifications, plans, and designs
- Visited construction sites with civil engineering staff to assess progress and confirm adherence to engineering plans, specifications, and standards

XYZ Company. City, country 1992 - 1995
SHIFT SUPERVISOR
- Supervised and coordinated activities of workers engaged in tempering, sawing, and cleaning metal preparatory to production of aluminum-alloy structural forms
- Studied production schedules and estimated worker-hour requirements for completion of job assignments
- Interpreted specifications, blueprints, and job orders to workers and assigned duties
- Established and adjusted work procedures to meet production schedules, using knowledge of capacities of machines and equipment
- Assisted workers in performance of tasks such as riveting, welding, bolting and chipping, using portable power tools

EDUCATION:

Name of educational institution. City, country 2005
AUTOCAD 2005 COURSE CERTIFICATE

Name of educational institution. City, country 1993
CONTRACTOR PROJECT SUPERVISOR CERTIFICATE

Name of educational institution. City, country 1982 - 1986
BACHELOR OF SCIENCE IN CIVIL ENGINEERING

LANGUAGES List of foreign languages

REFERENCES Available upon request.

9.9 Resumes for Specific Occupations

Situation

Some occupations require resumes with specific structures and information. Among such occupations are information technology (IT) and some regulated occupations. How exactly do these resumes differ from others?

Information

As an example of a resume written for a specific occupation, here are some of the different features that should appear in a resume you're preparing for an IT job.

For a software development position, for example, make sure your resume contains a section about your knowledge of programming. Name the section Technical Skills, or something similar, and include information about hardware, software, operating systems, and languages that you're familiar with. Also name the programming languages you know, versions you use, how many years you have used these languages, and when you last used them. For example:

Technical Skills

Operating Systems	Version	Last Used	Years of Experience
Windows	NT, XP, Server 2003	Present	8 years
Linux	Red Hat	2005	1 year

Languages	Version	Last Used	Years of Experience
Visual C++	5, 6	2000	3 years
Java	1.1 to 5.0	Present	5 years

Do not include old or outdated languages, and be sure to include the information that's best known in Canada. When describing your experience, you must show where you used these languages. If you named a language under Technical Skills, also mention it in your Selected Projects. If you don't, the employer may suspect that you've never actually used this language.

In the Experience section, describe the companies where you worked whenever possible. Name projects, specify their purposes, and describe your personal contribution, along with the tool you used. For example:

Experience
Selected Projects
New Software Product:
* Replication Engine for PointBase Database (7 months, 5 developers. JDK 1.1.x, 1.2, JDBC, JNI, Visual C++ 5.0, Rational Rose 98). PointBase is a pure Java relational database, supporting full SQL and JDBC standard with the goal to create a pure asynchronous transformational data replication engine working with PointBase.

Main Duties
* Developed about 200 classes, containing about 24,000 lines of Java code.
* Analyzed industry trends and competing products.
* Researched Java technologies related to the project, including JavaBeans, JDBC, JNI, RMI, Security, EJB and other Enterprise APIs.
* Prepared functional specification for the new product.
* Designed and implemented a fully functional prototype, using JNI to access legacy C++ application and JDBC to access the PointBase databases.
* Architected the pure Java product, using UML and Rational Rose.
* Implemented core components in Java.

If you are an IT specialist, you will likely have to write a few versions of a resume, customized for particular positions (such as a software developer, Q/A analyst, or business analyst) and technologies (user interface, server development, web). You may have broad experience, but if you put it all in one resume, you may be rejected because the employer will think that your knowledge in *their* area of interest is limited. Include only the skills most likely to be important to a certain employer or for a particular project.

IT resumes must be specific and use professional terminology.

Tip: When applying for an IT position, be ready to take a test at the interview, or have your skills assessed.

9.10 Typical Mistakes in Newcomers' Resumes

Problem

If you've sent out many resumes over a long period of time and you still haven't been invited to any (or many) interviews, it's probably because your resume doesn't work. It's easy to make a mistake in a resume when you're new to the Canadian job market. What are some of the typical mistakes that newcomers make when preparing a resume?

Solution

Aside from any specific problems in your resume, it may simply be that it is poorly written, containing bad grammar, spelling mistakes, and other English-language errors. When you are creating your resume, it is a good idea to have it checked by more than one person. Also, communicate what is important for the employer—based on the wording in the job advertisement—rather than focusing on what you like about yourself.

Having said that, below are some of the most common mistakes newcomers make in different sections of their resumes:

Objectives

- This section is sometimes omitted—but it's an important section. Employers need to see that you have objectives that fit with theirs!
- Sometimes applicants forget to name the specific position for which they are applying. Use the place you heard about the position to get the correct name. Or look on the National Occupational Classification (NOC).
- Some people include two or three positions at once. Instead, they should create and submit a separate resume for each position.
- Some applicants focus on a supervisory position, but the chances of getting a job like this as a newcomer are usually slim.

Experience and Education

- Sometimes applicants forget to include experience that relates to the position named in the Objectives section. They might include so much information about experience not related to the position that it's hard to find any experience that does connect with the job opening.
- Or perhaps they forget to show how their achievements in previous jobs will have a positive effect in the position for which they're applying. For example, an applicant who helped increase profit or reduce expenses should point out that they could do the same for a potential employer.

Immigrant Experience

Before he arrived in Canada, Bouzar was told that there were many jobs for engineers. He knew that companies would be hesitant to hire him at the level at which he had worked in Iran, but he thought he could quickly prove himself and work his way up. The problem was getting a start.

In Iran, a person's personal life is more important than their work skills and experience. So on his resume, Bouzar included all the personal information an Iranian employer would look for: religion, family background, age, gender, and height. He also included a photo. For three months he applied to every job posting he could find and was devastated when he got only two replies, neither of which was very serious.

After attending a resume workshop, he learned that the information he was including was not required and that it showed employers he didn't understand Canadian business culture. He rewrote his resume, keeping in mind what Canadian employers want. A short while later Bouzar found a job.

- Mature workers (usually considered 45 years and older) can be tempted to say they have over 25 years' experience. But this will not attract employers who are not interested in training someone unless they are likely to stay with the company for many years. Limit your career description to the last 10 years. And do not show the date of your college or university graduation if it was a long time ago.
- Some applicants emphasize their experience from their home country but not their Canadian experience. Canadian employers are most interested in Canadian experience. They want to know that you'll be able to understand and communicate with people in a Canadian context.
- Others may send their resume by e-mail without formatting it for e-mail. If this happens, the document will look completely chaotic when the employer receives it. This is not a good way to introduce yourself!

Tip: If employers receive a letter or resume with a candidate's age, gender, or religion, it puts them in a difficult situation. Canada has very strict laws about discrimination, so employers don't want to worry about a perceived bias. This means they may not read any further.

9.11 Writing a Top-Quality Cover Letter

Problem

It's standard practice in Canada to send a cover letter with a resume when applying for a job. If you've included all your education, skills, and experience in your resume, why do you also have to send a cover letter? And, how should you go about creating one?

Solution

More about You

While a resume lists your education, skills, and experience, a cover letter gives employers a sense of your personality. It will show them your communication style, demonstrate your language skills, and give you a chance to explain why you think you are better suited for the position than other candidates.

- Explain why you're interested in this company in particular. In doing so, you can show that you've done your research and are impressed with the firm.
- Be sure not to be too personal, and avoid using "I" and "me" where possible. Also, demonstrate a positive attitude. If you show negativity, it will reduce your chances of getting a job.
- Make sure the letter is no longer than one page.

Opening (Salutation)

If possible, address the letter directly to the person who is hiring ("Dear Mr./Ms./Mrs. ..."). If you do not know the person's name, write "Dear Sir or Madam" or "Dear Sir" or "Dear Madam." If you know only the person's title, you may write "Dear Personnel Manager" or "Dear Hiring Coordinator." (It's better to write to a particular department, not just to Human Resources.)

You and the Job: A Good Fit

In the Visible Job Market

If you are applying for a job in the visible job market, near the beginning of the letter, state where you found the ad. Name the newspaper or website, the date the ad was posted, and the ad number if one was shown.

Then, using the name of the position from the ad, write about how well your qualifications match the job requirements. You can even present this information in columns or a small table. Show the employer's requirements on the left-hand side and your matching skill on the right-hand side.

In the Hidden Job Market

If you're sending your application to a company in the hidden job market, give the name of the person who referred you to the company if that was the case. But do this only if the person gave you permission to use their name. Then, demonstrate your familiarity with the company and explain how your experience, skills, and education match their needs. Be sure to indicate any related work you've done or if you've worked for a similar company.

For any application (in the visible or hidden job markets), tell the employer when you would be available to start work.

How to End the Letter

At the end, ask for an appointment to talk to the employer at their convenience. Then add that you will follow up in the near future. For example, you could write, "I will call you at the end of this week to ensure that you have received this letter and to arrange an appointment that is convenient for you," or "I will follow up with a phone call during the week of July 21."

Before sending your cover letter, look it over slowly and carefully. Remember to sign above your typed full name and to include your resume.

Finding Examples on the Internet

Before you write your cover letter, look at some samples on the Internet. Search using the keywords "cover letter," "sample cover letter," and "cover letter" plus "example" or "model." Do another search using "cover letter," "job title," and "industry." This will help you with format and phrasing. If you are not entirely confident with your language skills, have a person with strong language skills read your letter before you send it to potential employers.

Tip: If you're employed elsewhere and do not want your current employer to know you're looking for a new job, indicate in the letter that your application is confidential.

Whether or not you indicate that you'd like confidentiality, be sure to include your full contact information (your full legal name, mailing address, phone and fax numbers, and e-mail address).

9.12 Distributing Your Resume

Problem

Once you've written your top-quality resume and cover letter, you can start sending copies to potential employers. How can you distribute your resume most effectively?

Solution

This can be an exciting stage in your job search as you discover new possibilities for employment. Start by picturing yourself doing a job you would enjoy. Then, write a list of the types of companies you'd be interested in working for. Of course, you may not be able to work at your dream job immediately. It's a good idea to prepare another list of positions you would be willing to take before the ideal job appears. Keeping these lists in mind, do some research to find actual employers who might be a good match for you.

Here's a list of places (organized under the visible and hidden job market titles) where you can send your resume during your job search.

The Visible Job Market

In response to job ads, send your resume exactly as instructed. Usually, employers request that resumes be sent by mail, e-mail, or fax. Some ads give an address where they want you to drop it off in person, however, and this is the best method of resume delivery. If you are fortunate, you may meet the hiring person when you deliver your resume; you could even get an informal interview on the spot.

The Hidden Job Market

- Companies who are hiring, but not advertising available positions
  - Find their contact information in business directories, in phone books, or on the Internet.
- Employment agencies according to their profile and the area they serve
  - Your selection of employment agencies should also depend on the position and wage you are looking for.
- Addresses of employers you've heard about through relatives, friends, and acquaintances
  - In this case, it is best to ask your contact to deliver your resume to the appropriate manager or to the human resources department personally.

- Online resume banks
  - Be careful in using this resource. It's the most passive method of job searching because you simply have to wait for someone to become interested in you. And, if you already have a job and your employer finds out that your resume is on the Internet, you could lose your current position before finding a new one.
- An employer or his representative at a job fair
  - This gives you a good opportunity to put your resume directly into your employer's hands. Sometimes you can even get a first interview immediately. However, at job fairs, employers receive many resumes in a short time, so it may be hard to make yourself noticeable compared to other applicants.
- Your own website
  - If you don't already have a job, this may help. However, a job bank would receive more traffic (viewers) than your website. And if you're already employed, your employer might learn that your resume is on the Internet and you could lose your current position. If you decide to display your resume on the Internet, it must be prepared in an appropriate manner (formatted in ASCII or plain text). (See 9.7 for instructions.)
- An organization where you want to work as a volunteer

Area of Distribution

Do not limit your field of search to one city. There is much more competition in large cities than in suburbs or smaller towns. So it's a good idea to distribute your resume throughout an entire province, or even in other provinces or territories.

How Many Resumes Should You Send?

It's not unusual to send 25 resumes or more before getting an interview. And if you do a mass mailing without careful selection of addresses, the probability of getting an interview will be less than 1 percent.

Tip: Avoid resume distribution agencies you may find on the Internet. They promise to send hundreds or even thousands of your resumes to addresses they have collected. However, this kind of distribution has a very poor chance of success. Your resume is likely to be treated as junk mail and weeded out by employers' spam filters.

Every resume you send out must be accurately targeted.

9.13 Why Didn't You Get an Interview?

Situation

What happens if you follow all the good advice, rewrite and improve your resume, try new tactics and approaches... and still don't receive any interested responses?

Information

Too Early to Worry?

First, think about whether or not you should really be concerned yet:

- How much time have you spent searching for a job—only two or three months?
- How many resumes have you distributed—15? 20?

If you answer yes to either of these questions, it's too early to worry. To get one interview, you may need to distribute 25, 50, or even 100 resumes.

But, if you've been conducting an active job search for more than half a year, have distributed 100 or more resumes, and have not been called for an interview, then, yes, it's time to rethink your approach.

Good Advertising, Good Quality

When you're looking for a job, you're actually selling a "product"—you. If you're not receiving any positive responses, you may have weaknesses in one, or both, of these areas: your advertising, or the quality of your "product."

Improving Your Advertising

Your resume and cover letter are key parts of your advertising campaign. If you have not received positive responses, look at these documents again:

- You may have overlooked a simple error.
- Your letter may put too much importance on experience unrelated to the position you've applied for.

- Re-read the advice in this unit and then read your resume and cover letter again. Have you omitted anything important?
- Look up more resources about how to prepare resumes and cover letters —and look for new models.
- Ask a trusted advisor to look at your resume and cover letter again.

Improving Distribution
- Have you applied to employers that are truly a good match for you?
- Have you applied to employers in a large enough geographic area, including employers outside of big cities?
- Have your applications actually arrived?
- Have you reminded contacts in your network that you're looking for work?
- Have you followed up after informational interviews (see 10.3), thanking interviewees for their advice?

Improving "Product" Quality
Improving yourself as a "product" is more complex. If your occupation is not in high demand on the Canadian job market, even the best resume will not work. The only way to change this is to improve your skills, education, and experience, including improving your English skills. Ultimately, you may need to consider changing careers.

Never Give Up!
Looking for a job in a new country can be discouraging. But don't give up. Do you spend 40 hours per week job hunting? Do you have a precise action plan and a journal recording all your activities?

If you're not yet taking these suggestions, start doing so now! And don't forget that it takes time to find the right job for you.

Tip: Imagine you're the person who is hiring and ask yourself if your resume looks professional. Would it convince *you* that you're the perfect person for the job?

9.14 Unit Summary

Key Words

on-screen: appearing or written on a computer screen

sans serif: (in printing) a typeface that does not have a short line at the top or bottom of some letters (Arial, Tahoma)

self-improvement: the activity of trying to improve your knowledge, social position, or character by your own efforts

Note: Entries taken or adapted from the Oxford ESL Dictionary.

Creating Your Canadian Experience

1. As a way of getting started on your resume, fill out the following tables with your history.

    Employment

Company	Date Started	Date Ended	Position	Duties	Achievements

Education

School	Date Started	Date Ended	Program	Course	Results

2. Take some time to think about each of the sections below as it relates to your career. Then fill out the chart as a way of getting started on your resume.

Objectives	
Highlights	
Experience	
Education	
Languages or Hobbies	
References	

3. In order to focus your resume for each position you apply for, complete the chart below every time you find an interesting job ad that you want to respond to. Comparing your skills and qualifications to the position you are applying for will allow you to target your resume towards what the employer wants.

	Your Qualifications	Position Requirements
Objectives		
Experience		
Education		
Skills		

4. List three people that you can ask to check your resume and cover letter for errors.

    a. _____

    b. _____

    c. _____

5. In a notebook or on your computer, create a sheet with the headings you see in the table below. Keep track of the resumes you send out and the responses that you get.

Date Sent	Organization	Position	How You Heard about the Opening	Response

Effective Interviewing

In This Unit

- How Do Interviews Work?
- Preparing for the Interview
- What Questions Will Be Asked at the Interview?
- Questions You Should Ask at an Interview

10.1 How Do Interviews Work?

Situation

Being invited to an interview represents a great success. Out of scores of applicants, you and a few others have been chosen to meet with your potential employer. What happens at interviews and how can you approach them successfully?

Information

Preparing for an Interview

When you are invited to an interview, do plenty of preparation. Be ready to answer questions about your interpersonal and communication skills, as well as your technical skills.

First, Second, and Third Interviews

The first interview is sometimes conducted over the phone by human resources. They will ask questions about your experience, job skills, and desired salary. Based on your answers, the interviewer will decide whether or not to recommend you for a second interview.

The second interview will likely be conducted by the head of the department in which you will be working. During this interview, you will be asked many of the same questions as in the first interview. As a newcomer, be ready to explain how your experience in your native country and in Canada will benefit your potential employer.

If there is a third interview, it is typically conducted by a vice-president or president of the company, who will decide whether or not to hire you and what salary you will be offered.

What Happens at an Interview?

The meeting begins with an exchange of pleasantries, smiles, and handshakes. There is often "small talk" about something other than the job.

The main part of the interview often begins when the interviewer says, "Tell us about yourself." In your answer, tell them about your experience, education, and skills.

During the next stage, the interviewer will tell you about the company and position for which you are applying. You'll then have an opportunity to ask questions.

In the final part of interview, salary will usually be discussed. Often, you'll be told that the final hiring decision will be made after other candidates are interviewed.

Peter's Personal Experience

I have gone to a number of interviews in Canada and have learned something new from each one. I now know that you should do some in-depth research before every interview.

First, you should find out who is going to interview you. For example, will it be the manager of the HR (Human Resources) department, the supervisor of the position you are applying for, or both? Based on my experience I'd say that HR staff usually ask questions about "soft" skills such as your interpersonal, organizational, and communication skills. And supervisors usually ask questions about your technical skills.

Second, you should learn as much as possible about the company and its culture. The more you know about the company, the more attractive you will be as a candidate.

Third, you should find out all you can about the position you are applying for. Don't restrict yourself to the information on the job posting. If possible, speak with a company employee who can tell you more about the position.

The more prepared you are for your interview, the better chance you'll have of getting the job.

Here are other things that might happen during the interview:

- Often, you'll be asked for references.
- The interviewer may look at samples of your work in your portfolio.
- You may be asked to take a test to check your professional skills.

After the Interview

It's a good idea to send a thank-you letter after the interview. If you don't receive a call within a week, make a "follow-up" call. You may learn that the position was taken by someone else or you may get a job offer.

Tip: One interview does not represent your last chance to get a job. It's one of many steps on the road to employment, where each disappointment teaches you how to be successful.

10.2 The Telephone Interview

Problem

If an employer likes your resume, he may conduct a telephone interview with you. It may be the first step towards an in-person interview. How should you conduct yourself during this interview? How can you to add to your value in the eyes of the employer?

Solution

Practice Makes Perfect

The best way to prepare for a phone interview is to rehearse. Ask a relative or friend to call you and ask (in the language of the real interview) some unexpected questions about your work history, skills, and **ambitions**.

Before giving an answer, you may repeat the interviewer's question. This will give you time to think, and it will show the interviewer that you've heard the question correctly. In your answer, be specific and use professional terminology. Add facts not included in your resume.

Once you've answered all the interviewer's questions, ask some questions about the job, including your place on the team and projects in which you are likely to participate.

After you've finished your practice interview, ask your friend or relative about the kind of impression you made based on your answers and telephone etiquette.

Pronunciation

Pronunciation is very important during a telephone interview. It's a good idea to prepare for an interview with a language teacher, or to spend time training with a tape recorder. Your voice should sound bright, clear, and confident. If you're not sure how to pronounce certain words, ask someone who knows.

Tip: If the telephone interviewer gives you an appointment for an in-person interview, write down the details in your notebook right away. Include the first and last names of the interviewer, along with the time and location of the interview. Don't rely on your memory alone for these details!

Employer Experience

Many employers start with a phone interview because it is a quick way to weed out some of the weaker candidates. Some employers find that people don't take phone interviews as seriously as in-person interviews. If the candidate is not ready, or if there is a TV or radio on in the background, the chances of getting an in-person interview will be greatly reduced.

It's also important to allow enough time for the call (at least 45 minutes). And if you're expecting a call on a particular day, you must make sure that you're at home to receive it. If the interviewer does not phone at the pre-arranged time, you should wait for the call.

A landline (or home phone) is preferable to a cell phone, as bad reception can hurt the flow of the conversation.

Telephone Etiquette

- Be polite.
- Think about what you're going to say, but try not to sound as if you're reading from a script.
  - Be ready to follow the conversation in the direction your interviewer takes it.
- Never begin the conversation with questions about salary or **benefits**.
- Be careful about the emotions you convey.
  - The goal of the telephone interview is to receive an invitation to a personal interview, not to express your feelings. Disappointment or irritation can be more noticeable in your tone of voice over the phone than in a personal meeting, so be sure to smile during the conversation. That will make you sound cheerful and pleasant.
- If the interviewer asks whether you have any questions, it means that interview is probably about to end.
- Once the interview is over, make notes about it.
- Write a thank-you letter and send it to the interviewer.

Problem

An informational interview is not about getting a job—at least not yet. It's an opportunity to ask a potential employer, or another contact, about their company or the industry in general. What are the advantages of informational interviews, and how can you set one up?

Solution

Advantages of an Informational Interview

By speaking directly with a potential employer, you'll find out a lot of information about their company and your field in a short time. Information you'll need to learn includes duties you would be expected to perform, education you require, and regions of Canada where your occupation is in demand.

Most people are happy to give informational interviews—people generally enjoy sharing their expertise and giving advice.

Who Should You Contact for an Interview?

In addition to potential employers, try to get interviews with the following people:

- An employment agency worker.
- A teacher at a local college or university.
- A counsellor at an employment resource centre.

How Can You Arrange an Interview?

Begin by searching for helpful contacts using your network. As well, look through business directories and "help wanted" ads. Contact the person you've found and ask for an informational interview.

If you phone, the receptionist will help you find the right person to talk to. In case you reach an employer directly, prepare a short script before you call. Here's one possible script:

- "Hello, my name is [your name]. [Name the person who referred you] gave me your name. I am a newcomer to Canada and worked in this field in my country, but I need to learn more about the occupation in Canada. Would you be able to speak with me at some point about this? It should not take more than 10 or 15 minutes of your time."

If a contact is unable to meet with you in person, ask if they could answer your questions by e-mail or letter.

Informational Interview vs. Job Interview

Informational Interview	Job Interview
You set up the interview with the potential employer.	The potential employer sets up the interview with you.
The purpose is to find information that will give you new opportunities and make your job search easier.	The purpose is to determine whether you are a good fit for the job that's available.
You are the interviewer asking the questions.	You are being interviewed and answering the questions.

Preparing for an Informational Interview

Before you go to the informational interview, prepare a list of questions specific to you. Here are some questions you could ask during an informational interview:

- What are the duties that must be performed by a [name a position]?
- What are the greatest challenges in this occupation?
- If I was to start as a [name a position], what would be my likely career path?
- What skills and qualifications do you think I need to reach my goal of working as a [name a position]?
- How can I obtain the necessary qualifications?
- Do you know other divisions or anyone else in the business community who might need someone with my qualifications?
- Which are the most rapidly growing companies in this field? Who should I speak to there?
- Are you planning any new projects that might create an opening at some time in the future?

Tip: During the informational interview, it may be possible to show your resume and portfolio to your interviewee and ask for advice on how to improve these documents.

10.4 Preparing for the Interview

Situation

Your interview preparation can determine your chances of getting a job and create a good (or bad) impression on your employer. In order to make a good impression, you'll need to prepare. What kind of preparation should you do?

Advice and Action Plan

Step 1—Learn the Basic Rules of the Interview

If you know the rules of the interview, you'll be more relaxed and self-confident. And self-confidence can help you get the job. In the next few chapters you will find answers to many questions newcomers often have about interviews. These include the following points:

- What questions you'll likely be asked—and how to answer.
- What you should take with you (e.g., resume, portfolio).
- What are the rules of etiquette (behaviour) for Canadian interviews.
- What are the main mistakes people make during interviews.
- What questions you should ask and how to talk about salary.

If you would like to learn more about any of these topics, enroll in a workshop at an employment resource centre (ERC) or in a Job Finding Club, or ask the people you know for advice.

Step 2—Study Your Potential Employer

Before you go to the interview, collect three kinds of information: general information about the company, information about the interviewer, and information about the position for which you are applying.

Information about the Company

Learning about the company will help you to better understand what they expect from their employees and what they are looking for in a candidate. It's a good idea to learn when the company was established, how many people it employs, and its past successes and future plans by looking at business directories, annual reports, trade magazines, and websites.

You may also be able to find out about the managers, and other people you might be working with. If you can find a friend or contact who works for the company, you may be able to ask questions about the day-to-day workings of the company, such as **dress codes**, and work environment.

Immigrant Experience

When Tsering came to Canada from the Philippines, she found that interviewers asked different questions than they did back home. Here, she discovered, a job candidate is expected to talk in detail about the company and the position they are applying for. They also expect you to describe how your skills will help the company. In the Philippines, interviewers generally wanted to know more about personal things such as your age, and health issues.

Once Tsering realized these differences, she did more research and thought more about how she would fit with the company's goals. Before long, she found a job with a company that suited her very well.

Information about the Interviewer

Once the interview is set up, ask politely who will be conducting the interview. Being interviewed by a Human Resources (HR) person or the manager you may be working for will affect the type of questions being asked.

Information about the Position

Knowing about the position ahead of time will allow you to focus your answers on the aspects that the employer feels are important. Start with where you heard about the job as this will likely be a great source of information. You may also want to look up similar positions at other companies.

- Determine the type of position (full-time or contract).
- What are the major responsibilities of the position?
- What is the company looking for in a candidate?

Step 3—Do a Practice Interview

- Ask friends or family members to act as your interviewer and have them ask you questions.
- Encourage them to throw in surprise questions.
- Ask them how you think you could improve.
- Think of mistakes you made in past interviews and correct them.

Tip: With good research and practice, you will be more calm and confident during the actual interview.

10.5 Effective Interview Behaviour

Situation

When you are being interviewed, your potential employer will be interested in learning about your personal qualities, as well as your skills. Through your conversation, she will be deciding how well you would fit into the team you could be working with. How can you make a good impression on your interviewer? What behaviours are effective at interviews?

Information

Your Appearance

- If you are in doubt about how to dress, simply wear a neat business suit or, for women, a businesslike jacket over a dress, skirt, or dress pants. It's important to appear neat and tidy.
- Don't wear anything that would make the interviewers pay more attention to what you're wearing than what you're saying.
- Check your appearance in a mirror before you leave the house and once more before you go into the interview.

Creating a Good First Impression

- Arrive at the interview about ten minutes before your appointment.
- When the interviewer first greets you, give him a self-assured smile and a solid handshake. Then say something like "I'm pleased to meet you."
- Sit down when you are invited to but not before.
- Look at the interviewer calmly and positively. Avoid glancing around the room.

Verbal and Non-verbal Communication during the Interview

- Your gestures and the way you hold your body (body language) count for as much as 70 percent of the first impression you make. Your tone of voice (whether you sound nervous or confident, for example) counts for 20 percent. What you actually say counts for only 10 percent!
- It's important to sit up straight and look calm. Avoid fidgeting with any objects.
- It's never acceptable to chew gum or to use a cell phone (be sure to turn your cell phone off).
- Avoid setting up a lot of appointments on the day of the interview. This way, you won't feel rushed. And never glance at your watch! The interviewer could interpret this as disinterest.

> **Tip:** At the interview, do not pretend to be something you are not. Be yourself! The employer is looking for the right candidate. But you are also looking for a job that is a good fit for you.

- Watch the interviewer to decide how to behave. If he or she is being casual, it would be a mistake to be too formal, and vice versa.
- Listen carefully to all questions. If the interviewer says something you don't understand, don't be afraid to ask for clarification.
- Be sure to maintain eye contact while answering questions and listening. In some cultures, this might be considered impolite. But in Canada, it indicates confidence and attentiveness.
- Show enthusiasm and a positive attitude.
- Answer questions with confidence.
- Don't be afraid of small pauses in the conversation. If necessary, take time to reflect on your answer before speaking.
- Keep your answers relatively short—about a minute long. But include specific examples from your education or experience to support your answers.
- After you've finished answering questions, be sure to ask some of your own.

Ending the Interview Well

- If salary is discussed, it will happen near the end of the interview. Don't appear too eager to talk about this. And decide before the interview exactly what amount you would agree to. That way, you'll be able to discuss salary clearly.
- During the interview, you may realize that this job is not for you. If this is the case, do not try to end the conversation. Wait until the interviewer indicates that the interview is finished.
- If you want the job but sense that you will not get it, be careful not to show your disappointment. However, you may ask how soon you can expect to hear a decision from the company.
- When the interview is finished, thank your interviewer politely for his consideration and say goodbye.

> **Tip:** It's completely acceptable to pause and think before answering a question. You may also ask the interviewer to clarify the question. Or repeat the question as you understood it and ask the interviewer if that is what they meant.

10.6 What Questions Will Be Asked at the Interview?

Problem

Interviewers will be impressed if you can answer their questions clearly and confidently. How can you prepare to make sure this happens?

Solution

The best way to ensure that you are confident in your responses is to think about possible questions ahead of time. Based on the chart below, brainstorm some questions your interviewers might ask. Then note points that you would include in your answers.

Questions	Answers
Tell me about yourself.	Briefly describe your post-secondary education, the courses you took, and your marks. Give a short work history of positions relevant to the job. Mention your devotion to your career. Emphasize your Canadian education and experience.
Where do you see yourself [a few] years from now?	Don't appear to be overly ambitious, but mention some possibilities for advancement. Point out that you'd like to have an interesting job with a salary that reflects your abilities and hard work.
What are your greatest strengths?	Describe strengths that relate directly to the position.
What is your greatest weakness?	Mention a weakness that can also be seen as a strength. For example, if you are a perfectionist, you should say that. Mention that English (or French) is not your native language but that you're working hard to improve it.
What would be your ideal job?	Mention that you like work that challenges you or that gives you the chance to take initiative and show your creative abilities.
What do you think you can contribute to this company?	Describe how you think your skills can improve or complement the efficiency and profits of the company.

Questions	Answers
What do you know about our company?	Talk about information you discovered during your research and describe where you found the information, if that would impress your interviewer.
You seem overqualified (or under qualified).	Say that you would be satisfied with the job you are applying for and that you look forward to the chance to show your abilities.
Tell me about something you've done that demonstrates initiative.	Describe an experience you've had since coming to Canada.
Do you work well with others?	Give examples to demonstrate that you are a good team player—from your Canadian experience if possible.
What major problems have you faced in your career and how have you solved them?	Focus on a problem that you solved with special skills or that resulted in an award or other recognition.
What did you like most about your last job and your last manager?	Avoid saying anything bad about your previous employer. Praise them for encouraging you or for giving you opportunities.
Why did you leave your last job?	Explain that you had no prospect for growth, that you earned a new degree, or that you left in order to come to Canada.
In what area would you most like additional training if you get this job?	Mention something that would help you perform your new job even better. Always be eager for opportunities for self-improvement.

Employer Experience

One of the most common mistakes that people make in interviews is talking too much. It's understandable because they are likely excited and nervous, but it can create a bad impression. It's important to listen to the question carefully and then answer only it. Offer plenty of detail, but don't say anything unrelated to the topic.

To make sure you've answered well, refer to the question at the end of your response. Or ask the interviewer directly if you've answered the question they asked.

10.7 How to Answer Behavioural Questions

Problem

Behavioural questions are designed to help the interviewer see how you would act in a difficult or complex situation. For newcomers, these questions can also indicate how your ethics and culture fit with Canadian business operations. The employer will be trying to determine how your behaviour might improve human relations and productivity, and how it might cause problems. How can you prepare for these questions to present yourself in a positive way?

Solution

How to Recognize Them

Behavioural questions usually begin with something like, "Describe a situation in which you..." or "Give me an example of a time when you..." These questions can be about your ability to resolve conflicts; your management style; how you've attracted clients; how you've succeeded in difficult situations; what major mistakes you've made and what the results were; or why you left a previous job.

Immigrant Experience

Tsering has learned that Canadian interview standards are very different from those in the Philippines, where, to make things even more confusing, Tsering had been the interviewer and not the interviewee!

She has made some changes to the way she behaves in an interview. She maintains eye contact with the people speaking to her, she tries to relax and enjoy the flow of the conversation during an interview, and she doesn't give too much personal information. While employers back in the Philippines were interested in personal details, Tsering has learned that in Canada it is considered inappropriate and, in some cases, illegal for employers to ask questions of a personal nature.

Now that she has a better grasp of etiquette for job interviews, Tsering feels more confident about herself as an interviewee.

With these questions, the interviewer wants to learn about problems that occurred because of an interviewee's incompetence or lack of planning skills, or how well they dealt with unexpected developments.

How to Answer Them

Show that you used your best qualities to create the best possible solution to the problem. Describe the lessons you learned. And try not to be vague or general. Describe specific situations from your past.

The information you give the interviewer must match the education, experience, and skills you included in your resume. So before going to the interview, re-read your resume carefully and prepare several stories about your past work based on it.

Your stories should take only two or three minutes to tell. And they should be structured in this way: first describe a problem that matches the question the interviewer asked. Then tell your story, including explanations for your actions. End with the results of your decisions. Or reverse this structure, starting with the results: "I achieved outstanding results by acting promptly and carefully when …"

Write your stories, have a language expert review them, and memorize them. But try not to sound rehearsed!

Sample Question	Answer
Describe a case where you disagreed with your boss.	I asked the head of our department to give me an additional worker so I could finish my work on time. He said he couldn't spare anyone, so I had to manage by myself. I did not want to have a conflict with the boss, so I left upset. To speed up the project, I worked overtime, including weekends. The boss noticed I was still there when he went home, and he had to give me a special pass to work on the weekends. After several days, he approached me and asked how the work was going. I'd been waiting for this question and explained to him patiently and in detail what was completed and what still had to be done. He understood that this work was too much for one person and gave me the assistant I'd requested.

Tip: After telling your story, you can ask the interviewer if you've properly answered her question.

10.8 Questions about Immigration and Culture

Problem

Newcomers face extra challenges in interviews simply because they are "new." That is, if you're a newcomer, interviewers will not be familiar with your culture. They may find your speech or gestures difficult to understand and this may make them doubt that your skills, education, and experience will fit with Canadian standards. How can you help your interviewers trust you and your abilities?

Solution

Show Convincing Documentation

Show samples of your work and your diplomas (translated into English by a professional translation service). Provide an evaluation certificate from an official foreign credentials evaluation service (see 1.6). This will demonstrate that your foreign credentials match Canadian ones. Obtain a Canadian certificate, licence, or diploma in your field and present these at interviews.

Give Good References

If you give a reference from your home country, it's best if this person speaks English (or French if you are in a French-speaking area). The ideal references to give, however, are Canadian references. If you know someone who works at the company to which you're applying, present them as a reference. Include a Canadian who lives relatively nearby: an English teacher; a co-worker or supervisor from a place where you volunteer(ed); a landlord; or any reliable Canadian friend who is not a newcomer.

Ask to Be Tested!

If you think the interviewer might not trust your knowledge, politely suggest an immediate test of your skills (do not do this in a challenging manner). The test could involve answering questions or otherwise demonstrating your ability.

- For example, if you're applying to be a secretary, you could ask to input a document and then do it quickly and without mistakes. If you are a draftsperson, you could do a sketch, either manually or on a computer (which would also show your ability to use the software).

Answer Questions with Confidence

Answer interview questions confidently and briefly. Demonstrate your international work experience by referring to specific examples. The examples should prove that you performed the same duties as those required in the job. Describe times when you were faced with serious problems and indicate how you solved them. Emphasize your ability to work as part of a team, reach compromises, and solve conflicts.

The interviewer may be concerned about how your culture could affect your behaviour on the job. You may be asked how you would act in a certain situation.

Sample Question: If you have an innovative idea on how to improve business, what actions would you take?

    (a) tell colleagues about the idea
    (b) talk about the idea with your manager
    (c) present the idea at a staff meeting
    (d) not share the idea with anyone

In Canada, the best answers would be (b) and (c).

To learn about desirable behaviour in Canadian workplaces, attend employment resource centre workshops.

Deal with the "Overqualified" Response

It's unlikely that your first job in Canada will be at the same level you worked at in your home country, so it's more practical to apply for a lower position. For example, an internationally trained engineer might find employment as a technician.

In your resume and interview, present yourself according to the level for which you're applying. Otherwise, you might be considered overqualified.

Answer Questions about Your Culture

Along with the work-related questions, you may be asked culture-related ones. You might be asked why you immigrated to Canada, or if you expect extra time off for religious or cultural holidays. At some workplaces, you may be expected to change your style of dress. Be as flexible as you can without betraying your religious or cultural principles.

10.9 Recognize and Deal with Illegal Questions

Situation

Interviewers in Canada tend not to ask questions about a candidate's personal life. This is because many questions of this nature are illegal in Canada. Exactly what questions are illegal, and what should you do if an interviewer asks you such a question?

Information

What Kinds of Questions are Illegal?

In many cases, questions that ask for personal information are illegal in Canada. For example, questions about age, state of health, marital status, presence of children or parents, religion, nationality, and home ownership are illegal.

Questions are often asked in a veiled form (in a manner that is not obvious). For example, the interviewer may attempt to learn your nationality by saying, "What an interesting surname! What language is that?" Or, they may try to find out your age by asking, "What year did you graduate from school?" You may not object to answering any of these questions, but if you feel that it would not be in your best interest to answer them, you should know that you are not legally required to do so.

If you are asked an illegal question, try to understand why the interviewer may be asking it. Often, these questions are in the interest of work. For example, asking a woman if she has children might really be to find out about her availability for business trips or overtime work.

Questions about health may not be illegal if they are related to whether or not you have the physical ability to carry out your assigned tasks. If the job requires carrying heavy weights, for example, and you have arthritis, you would not be a reasonable candidate for that position.

Taking It Online

Website Name	Website Address
Canadian Human Rights Commission	www.chrc-ccdp.ca/default-en.asp

If the interviewer wishes to learn whether or not you have a family, they may ask for a name, address, or phone number of the relative they should contact in case of emergency. In this case, you can simply give a person's name and phone number without specifying a degree of relationship.

Regarding a question about your age, you might simply choose to answer that you have enough education and experience to cope with forthcoming work.

Three Ways to Deal with These Questions

1. You may directly answer the question—it is your choice. However, you should ask yourself whether or not the answer will hurt your chances of getting the job.
2. You can refuse to answer such a question. This is not likely going to work to your advantage, but you have the right to refuse an answer if you feel it's necessary.
3. You may answer indirectly. In this method, you do not have to openly recognize that the question is illegal; this allows you to avoid confrontation and give the impression that you assume the interviewer's curiosity is purely work-related.

The third method—answering indirectly—is the best. For example, if you are asked if you are a Canadian citizen, you can answer, "You probably want to know if I have the right to work in Canada. Yes, I do." As an indirect answer to a question about children, you could simply respond that if it is necessary, you are ready for business trips and are prepared to work overtime.

Be ready for illegal questions and try to answer them easily without displaying frustration or uncertainty. If the interviewer asks illegal questions repeatedly and presses you for answers, it may be a good time to evaluate the ethics of the interviewer and the company.

Tip: If a question seems illegal but you're not certain it is, you have the right to ask the interviewer how the question relates to the job for which you are applying. This would be a relevant and understandable response.

10.10 Questions You Should Ask at an Interview

Problem

Near the end of an interview, job applicants are usually asked if they have questions for the interviewer. It's important to prepare these questions before the interview. So, what should you ask and how should you prepare?

Solution

Why Ask Questions?

It is absolutely necessary to ask questions at the interview. Doing so benefits both you and the employer. Your questions help the interviewer understand what is important to you, and the interviewer's answers will help you decide whether this is the right job for you.

Preparing Questions in Advance

Prepare your questions in advance so you don't appear indecisive during the interview. Write them down in a notebook and take it to the interview.

- You should ask questions about your future duties, the structure of the company and department where you would be working, and trends in the industry.
- The questions you ask will depend on the type of interview.
  - With a human resources manager, ask about daily routines, business hours, overtime hours, holidays, and why the position has become available.
  - With the head of the department, you might ask questions about your field of work to show your competence and confidence.
- The number of questions you ask depends on you. Three to five questions are ideal, but prepare more than this, just in case. Some of your questions will likely be answered during the interview itself.
- Your questions should be open-ended. That is, they should require full answers, not just a "yes" or "no."

- Questions about what you can do for the company will impress the interviewer more than questions about what they can do for you.
- After asking a question, give the interviewer time for the answer—and don't interrupt him.

Sample Questions
Here some questions you may want to ask.

- What are the main responsibilities of the position?
- What are my first priorities when I start the job?
- What are the company's goals and how might I contribute to achieving them?
- Why was this position created?
- What kind of training or educational opportunities does the company provide for staff?
- Can you tell me what the next step in the hiring process will be?
- When should I expect to hear from you?

Questions about Salary
The most complicated question is about salary. If salary is the most important factor in your job search, then be sure to indicate your salary expectations in your cover letter. Then, when you are invited to the interview, you can ask this question.

Otherwise, the question about salary should wait until the interviewer asks you about it or until you actually receive a job offer.

Tip: Try to avoid asking questions about information that's already available in company brochures or on a website. Ask questions that build on this information or ask about other issues that will help you and the interviewer decide whether or not you're a good match.

Situation

After the interview, days may pass before you find out whether or not you got the job. What should you do while you're waiting to hear from your potential employer?

Information

Take Notes about the Interview

Right after the interview, make notes about the impressions you got from it. You may want to include the following items:

- What questions the interviewer asked you.
- What you liked and disliked about the interview and about your performance.
- The questions you feel you didn't answer well.
- The information you learned about the company.
- The duties you'll perform if you get the job.
- Any questions asked by the interviewer that seemed unexpected, difficult, or illegal.
- Additional items that caught your attention during the interview.

Employer Experience

Candidates can improve their chances of getting a job by asking, at the end of the interview, when the employer expects to make their decision. Employers like to see that candidates are thinking about the next steps in their job search. Also, ask how you should follow up. Should you phone or send an e-mail? Different employers may have definite preferences.

Either way, when you follow up, do not just say thank you. Tell them that after hearing about the job in more detail, you are even more interested in the position and feel even more that you are suited for it. To prove this point, refer to some items that were discussed in the interview. If done correctly, a follow-up call or e-mail will help the employer remember you as a good candidate.

In your notes, include the name of the interviewer, her position, and who will decide whether or not you get the job. Don't wait until you get home to make these notes. You'll likely forget some important details by that time. Stop at a coffee shop on your way home and write your notes there.

These notes will be useful when you prepare for other interviews, or if you have a second interview with the employer you just met.

Send a Thank-You Letter

Sending a thank you letter right after the interview will help your potential employer remember you. And it will show that you are attentive and that you do things on time. If you had more than one interviewer, send a thank you letter to each of them.

Here are a few things to include in the thank-you letter:

- Be sure to thank the interviewer for her time.
- Always refer to two or three points discussed during the interview that made you want to work for the company.
- You should describe skills, education, and/or experience that you feel you should emphasize now because of items that were discussed during the interview.

Follow Up with the Employer

If the interviewer promised to tell you their decision within a week but you have not heard from them by then, you may phone or e-mail to find out the result. Politely ask what the result was or ask about when the decision will likely be made.

Even if you think you'll likely be hired for this job, continue your job search.

Tip: If you do not get the job, it is acceptable to write to the employer asking them for the reasons behind their decision. Do not show disappointment. Just let them know that you would like to improve your chances for your next job application. Thank the employer again for their interest and ask them to contact you if they have another job opening.

10.12 Negotiating a Job Offer

Situation

Receiving a job offer for a position you like—or need—may be one of the best events since your arrival in Canada. But some important details still have to be taken care of. Notably, the company hiring you must give you a written job offer that includes information about working conditions. If the company is large, you will receive this document from the Human Resources (HR) department. What should the job offer contain, and how should you respond to it?

Information

By the time a company sends you a job offer, they have invested a lot of time and money in looking for the right person. So your potential employer will be hoping that you'll accept. You do not need to accept the exact offer they give you, though. It's usually possible to negotiate some items.

Here's the information you'll find in most job offers:

- Salary, benefits, and **probation period** (During the probation period, your ability to perform the job will be assessed. If you cannot perform its duties, you will be dismissed. Not all jobs require a probation period.)
- The name of the department where you would work and description of your duties
- Starting date and definition of the job as full-time, part-time, temporary, or permanent
- Length of the workday and workweek

The offer may also contain:

- Opportunities for growth and improvement of your skills
- Conditions of overtime, paid vacation, and holidays
- Staff regulations
- Employee's responsibility not to disclose confidential information

A Note about Benefits

Good benefits can make a lower salary more attractive or a high salary very attractive! Here are some benefits you might receive as part of a job:

- Health insurance (beyond government-based health insurance), dental insurance, and pension fund deductions
- Life and disability insurance

- **Profit-sharing** plan
- Company vehicle or free parking
- Flexible work hours

Negotiating a Job Offer

- If you think the job offer you receive is reasonable, sign it and return it to the company. And, of course, tell the person who wanted to hire you that you've accepted their offer!
- If you're not sure about accepting, ask the company for a bit of time to discuss the offer with advisors and family. But don't spend too much time doing this!
- If another company has offered you a job at a higher salary but you'd prefer to work for *this* company, let this company know. They might be able to offer you a better salary or benefits.

Salary Negotiations

If the salary in the job offer is lower than you expected, the employer may feel that you will take time to get used to Canadian workplace culture—at their expense.

What should you do if you want to work at this company but the salary is lower than you'd like? Here are some strategies that you may want to consider using:

- Ask for your salary to be reviewed within three to six months (salaries are often not reviewed until a year after hiring).
- Ask for an increase to benefits or other non-salary perks such as vacation time. You may also ask the employer to pay for upgrading courses, to reimburse mileage expenses, or to provide a better compensation package in case you are laid off.

How to Say "No"

If you decide not to accept the job offer, your refusal should be polite and you should give reasons for your decision. Also, tell the company that you'd like to hear about any future job openings that better suit your skills, education, experience, and desired salary.

Tip: Job offer negotiation is common, and employers usually try to be understanding and flexible. Don't hesitate to ask questions, and be determined enough to get the job and salary you need without being too demanding!

Situation

During the interview, the potential employer will consider your suitability based on three factors: your personality; your skills, education, and experience; and how well you would fit with the team. If you aren't hired, it's important to find out why. Did you make mistakes during the interview? How can you improve for the next time?

Information

If you don't get a job, it may be that you and that company were truly not a good match. However, it's possible to make interview errors that prevent you from being hired. Even if this happens, the experience can be a positive one. Use the following chart to review your interview. Work on any "no" answers to do even better on your next interview!

Did You . . .	Yes	No
Arrive at the interview on time?		
Shake your interviewer's hand upon greeting?		
Smile and greet your interviewer in a friendly way?		
Wait to be invited to sit down before doing so?		
Show a positive and friendly attitude?		
Make eye contact when talking?		
Appear calm?		
Have a good flow of conversation?		
Say positive things about a previous job or manager?		
Pay attention?		
Let your interviewer know you were familiar with the industry?		
Understand the questions?		
Answer questions briefly but completely?		

Did You . . .	Yes	No
Express interest in working for this company?		
Show your knowledge of the company?		
Provide detailed examples of your experience?		
Use relevant technical terms?		
Communicate your long-term plans?		
Describe what you could offer the company?		
Let the interviewers know you were willing to take on challenges?		
Remain positive throughout the whole interview?		
Shake the interviewer's hand upon leaving?		
Thank the interviewer when you left?		
Say goodbye politely?		

Employer Experience

Some people are shy about asking questions if they don't understand instructions or if they don't hear them clearly. But it's important to ask questions like these! One newcomer with excellent skills was interviewed for an administrative position. The interview went very well. The next day she returned to the office for a second interview. The staff wasn't expecting her, however, and there was some confusion while they looked for her interviewer of the previous day. Surprised to see her, the interviewer explained that he had asked her to *call* him back, not to *come* back to the office. As a result of this mix-up, the interviewer did not hire the applicant because he felt her communication and listening skills were not good enough.

If she had asked a question to clarify this situation, she might have gotten the job!

Remember, the interviewer's decision depends on how you perform during the interview. So, the invitation to the interview is your doorway to success. That's why it's important to walk through that doorway with confidence and understanding of how you should act and what you should say.

Tip: Look at yourself from the interviewer's point of view and ask yourself, "Would I hire this person?"

Key Words

ambition: the strong desire to be successful, to have power, etc.

benefits: extra payments or services that are given to an employee in addition to his/her salary

dress code: a set of rules explaining what types of clothes people are allowed to wear in a particular place

probation period: a period of time at the start of a new job when you are tested to see if you are really suitable

profit-sharing: the system of dividing all or some of a company's profits, usually between employer and employee

Note: Entries taken or adapted from the Oxford ESL Dictionary.

Creating Your Canadian Experience

1. Take some time to find answers to the questions below about the company you are going to be interviewing with.
   Tip: Start on the company's website, but then also search in local newspapers as well as any trade magazines or industry websites.

Questions	Answers
What do they do? Come up with a list of products and services.	
Who is their biggest competition and how does it differ?	
What is the structure of the organization?	
What are the recent trends in the industry?	
How do they treat their employees?	

2. Take some time to find answers to the questions below about the position you are interviewing for.
   Tip: Start by looking where you first heard about the position, and then try looking on the NOC and Job Futures websites.

Questions	Answers
What is the title of the position?	
What skills are required?	
What skills are recommended?	
What are the main duties for the position?	
What is the average rate of pay?	

3. Come up with a list of 10 questions that you may be asked in an interview. Find a relative or friend to ask you these questions in a random order. We have started you off with a few questions from 10.6. Add two more general questions, two industry-specific questions, and three that are specific to the position based on the description ad.

    1. Tell me about yourself.

    2. What are your biggest strengths?

    3. What is your biggest weakness?

    4. _____

    5. _____

    6. _____

    7. _____

    8. _____

    9. _____

    10. _____

    Note: When you are practising, make sure to practise not just what you say in an interview, but how you say it (pay attention to posture, eye contact, and speaking with confidence).

4. On the Internet, research three companies in your industry where you could do informational interviews.
    Tip: Search using keywords "[your industry]" + "[your city]" to see what companies are in your area.

Company	Contact Person	Contact Information

5. Answer the behavioural interview questions below. Keep in mind that your answers should have three parts. The situation, the actions you took, and the results of those actions.

Questions	Answers
Describe a time when you dealt with a stressful situation and handled it well.	
Give an example of a time when you used your judgment and logic to solve a problem.	
Talk about a time when you saw a problem coming and did something to prevent it.	

6. Looking over 10.10, come up with a list of ten questions that you can ask at interviews. Try to include some about the company in general, and some about the specific positions you are interviewing for. Leave questions about salary and vacation time/days off for second or third interviews.
   Note: It is good to have at least ten questions prepared, as many will already be answered during the interview.

   1. _____

   2. _____

   3. _____

   4. _____

   5. _____

   6. _____

   7. _____

   8. _____

   9. _____

   10. _____

7. Create three lists of the key factors that need to be negotiated for a job offer. Make the first list your wish list, the second is a realistic list, and the third is your "bottom line."

Categories	Wish List	Realistic	Bottom Line
Salary			
Benefits			
Vacation time			
Job title			
Future prospects			
Other			

Internet Resources

In This Unit

- A Look at the World Wide Web
- Learning Internet Job-Hunting Skills
- Job Search Engines

11.1 A Look at the World Wide Web

Situation

The Internet (or World Wide Web) is a vast resource filled with countless websites that can be accessed 24 hours a day, 7 days a week. And with e-mail, potential employers throughout Canada can be contacted within minutes. How can you use the Internet effectively in your job search?

Advice and Action Plan

A Speedy and Inexpensive Research Tool

- The Internet can be accessed free of charge, apart from payment for an Internet account. If you don't have your own computer and account, you can access the Internet for free at public libraries and employment resource centres (ERCs).
- If you don't know how to use the Internet, take a workshop free of charge at a public library or an ERC.
- Most companies, government agencies, and educational institutions have their own websites.
- You can subscribe to free newsletters and use free dictionaries and online translation programs.
  - Note that the quality and accuracy of Internet translation programs cannot be guaranteed. It's a good idea to avoid using online translation programs for legal or business documents.
- Provincial and federal governments in Canada have a great amount of material to help newcomers adjust to life in Canada. See, for example, the website for Citizenship and Immigration Canada (CIC).

Tip: Information on some websites may be outdated or inaccurate. If you use the Internet for research, be sure to use good-quality sites (see 11.3). When in doubt, **double-check** website information with reliable published sources.

> **Tip:** Look for websites in your native language. These might include sites posted by others from your country of origin. And they might include useful tips about adapting to life and the job market in Canada.

A Source of Job Ads

- Employers publish job ads on the Internet.
- Internet job banks and resume banks link candidates with potential employers (see 5.5, 5.6, 6.9, and 11.2). Services such as Job Alert will send you e-mails about job openings as soon as they're posted.
- You can create your own website to advertise yourself or your business.
  - Remember, though, that if you already have a job and you post a resume on your website, your current employer could see the resume. You could lose your current job!

Fast, Effective Communication

- Through e-mail, job applicants can distribute hundreds of resumes throughout the country.
- Many websites are interactive. That is, you can send an e-mail through the website to ask a question about information you found there.

Taking it Online	
Website Name	**Website Address**
CIC	www.cic.gc.ca

11.2 Internet Job-Searching Help

Problem

Many government and public organizations in Canada offer information on the Internet about programs that help newcomers adapt to life in Canada and find jobs. On which websites should you look for assistance?

Solution

Job Searching

- The Human Resources and Social Development Canada (HRSDC) website covers all aspects of employment in Canada. It includes several useful links.
  - A link to the Service Canada website includes sections like Newcomers to Canada, Looking for a Job, Starting a Business, and Find a Service Canada Centre Near You. (For more about Service Canada, see 7.1.)
    - Note that in Service Canada's Job Bank, the Job Search option leads to the job title, province, and city where a person might be looking for employment. Useful sections include Job Match, Job Alert, Resume Builder, and Career Navigator. (For more about Job Banks, see 5.5 and 5.6.)
  - A link to the National Occupational Classification (or NOC, which is under the letter "n" in the HRSDC's A–Z index) contains about

Taking It Online	
Website Name	**Website Address**
Canada Language Council	www.c-l-c.ca
CIC	www.cic.gc.ca
FCRO	www.credentials.gc.ca
Going to Canada	www.goingtocanada.gc.ca
HRSDC	www.hrsdc.gc.ca
Integration-Net	www.integration-net.ca
NOC	www5.hrsdc.gc.ca/NOC-CNP/app/index.aspx?lc=E
CICIC	www.cicic.ca

40,000 job titles. Two useful sections on this website are Occupational Descriptions and the Index of Titles.

- The Foreign Credentials Referral Office (FCRO) website provides information about evaluation of credentials obtained outside Canada. It also indicates where to obtain licences for occupations that are regulated in Canada. (For more on the FCRO, see 8.8.)
- The Canadian Information Centre for International Credentials (CICIC) provides information similar to the FCRO site.
- The Settlement.org website includes a helpful document about how to search for jobs on the Internet called *The Canadian Labour Market Online: An Internet Guide for Internationally Trained Professionals and Tradespeople* (published by the New Canadians' Centre in Windsor, Ontario).

Adjusting to Canada

- The Citizen and Immigration Canada (CIC) website offers information about your first week in Canada. It also includes sections on advice for newcomers, programs for newcomers, finding help in your community, key information sources, and communities across Canada.
- The Canada Language Council website lists officially approved English- and French-language programs in Canada.

Job Searching and Settlement

- The Going to Canada website is divided into eight main sections: Welcome to Canada, Get to Know Canada, Move to Canada, Live in Canada, Immigrating to Canada, Working in Canada, Visiting Canada, and Studying in Canada.
- The Integration-Net website covers topics such as adjusting to life in Canada, finding help in your community, finding reliable sources of information, finding out about education assessment, and finding a job.

Tip: Wherever you settle in Canada, information is available for your region. The best way to find it is by entering words like "immigrant," "information," and the name of your province or territory in an Internet search engine.

11.3 Learning Internet Job-Hunting Skills

Problem

At any time, you can log on to the Internet and find hundreds of job postings. But it takes skill to focus on the jobs that might be suitable for you. How can you avoid wasting time on websites that won't help you?

Solution

There are two ways to look for jobs on the Internet. You can go directly to an Internet job bank or other job-searching website (see 11.4), or you can do a general search through a **search engine** (such as Google or Yahoo).

General Searches on Search Engines

At present, the most popular search engine is Google because it's simple to use, thorough, and fast. But even Google needs to be used with skill. For example, if you enter "employment" in the Google search box, you'll get more than a quarter billion results. It would take a lifetime to visit that many sites, so you need to narrow down your search.

- The more keywords you use, the fewer results you'll receive. Entering "Canada + employment + newcomer" will bring the number down considerably.
- Then, if you add the name of your occupation, the number of results will become even more manageable. Entering "Alberta + employment + newcomer + pipefitter" will reduce the number to just over 200.
- If you can't find what you want within the first 50 results, refine your search by changing your keywords.

Rules for a Successful Search

Near any search engine's search box, there's a Help section. This section will give you some rules for performing a successful search. Here are some of the rules you'll find:

- If all of your keywords are in quotation marks, the search engine will search only sites that contain the exact phrase you entered (the same words in the same order). For example: "Office clerk job in Toronto" will certainly narrow your search.

- If you want to look only at sites that contain a certain word or phrase, type a plus sign (+) before the word or phrase.
- If there is a word you do not want, use a minus sign (-). For example, if you do not want to waste your time looking at American job sites, you can use the minus sign to exclude certain results, as in "-US" or "-USA."
- Other searches can be done using the Advanced Search command located near the search box in most search engines. For more information, input the keywords "Boolean Advanced Searching."

Assessing Your Internet Search Results

Here are some factors to think about when you're deciding whether or not to trust a particular website:

- Who is the owner of the website—a government? A public or private organization? An individual? Contact information, such as a phone number and address, should be provided on the website.
- Information will be more relevant if the website was posted in Canada.
- Websites that have poor quality in other areas likely don't have accurate, or updated information either. Poor-quality websites contain obvious spelling or factual errors, design flaws, or broken links.
- Does the website have a bias, such as a commercial or political purpose? If so, its information may be less reliable.
- A site is more likely to be trustworthy if it has links to or from other sources you trust.
- Check some of the information from the website on other sources to see if it is reliable.
- A website should contain its own information. It should not consist only of links.
- A website that requires payment for its services is not necessarily untrustworthy. But do not give personal information or your credit card number unless you are certain that the website owners are reliable.
- Do not trust a site that guarantees you job interviews for a fee. If a site offers services that seem too good to be true, they probably are!

If you're not sure that you trust a particular job-related website, ask for advice from a counsellor at an ERC.

Tip: Spend more time thinking of effective keywords and you'll spend less time on your Internet search.

11.4 Job Search Engines

Problem

Job search engines contain job ads and other information about employment. How can you find and use the most helpful job search engines?

Solution

- Workopolis—the largest Canadian job search engine:
  - It's run by two Canadian media companies: Toronto Star Newspapers Ltd. and Gesca Ltd.
  - The site offers more than 50,000 job ads per day.
  - Job listings can be located using a keyword search or one of the following options: By Location, By Date, and Now Hiring.
  - It has an Ask a Career Advisor section where you can send questions through the website to an advisor.
- Job Bank, run by Service Canada—the second-largest Canadian job search engine:
  - To find jobs in Nova Scotia, for example, type "Nova Scotia" in the search box, along with the name of the position you are seeking. Then click Search. This will give you positions available throughout Nova Scotia.
  - Job Bank also has these helpful options: Job Match, Job Alert, Resume Builder, Job Search Tips, Student Job Search, and Career Navigator.

Taking It Online	
Website Name	**Website Address**
All Canadian Jobs	www.allcanadianjobs.com
Job Bank (Service Canada)	www.jobbank.gc.ca
Eluta Canada	www.eluta.ca
Monster	www.monster.ca
T.O. Jobs	www.tojobs.com
Workopolis	www.workopolis.com

- Monster—contains over 25,000 Canadian job postings:
  - You can find job ads across Canada by entering keywords, searching by category, and searching by location.
  - You can also create your own account and visit Resume Centre, Interview Centre, Self Assessment Centre, and Career Centre.
- All Canadian Jobs—contains more than 50,000 job ads:
  - Type the job title and location in the search box and find job ads related to your occupation. You can also post your resume on this site.
- Torontoworking.com—has more than 20,000 job ads:
  - To use this site, type the keyword for your occupation and the city and province. The site lists newly posted jobs and jobs by industry.
- Eluta Canada—created in 2006 by Mediacorp Canada Inc.:
  - Type the keyword for your occupation, along with the location. Then click on Find Jobs. At the end of your search results, you'll see a link that says E-mail. If you use this option, you'll receive e-mail notification of jobs that match your search criteria.

Staying Current

Job-search websites appear and disappear from the Internet, so it's a good idea to keep looking for new ones.

Tip: If you use a job search engine every day, you'll continue to find new opportunities all the time.

11.5 Using Job Alert

Situation

Using job search engines every day is one way to keep updated about job opportunities. But it's also easy to miss new postings, so the providers of job search engines often offer Job Alert, or a similar service, to make sure you find out about new positions as soon as they're available. How do Job Alert and similar services work?

Information

How Does Job Alert Work?

Many job banks will tell you about new job postings by e-mail if you sign up for Job Alert or a similar service. (Other names for this type of service are Career Alert, Job Search Agent, and Career Agent.)

The service is almost always free. To sign up, first register on the website with the Job Alert service. Then indicate which industries and positions you're interested in. That's all you need to do. After that, the job bank will send you e-mails about new positions that match your interests.

What if You Don't Have a Computer?

You do need an e-mail address to use Job Alert, but you don't have to have a computer. Some job banks offer you a private mailbox for e-mails on their own website, or you can obtain your own free e-mail address on Yahoo, Hotmail, or a similar provider.

In either case, you can pick up your e-mails on any computer that you can access—for instance, at the library or an employment resource centre (ERC).

A Warning: Choose Your Job Bank Carefully

When you register for a Job Alert–type service, you will be asked to give some personal data. Some job banks ask only for your name and e-mail address, along with a username and password. Others require your home address, postal code, and phone number.

If you provide personal information online, it may end up with a different group of people. As a result, you may receive "junk" e-mails (or SPAM) saying things like "You've won a million dollars!" or "Get rich working at home." If your registration included your home address and phone number, you may receive other types of junk mail, too. So it's important to use only job banks with good reputations—for example, the ones mentioned in this book. No matter which one you sign up with, it will not likely guarantee that your personal information will stay with them. They'll probably require you to sign a contract that includes wording like the following (sometimes called "disclaimers"):

- "The website owner promises not to transfer your private data to any other party."
- "The website owner cannot guarantee that no one can or will take advantage of your data."
- "When giving your personal data online, you are at risk and only you bear the responsibility for possible consequences."

Tip: Job Alert is only one tool for finding employment. Don't rely on it to do all your job searching for you! Keep up your own active job-searching campaign.

11.6 Unit Summary

Key Words

double-check: to check something again, or with great care

search engine: a computer program that searches the Internet for information, especially by looking for documents containing a particular word or group of words

Note: Entries taken or adapted from the Oxford ESL Dictionary.

Creating Your Canadian Experience

1. Search the Internet for job banks in your city or industry. Sign up for three different Job Alert–type services.

   Website Name and Address: _____

   Website Name and Address: _____

   Website Name and Address: _____

2. Record the number of "hits" you get for certain keywords. (Most search engines will tell you the number of hits—websites that match your search—at the top of the results page.)

Search	Your Province	Your Occupation	Job Agency	Newcomers
Results				

Search	"[your province]" + "[your occupation]"	"[your occupation]" + job agency	"[your province]" + job agency	"[your province]" + newcomers
Results				

Search	"[your province]" + "[your occupation]" + newcomers	"[your occupation]" + job agency + newcomers	"[your province]" + job agency + newcomers	"[your province]" + "[your occupaton]" + job agency + newcomers
Results				

3. Try searching using other combinations of words that relate specifically to you, your industry, or your city.

Search				
Results				

Search				
Results				

4. Make a list of three places that you can get computer training. Also, write down what kind of training it is and when the courses are offered. Tip: Search the Internet using keywords "computer training" + "[your city]," or ask at your local library, employment centre, or newcomer centre.

Location	Type of Training	When Offered

Section 3

You're Hired—Now What?

Choose a job you love and you'll never
have to work a day in your life.
—Confucius

How to Start and Maintain a New Job

In This Unit

- Understanding Employer Expectations
- Workplace Culture and Etiquette
- Build a Working Relationship with Your Manager and Co-workers
- Dealing with Conflicts at Work

12.1 Understanding Employer Expectations

Situation

Getting a new job is exciting but it also brings challenges. Most new employees will feel some concern about performing well enough. And if you're a newcomer, you might have anxiety about working with a new language and in a different culture. Understanding what most employers expect is the first step to lessening any anxiety.

Information

Expectations will vary depending on the employer and the job, but the following chart shows some expectations that most Canadian employers would have.

Expectations	
Honesty	Employers expect **honesty**. For example, if you are given a task that you cannot complete accurately and on time, tell your boss immediately. If you promised him or her that you'd use the "know-how" you brought from abroad, you'll need to show that you know how! The employer will also expect you to be careful and honest when using company property.
Responsibility	Employers expect **responsibility**. This means that when you agree to complete a task, you should finish it on time and avoid making excuses or blaming others for your mistakes. If you are a team leader, you must take responsibility for the completion and quality of your team's work. Good attendance is also highly valued.
Productivity	**Productivity** refers to the speed and effectiveness of your work. When you start your job, most employers will understand that you need some time to learn. But quite soon, your productivity is expected to grow. If you're on a probation period and your employer thinks you have not been productive enough by the time it ends, he or she may decide that the job is not for you.
Competence	**Competence** is the ability to use and share knowledge and skills needed for the job. Your competence is also proven by your ability to work with little supervision. Do you know Canadian rules and standards as they apply to your field? Do you understand technical drawings and language, if these are needed for you work? Can you propose new ideas and prove their benefits?
Communication Skills	Canadian employers look for workers with good **communication skills**. This is because you need to interact well with co-workers. While working in a team, you will be expected to share your knowledge and expertise as

Expectations		
	well as respect the thoughts of others. The ability to manage and resolve **conflicts** is important, especially if your team includes people from countries with different languages, customs, and beliefs.	
Personal Appearance	Your **personal appearance**—appropriate dress and hygiene—are important in the workplace.	
Positive Attitude	A **positive attitude** is vital. Employers prefer optimistic employees because they make the most of opportunities. If something bad happens, employers will know you can use it to learn how to change things so it doesn't happen again.	

Employer Experience

The vice-president of a large company hired a woman as an assistant even though she had no Canadian experience. She felt her skills and language level were strong enough and that her lack of Canadian experience wouldn't be a problem.

One day, during her assistant's first week on the job, the vice-president asked her to hold her calls while she was in a meeting. But the phone rang a few minutes later, interrupting her meeting. It was her son calling. So the vice-president assumed her assistant had put the call through because it was from a member of her family. In the following days, however, her meetings were interrupted several more times by the phone. And the vice-president noticed that other duties she considered simple were done incorrectly. Frustrated, she decided to speak with her new employee.

She learned that her assistant was unfamiliar with some informal workplace language and was too nervous to ask the meaning of the words. So, even though her English was very good otherwise, this led to confusion and errors. The new assistant was very fortunate. Her new boss took the time to clarify terminology. And the assistant learned to ask for clarification when she was unsure of a term.

Tip: If your company has an **employee handbook**, take the time to read it. The more you know about your organization, the more you can contribute.

12.2 Workplace Culture and Etiquette

Situation

Etiquette (expected behaviour) varies from country to country, so everyone coming to Canada faces different challenges in adapting. Because Canada is a multicultural society, many cultural behaviours are accepted. However, you do need to follow some basic rules of Canadian etiquette in the workplace. What are these rules?

Information

Greetings and Goodbyes

- In casual meetings, there are two versions of greetings: the more formal greeting (such as "Good morning" or "Good Afternoon") and the less formal one (such as "Hello" or "Hi").
  - The answer to any greeting is usually "Hello, how are you?"
  - The other person's answer will usually be "Fine, thank you" whether or not the person feels good or bad. These polite greetings do not reflect genuine concern. Neither do polite farewells. For example, the farewell "See you" or "See you later" only means goodbye. It doesn't mean the person really plans to meet with you again.
- Your first meeting with your employer or a co-worker usually begins with a handshake. If someone offers you a hand, it should be shaken firmly and with confidence. While shaking hands, make eye contact and smile.
- Apart from handshakes, Canadians do not generally like being touched or embraced by people they don't know. In some cases, unwanted touching can be wrongly understood as sexual **harassment**.

Addressing People by Name

- In Canada, a person's first name is used more frequently than their second one. So if someone tells you to call them by their first name, you should do so even if the person is your manager.
- At a first meeting, however, it is better to address a person as Mr. or Ms., and their last name until they ask you to call them by a different name.

Verbal and Non-verbal Communication

- When speaking with people you do not know well, you should not ask them about their age, salary, or religion. Instead, talk about the weather, sports, movies, work, or family (this is called "small talk"). You can describe the traditions of your country, culture, or national cuisine and ask about the same in Canada.

- When standing and talking, the best distance to keep between yourself and the other person is about 50 cm (an arm's length). Standing too close is considered impolite. Standing farther away can be seen as shyness or disinterest.
- During a conversation, if you look into a person's eyes often, it means you are interested in the conversation. But if you look away often, it indicates discomfort or boredom. If you avoid eye contact while answering a question, you may be suspected of lying.
- Interrupting a person in the middle of a sentence and suddenly changing the topic are both considered impolite.

Punctuality

Canadians place great importance on being on time, so do not arrive late. If you have an unexpected delay, phone to say you will be a bit late.

Teamwork

- Teamwork is valued highly in Canada. When asked to work on a team, present your ideas willingly but do not force them on people. Ask questions to be sure the other team members understand your idea.
- Canadians do not like strong debates in the workplace. Even during disagreements, they prefer to speak calmly, without raising their voices. If there is conflict between colleagues, they will have a private, face-to-face conversation. That way, they can try to understand each other better (conflict often arises from a lack of understanding).

General Work Procedures

- Arrive at work on time and do not leave early.
- Do not use working hours for personal tasks.
- If an urgent personal matter prevents you from going to work or requires you to leave work early, tell your manager immediately.
- If you need to take time off for a personal matter, try to give two weeks' warning. When you return, give your manager any documents he or she may have requested to confirm your right to absence.

Tip: Employment resource centres (ERCs) regularly hold lectures and seminars about Canadian workplace culture and etiquette.

12.3 Emotional Intelligence

Situation

Recent research has shown that the most intelligent people do not always have the best careers. A person's intelligence quotient (IQ) is not as important as their emotional intelligence quotient (EQ). What exactly is emotional intelligence, and how can it affect your career?

Information

The History

In 1990, psychologists Salovey and Mayer showed that IQ, by itself, cannot predict how well a person will do in the workplace. Career success, they said, depends more on emotional intelligence. When measured, this is called "emotional intelligence quotient" (EQ) and it depends on the following points:

- A person's ability to monitor their feelings and emotions is noted.
- The ability to monitor the feelings and emotions of the people around them is tested.
- Also tested is the way a person uses this information to guide their responses.

About EI and EQ

A person with a high EQ is skilled at understanding the reasons for people's emotions and the consequences of those emotions.

- When speaking with a client, you will likely be more successful if you use your EQ to understand the client's motivations. If you understand what drives them, you will know how to approach them successfully.
- When you're new on a job and are getting to know colleagues, a high EQ will help you understand their emotions. Understanding their feelings will help you work with them more effectively.

Taking It Online	
Website Name	**Website Address**
Institute for Health and Human Potential	www.ihhp.com

Tip: Most people can tell whether or not they have a high EQ. Do you think you're good at understanding other people's behaviour? Find out if your understanding of yourself matches with your EQ score.

If your manager is in a bad mood, is it because you made a mistake? Or did he have a quarrel with his wife, followed by traffic jams on his way to work?

EQ also involves looking at your own emotions. If you are under stress, how will that affect the quality of your work? Through understanding the reasons for, and consequences of, your emotions, you are more likely to behave correctly. And a manager will always prefer an employee who is **self-controlled**, doesn't get angry about minor problems, and is capable of adjusting not only to his own, but anothers' emotions.

A high EQ allows a person to use emotions effectively. Showing enthusiasm, interest, sympathy, or other positive emotions will likely create a good impression on your employer and co-workers. Emotional skills will also help you to solve conflicts and convince people to consider your ideas —this will improve your chances of promotion.

Find Your EQ

Some large companies use expensive tests to learn the EQs of potential employees. But you can test your own EQ free of charge using tests in a book by author Mark Davis called *Test Your EQ*. These tests are divided into chapters on recognizing emotional states, understanding emotions, regulating and controlling emotions, and using emotions effectively.

This book also includes exercises in self-training and self-control to help you raise your EQ. An EQ test is also available on the Internet at the website of The Institute for Health and Human Potential.

12.4 Your First Days at a New Job

Problem

Your first days at a new job can be a great adventure. But they can also be stressful as you try to make the best possible impression on your manager and co-workers. What should you do during your first days at work in order to make a good impression?

Solution

Getting Ready to Go to Work
- Dress in a businesslike way. You might be able to dress more casually later on, but at first you need to look your very best.
- Leave early enough that you will arrive at work slightly early.

Meeting and Greeting
- When your manager greets you, smile, shake his hand with confidence, and express your enthusiasm for the new job.

What You'll Need to Learn
- On your first day, you'll likely be gathering information more than working. You'll also learn about the daily routine and the names of your co-workers. It's a good idea to write names down so you don't forget them.
- Spend some time learning more about the company and its competitors.
    - Read the most recent annual reports or booklets describing the company.
    - Become familiar with the company's structure. Who are your co-workers? Who are the supervisors, clients, and vendors?
    - Find out where, when, and how business meetings are carried out and which ones to attend.
    - If there are safety rules, ask to see them and study them carefully. Ask who is responsible for workplace safety, where he is located, and what his phone number is.
    - If there is a trade union, find out how to become a member.

Tip: Now that you have a job, do not forget to thank anyone who helped you find it!

- Attend any **orientation sessions** for new employees.
- Obtain an employee handbook and learn about company policies and ethics—including any vacation days, sick days, and benefits.
- Find out more about your department and team, and learn about any personal duties and obligations.
- You'll likely notice things that could be done differently, based on your experience in your home country. But don't offer advice yet! After you've shown that you can do your job, your co-workers and manager will be more likely to accept your advice.
- After the first few days, you may feel you need more training to do your job well. If the company does not provide this training, find out how to get this education yourself.

Your First Assignment
- When your manager gives you your first assignment, make sure that you understand it completely. Write the instructions down and then repeat them back to your employer and ask if you understood them correctly.
- If your work is part of a larger project, ask who you will be working with and how you will communicate: face-to-face meetings, video conferencing, phone, or e-mail?
- Use a notepad to write down tasks, deadlines, meetings, action plans, ideas, and questions.

Nina's Personal Experience

My first job in Canada was working as a customer service agent at a call centre. After three days of in-class training, we started to make calls. I was so nervous about speaking to people I didn't know that I couldn't carry on a proper conversation. People hung up on me after just a few seconds. I felt terrible.

My supervisor came over and asked me if I felt comfortable with the job. She said, "Telemarketing is really quite challenging. Do you think you can do it?" I'd made very few cold calls in Chinese and even fewer in English. I didn't feel very confident about my language skills, but I decided I *had* to prove myself by my actions. I worked very hard to remain positive and somehow, surprisingly, my confidence came back. By the middle of that day, I made my first sale! I soon became one of the top producers of our sales team.

12.5 Build a Working Relationship with Your Manager

Problem

Perhaps you met your new manager during the job interview and she chose you above the other candidates. In some cases, however, you will meet your manager for the first time during your first day on the job. How can you build a good working relationship with your manager, and why is this so important?

Solution

A great deal about your job depends on your manager. She gives you assignments, evaluates your work, and will likely assess whether or not you will continue to work for the company after your probation period. This is why it's important to understand your manager and work well with her.

Immigrant Experience

When Bouzar started at his first job, he faced two new cultural practices. The first was about gender issues in the workplace. Bouzar was from Iran, where women have little or no power. Now he had three supervisors—and all were women. But Bouzar had read about gender issues, so he thought he was prepared. He decided to treat his supervisors just as he would treat a male boss in Iran. He tried not to bother them too much, and quietly did his work.

At his three-month review he was confronted with a second cultural difference. One of his supervisors told him she was not completely satisfied with his work. Bouzar was confused. He'd been respectful and had tried not to bother anyone with questions. The supervisor explained that in Canada it's important to show initiative and to ask for more work than is assigned. As a result, Bouzar decided to take more initiative while maintaining a high level of respect for his female superiors.

Understand Your Manager

A good manager will introduce you to your team and explain the best way to perform your first assignment. She'll also tell you how to work more efficiently, how to get the company to pay for your training, and how to interact with co-workers.

- Carefully think over your first assignment.
  - Do you have enough information to complete the job? If not, where can you find it? Ask in advance how often you will meet with your manager to discuss any problems. Would she prefer to meet with you in person, by phone, or through e-mail? Will you be working on a team?
  - Ask for any tools you feel are necessary—for example, software that must be installed on your computer. Prepare a detailed plan of action and schedule.
  - Ask your boss for a second meeting to report results. Ask for assistance if you think you cannot finish on time.
- If you do not agree with your manager, do not immediately take your concerns to upper management.
  - Try to understand your manager's opinion. Suggest a solution to any problems. For example, if you think you won't finish on time, explain that you *will* finish on time if you have assistance.
- Every manager treats employees differently (has a different management style).
  - If your manager is friendly, it does not always mean she likes you, and a sharp tone does not always mean that she's unhappy with your work. Talk to colleagues who've known her for a while. They'll likely give you advice.
- In some workplaces, the initiative of workers is welcome or required. In others, if you show initiative, your manager may think you are questioning her authority and you could lose your job.

Tip: Ask your manager about his needs and expectations. When you succeed, your manager will be proud of you and the direction he gave.

12.6 Build Good Relationships with Your Co-workers

Problem

As an employee, your skills and knowledge will be valued highly. But your relationships with co-workers are also key to your success. In Canada, more people lose their jobs because of bad relationships than because of poor job performance. As a new employee, it can be a challenge to fit in with everyone. What can you do to help this process?

Solution

Make a Good First Impression

- From your first day, try to remember the names of your colleagues. As a helpful tool, you could draw a map of the office showing the names of people and their locations.
- Communicate with your colleagues. Invite them to lunch. Take in pastries or breakfast as a welcome to everyone.

Be Professional

- Leave your home and family problems outside the workplace doors. No matter how you felt leaving home in the morning, greet your co-workers with a friendly smile.

Fit In with a Team

- After joining a new team, you may find smaller groups of friends within it. Try to avoid joining these smaller groups (cliques) and do not repeat gossip you hear at work.
- When a new team is formed or a new member (you) is added, a power struggle often starts. Your goal is to get through this stage as quickly as possible and to start effective teamwork.
- Try to understand the duties of each team member. Learn their strong and weak points. Be ready to help them in areas where you are stronger and ask them for some help—but not too much!—in areas where you are unsure.

Be Open to Learning

- Choose your most skilled and friendly co-worker and ask him or her to be your mentor. Most people will be happy to help.

- Don't hesitate to ask questions, but be careful not to ask the same person all the time. And don't expect anyone to rescue you. As much as possible, solve problems on your own.
- Use every opportunity to learn something new.
- Speak 20 percent of the time and listen 80 percent of the time.
- Avoid saying, "But that's how we did it at my previous job."
- Once you understand your new environment and are accepted by the team, you might offer some advice based on a previous job.
- If misunderstandings arise, try to clear them up immediately. And if you've made a mistake, admit that you were wrong and say that you're willing to keep learning.

Be Respectful
- Help your co-workers when needed—but remember to do your job first!
- Show respect for managers and co-workers at all times.
- If a co-worker from another culture surprises you with their cultural behaviour, do not criticize him or her for that.
- Your own culture might accept behaviours not considered acceptable in Canada. Make sure that co-workers don't misunderstand your words and actions.
- Many companies celebrate only Canadian holidays. Participate in them. If you need time off for your own holidays, ask for permission from your manager.

Rules for Successful Work Relationships
- If someone has a problem with you and confronts you, take time to cool off before you respond.
- If someone has done well, compliment them.
- Thank anyone who compliments you on a job well done.
- Don't complain too much. People might think you're a whiner.
- Never discuss your salary with your co-workers.
- Don't pretend to know everything. Be open to learning from others.
- Don't get involved in, or repeat, workplace gossip.
- Don't tell jokes about sensitive subjects such as sex, religion, or race.
- Take part in after-hours work activities to build relationships.
- Take responsibility for mistakes immediately, and find a way to fix them.
- Avoid workplace romance, as most companies do not allow it.

Tip: When you're starting your new job, work hard on even the most routine and boring task. Your co-workers and manager will be happy and you'll become very valuable to the company!

12.7 Conflicts at Work

Problem

Conflicts occur at work when people, or groups of people, have goals or personalities that do not fit well with each other. Differences can also occur because of age, experience, gender, character, or ambition. In Canada, conflicts can also arise between people of different cultures. What is the best way to behave if you're involved in a conflict at work?

Solution

Here are three of the most common conflicts that take place at work—with advice on how to resolve them. With practice, you can become efficient at resolving conflicts at work and in your personal life.

Workplace Conflicts		
Conflict	**Possible Reasons**	**Possible Solutions**
Between You and Your Boss	You may have a problem with your manager for several reasons: • You've been forced to work overtime. • You've been asked to do work that is not in your job description. • You have not received an expected promotion or salary. • You feel your manager is rude, dishonest, or too critical.	• Do not complain to higher management immediately. This will just increase the conflict and the results will not usually be good. • Try to understand your manager and discuss the problem. • Try to find a **compromise**. Perhaps you are to blame for the conflict and you don't know it. For example, you may have made a crucial mistake. • If the conflict cannot be resolved and you are under a lot of stress, speak to your Human Resources (HR) department. At worst, ask to be moved to another department.
Between You and a Co-worker	A conflict with a co-worker could arise because of the following: • A disagreement about the best way to carry out a task. • A disagreement about who will work on specific parts of a project.	• Choose a suitable time and place (over coffee or lunch) to talk one-on-one with the person with whom you had a disagreement. Maybe this misunderstanding can be settled easily through communication.

Conflict	Possible Reasons	Possible Solutions
	• A disagreement about who should be rewarded for good work or who should take responsibility for mistakes. • Rivalry, gossip, or disrespect (occasionally about culture).	• If you are at fault and ready to admit it, apologize. A simple apology can resolve most conflicts. • It may help to bring in a third person, such as a Human Resources employee or a mutual friend, as a peacemaker. • If a problem is too large for you to resolve between you, your manager should help.
Between You and a Client	If you work directly with clients, conflicts will likely happen at some point. This can happen if the following occur: • There's a miscommunication about an agreement or promises. • The company or your co-workers can't deliver on your promises to the client. • The client expects more than is reasonable. Remember that a happy client can bring you two or three potential clients, but an unhappy client can really hurt your business.	• Listen to the client closely. Do not show anger or impatience, even if he makes unreasonable claims. • Repeat the client's concern in your own words so he knows that you've listened closely and have understood. • Resolve the problem immediately if you can. If this is not possible, get a name and phone number and say that you'll be in touch soon (perhaps after discussing the problem with your employer). • Do not promise anything if you're not sure you can keep your word. • Try to make sure the client is satisfied before you end the conversation.

Tip: If you're having a conflict at work, remember that you're not alone. Though one person may be unhappy with you, others will likely support you. But if no one takes your side in a conflict, you may be wrong.

12.8 Manage Your Career

Situation

For most newcomers, their first job is one or two levels below their level of qualification. If you are in this position, you have used a good strategy. It's better to take almost any job in your field, just to get started, than to hold out for your ideal job (which you may never attain without some Canadian experience). After a while, however, you'll want to get a promotion. How can you manage your career to make sure you move to a higher level?

Advice and Action Plan

The First Three Months

The first three months at your new job is often a probation period (unless you're in a field that doesn't require a probationary period). At the end of this period, your work will be assessed and the employer will then decide whether you may or may not stay at the job. Below are several things you'll want to do during your probationary period.

- Work as hard and as well as you can in job performance and in building relationships with co-workers.
- Decide if you need to upgrade some of your skills. If you do, ask your company if you may take a course in this area. For example, you may need to learn a new computer program or new laws governing your business.
- Work on gaining the trust of your manager and co-workers while you learn Canadian culture and ethics in the workplace.
- When you meet with your manager, ask how you can improve your work habits or skills. In a diary, record your efforts to improve, and the results of those efforts.
- Find out exactly what your manager expects of you. Then set goals for the next week, month, and three months. Double-check with your manager to make sure you understood his expectations. (If you do a good job at something but it's not what he wanted, you may fail your probationary period!)

- Ask your co-workers about things you're not sure of. Is it acceptable to talk about non-work-related topics during work hours? How much initiative should you take?
- Make an effort to fit in with your team. Go out for lunch with them and participate in after-work activities with co-workers.

Once You've Settled In

After you've passed the probationary period, make a plan for developing your career. For example, set a two-year goal and plan the steps you'll need to take to reach your goal.

Next, get ready for your first performance review (this usually happens six to twelve months after you were hired). Ask for a copy of the form that your manager will use to judge your performance. You may likely be judged in areas like the following: quantity of work done, cooperation with manager and co-workers, personal appearance, attendance, and punctuality.

If It Isn't Working Out

At some point, you may feel you need to leave the company. This might happen if you realize you will not likely be promoted or receive a salary increase. You might also want to move to a different job if your manager won't support your efforts to improve yourself or if there are lay-offs or other kinds of distress within the company.

It is proper etiquette in Canada to warn your company before you leave. Usually, two weeks' notice is required. But if you are participating in a project, try to finish it or transfer it to another person. This way, the company will not have to struggle when you leave.

Remember that it's best to begin searching for new work before you quit your current job!

Tip: If you need to move to a different city or region to advance your career, consider doing so. But also think of the personal consequences of leaving your current community.

Key Words

compromise: to reach an agreement in which each side gets something it wants and allows the other side to have something it wants

conflict: a fight, argument, or disagreement

employee handbook: a small book that gives useful information and advice about your job and/or company

harassment: the act of annoying or putting pressure on somebody, especially continuously or on many different occasions

orientation session: a meeting that helps you become familiar with something new

self-control: the ability to control your emotions and appear calm even when you are angry, afraid, excited, etc.

Note: Entries taken or adapted from the Oxford ESL Dictionary.

Creating Your Canadian Experience

1. In 12.1, you read about business qualities. After a week on your new job, use the chart below to tell how each quality could relate to your new position.

Honesty	
Responsibility	
Productivity	
Competence	
Communication Skills	
Personal Appearance	
Positive Attitude	

2. Discuss your answers in one of the above areas with a friend.

3. Write down three culture or etiquette standards that you noticed at your new job, but were unsure of. Find a friend, teacher, or colleague that you feel comfortable with and discuss them.

    a. _____

    _____

    b. _____

    _____

    c. _____

    _____

4. Search the Internet for places where you can take free IQ and EQ tests. Record your scores in the table below; take notice of your strengths and weaknesses.

Tip: Using keywords "free IQ test" or "free EQ test" in an Internet search engine should give you some tests to choose from, but be careful of websites that try to charge you for them.

Test	Score	Strengths	Weaknesses
IQ			
EQ			

5. Now that you are employed, it is important to continue to think about advancing your career. Write some realistic goals below.

Categories	6 Months	1 Year	2 Years	5 Years	10 Years
Salary					
Position					
Responsibilities					
Other					

Your Rights at Work

In This Unit

- Canadian Employment and Labour Standards
- Wages and Salaries
- Health and Safety Rules in the Workplace
- Trade Unions in Canada

13.1 Employment and Labour Standards

Situation
Everyone who has the legal right to work in Canada is protected by
Canadian labour laws. These are based on employment and labour
standards that contain rights and responsibilities both for employers
and employees. What are these standards?

Information

Canada Labour Code
Employees of the federal government are subject to the Canada Labour
Code, as well as individuals who work for banks, air transport companies,
broadcasters, shipping companies, or other industries that are considered
to have an effect beyond the scope of a single province.

Among other things, the code details the rights and responsibilities of
employers and employees, workplace health and safety expectations, and
the complaint resolution process.

Provincial and Territorial Standards
For the most part, provinces and territories establish and enforce their own
employment **legislation**. About 90 percent of employees are covered by this
legislation and standards vary across the country. Employment legislation
addresses topics such as work hours, pay, and termination of employment.

Within each province and territory, there is generally a ministry or
department of labour which governs employment matters. A website for
your area will provide detailed information about employment legislations,
as well as contact information for someone who can assist you with any
employment-related questions you may have.

The Human Rights Act and Employment Equity Act
In every province, Canada's Human Rights Act protects the rights of
employees. This act forbids workplace discrimination by race, origin, skin
colour, religion, age, sex, sexual orientation, marital status, family status,
disability, or conviction for which a pardon has been granted.

In addition to administering the Human Rights Act, the Canadian
Human Rights Commission also enforces the Employment Equity Act,
which is a measure to ensure equality within the workplace. If employees of
federally regulated organizations believe that their rights are being violated,
they should contact the commission.

There are also provincial and territorial human rights agencies, which have their own human rights acts. If workers in non–federally regulated organizations encounter problems regarding their rights at work, they can contact these agencies for advice. A list of these agencies can be found on the Canadian Human Rights Commission's website.

Source: HRSDC, Canada Labour Code (www.hrsdc.gc.ca/en/lp/lo/ohs/publications/ overview.shtml).

Online Information
More information about the Canadian laws and standards, and region specific information, can be found at the following websites:

Federal Resources
- Canada employment and labour standards—canadaonline.about.com/ od/labourstandards/Canada_Employment_and_Labour_ Standards.htm
- Canadian Human Rights Commission—www.chrc-ccdp.ca
- Canada Labour Code—laws.justice.gc.ca/en/L-2

Provincial Resources
- British Columbia—www.labour.gov.bc.ca/esb
- Alberta—employment.alberta.ca/cps/rde/xchg/hre/hs.xsl/1224.html
- Saskatchewan—www.labour.gov.sk.ca
- Manitoba—www.gov.mb.ca/labour/standards/index.html
- Ontario—www.labour.gov.on.ca/english
- Quebec—www.cnt.gouv.qc.ca/en/index.asp
- Nova Scotia—www.gov.ns.ca/enla/employmentworkplaces
- New Brunswick—www.gnb.ca/0308/index=e.asp
- Newfoundland and Labrador—www.hrle.gov.nl.ca/hrle
- Prince Edward Island—www.gov.pe.ca/commcul/lair-info/index.php3
- Yukon—www.community.gov.yk.ca
- Northwest Territories—www.ece.gov.nt.ca
- Nunavut—www.gov.nu.ca

Tip: Review the employment standards that cover your province or territory. If you don't understand some of the material, ask at an employment resource centre or your trade union.

13.2 Hours of Work and Overtime

Problem

Many newcomers are concerned when employers expect them to work overtime. What is considered to be a normal workday in Canada? What is a normal workweek? Can employers force you to work on weekends or holidays?

Advice and Action Plan

Provinces and territories generally have standards that determine the maximum length of the workday in Canada, but the laws are different from province to province. Links to employment standards and rules for all provinces and territories can be found on the Going to Canada website (www.workingincanada.gc.ca).

Workday and Workweek Length

Below is a chart that shows the regulations by province. Look it over to see what the rules are in your province, but be aware that there are exceptions to these numbers depending on your occupation. Check employment and labour standards in your area to find out what applies to you.

Province	Workday	Workweek
BC	8 Hours	40 Hours
AB	8 Hours	44 Hours
SK	8 Hours	40 Hours
MB	8 Hours	40 Hours
ON	8 Hours	40 Hours
QC	8 Hours	40 Hours
NS	No standard	48 Hours

Province	Workday	Workweek
NB	No standard	44 Hours
NL	No standard 14 hours max.	40 Hours
PEI	No standard	48 Hours
YT	8 Hours	40 Hours
NT	8 Hours	44 Hours
NU	8 Hours	40 Hours

Overtime

- For overtime work in most provinces and territories, employees must be paid a **time-and-a-half wage**.
- In some cases in certain provinces, an employee can receive extra time off instead of (in lieu of) overtime pay.
- In some provinces, in cases like production emergencies, hospital emergencies, and natural disasters an employer can sometimes force you to work overtime without your agreement.

- In some provinces salaried employees are excluded from overtime pay, but in others even salaried employees must be paid overtime.
- Look on your province's website to see regional differences.
- An employer may ask you to sign an agreement that says you can work hours different than employment standards laws. You do not have to sign, but weigh the pros (extra money, relationship with your employer) and cons (longer workdays and workweeks).

Days Off

There is no law in Canada that forbids working on Sundays or on the night shift (in some provinces, employees in certain professions may refuse to work on a Sunday if they give sufficient notice). The employee receives no additional payment for working on Sundays or at night. There is also no law forbidding work on the night shift alone. And no law requires your employer to transport you home at the end of the night shift. Retail workers, however, are allowed to demand Sunday off for religious reasons.

Vacations

Across most of the country, after an employee has worked full time for one year, the employer is required by law to give him a two-week paid vacation. These vacation days may be taken all at once or in smaller amounts.

There are nine public paid holidays (called "statutory holidays") per year in most of Canada. The dates of these holidays are below.

Holiday	Date
New Year's Day	January 1
Family Day	The third Monday in February
Good Friday	The Friday before Easter Sunday, falling between March 19 and April 23
Victoria Day	The last Monday on or before May 21
Canada Day	July 1

Holiday	Date
Labour Day	The first Monday in September
Thanksgiving	The second Monday in October
Remembrance Day	November 11
Christmas Day	December 25
Boxing Day	December 26

In addition, each province has a few holidays of its own. In order to obtain extra pay for working on those days, the employee must have worked at the company for no less than three months.

13.3 Wages and Salaries

Situation

It's exciting to get a new job, but it is important to know the legal side of wages and pay. What rules do employers have to follow concerning paying employees?

Information

Wages and Salaries

You may hear the terms "wage" and "salary" used interchangeably, although they do not refer to exactly the same thing. While a wage is the amount a person makes per hour of work, a salary is the amount a person makes over the course of a year.

Minimum Wage

Employment standards acts across Canada set the minimum hourly wage (known as "minimum wage"). All employees must receive this amount or more, with a few exceptions. A number of organizations in Canada believe it should be increased to $10 per hour.

Minimum Wage by Province (as of April 1, 2008)					
BC	$8.00	QC	$8.00	PEI	$7.50
AB	$8.40	NS	$7.60	YT	$8.58
SK	$8.25	NB	$7.75	NT	$8.25
MB	$8.50	NL	$8.00	NU	$8.50
ON	$8.75				

Minimum wage rates still apply for part-time (less than 30 hours) and for temporary jobs.

Employees who work on commission calculate their hourly wage by dividing it by the number of hours spent working. The result must not be less than the minimum wage. If meals and lodgings are provided, the employer has the right to deduct that amount from the wage.

Separate wage rates apply to students who work during school and college or university vacations. And a few service industry occupations may receive a lower wage and be expected to make up the difference in tips.

People who pick crops may be paid depending on their productivity, and those who provide live-in nanny care may see some of their wages go to pay for their accommodations.

Equal Pay for Equal Work

Each province and territory, other than Nunavut, has equal pay legislation included in either its employment standards or human rights legislation. Men and women who perform the same duties with the same skill are expected to be paid the same rate. If employees feel they are not being fairly compensated, they can begin the complaint process that has been established by their jurisdiction's legislation.

With a few exceptions, an employee's right to equal pay in relation to other employees only applies if they work in the same establishment. A difference in pay will often be justified by a **seniority** system, merit system, skills shortage, or another factor not based on gender.

Sometimes employers try to pay lower wages to newcomers. This is discriminatory and may be a violation of your jurisdiction's employment standards legislation. If you think your employer is in violation, follow the complaint process for your area.

Timing of Wage Payments

Employers are required to pay their workers regularly and to issue a statement of earnings. This statement must include the name of the employer and employee, the pay, and all deductions for the given period, the number of working hours, and the age of worker (if she is under 18 years). Documents about payment must be kept by employers for two years.

If wages or salaries are not paid on time, employees have the right to apply to the ministry in charge of labour in their province or territory. The ministry can make the employer pay the wage or salary owed. In some cases of serious violations, the employer may be fined or jailed.

Wage and Salary Increase

If an employee has performed well, she usually receives a pay increase at her annual employee performance review.

Tip: If an employer does not agree to increase your wage or salary, you can ask for another form of financial reward—for example, a one-time bonus, payment of mileage (gas and "wear and tear" on a vehicle) for your rides to work, or payment for trip abroad.

13.4 Vacation Time

Situation

Most employees in Canada are entitled to vacation time and some are allowed special leaves. As an employee, what vacation time and leaves can you expect to have?

Information

Vacation time is governed by the Canada Labour Code and provincial and territorial standards (see 13.1).

Usually, employees are allowed to take time off whether they work full- or part-time. And vacation time that is taken is included in an employee's working period. This means the time counts towards seniority, vacation, and salary, as if the employee had been on the job all the time.

Vacations

- After an employee has worked full-time for one year, the employer is generally required to give him at least two weeks' paid vacation.
- If you have worked at a company for less than one year, you are not legally entitled to vacation time. But you can usually negotiate either paid vacation or vacation pay for the portion of the year you did work.
- Employers will often allow vacations to be taken a few days at time. But this must be negotiated. Vacation pay is also usually negotiable (instead of vacation time).
- The employer has the right to determine the timing of your vacation. For example, if November is the busiest month, the employer can refuse to allow vacations in November.

Although, legally, employees need to give up to four weeks notice of a vacation, it is a good idea to give an employer as much notice as possible. Another good reason to do this is to ensure that you get the time off that you want. In the summer months, when children are not in school, many people want the same weeks off.

> **Tip:** Employers may sometimes prefer giving extra vacation time instead of increasing an employee's salary. Keep that in mind when negotiating your contracts.

Jurisdiction	Length of Vacation	Notice Required	Amount of Vacation Pay
Federal	2 weeks; 3 weeks after 6 years of consecutive employment	2 weeks	4 percent of annual wages; 6 percent after 6 years
BC	2 weeks; 3 weeks after 5 years of consecutive employment	Not specified	4 percent of total wages earned in the year of employment (if at least 5 calendar days of employment have been completed); 6 percent after 5 years
AB	2 weeks; 3 weeks after 5 years of consecutive employment	2 weeks	4 percent of annual wages; 6 percent after 5 years
SK	3 weeks; 4 weeks after 10 years of employment	4 weeks	$3/52$ of total wages earned in year of employment; $4/52$ of total wages if entitled to 4 weeks of annual holidays
MB	2 weeks; 3 weeks after 5 years of consecutive employment	15 days	2 percent of wages earned in first year of employment for each week of vacation
ON	2 weeks	Not specified	4 percent of wages earned in applicable period (normally 12 months)
QC	2 weeks; 3 weeks after 5 years uninterrupted service (1 additional week in special cases); one day per month (to a maximum of 2 weeks) for those with less than 1 year uninterrupted service	4 weeks	4 percent of gross wages during reference year; 6 percent if entitled to 3 weeks, special provisions for sickness, accident, or maternity leave
NS	2 weeks; 3 weeks after 8 continuous years of employment	1 week	4 percent of wages; 6 percent after 8 years of continuous employment
NB	2 weeks or 1 day per month worked during vacation pay year (whichever is less); 3 weeks or $1\frac{1}{4}$ days per month worked during a vacation pay year (whichever is less) after 8 consecutive years of employment.	1 week	4 percent of wages earned in vacation pay year; 6 percent after 8 years
NL	2 weeks; 3 weeks if after 15 consecutive years of employment	2 weeks	4 percent of wages earned during 12-month period; 6 percent after 15 years
PEI	2 weeks	1 week	4 percent of wages
YT	2 weeks	Not specified	4 percent of annual wages earned in one year of employment (if employee has been continuously employed for a period of at least 14 days)
NT/NU	2 weeks; 3 weeks after 6 years of employment (continuous or accumulated over past 10 years).	Not specified	4 percent of wages; 6 percent for an employee entitled to 3 weeks of vacation

Source: Human Resources and Social Development Canada.

13.5 Special Leaves

Situation

Sometimes things happen in people's personal lives that require them to spend some time away from work. Most employees in Canada are entitled to some special leaves for cases such as these. As an employee, when are you entitled to this leave?

Information

Special leave time is governed by the Canada Labour Code and provincial and territorial standards (see 13.1).

Three types of leaves (time off) are described in this chapter. Usually, employees are allowed to take this time off whether they work full- or part-time. And time taken for these approved leaves is included in an employee's working period. This means the time counts toward seniority, vacation, and salary, as if the employee had been on the job all the time.

Maternity and Parental Leave

Time off is provided for a woman to have a baby (maternity leave) and for a mother, father, or guardian to take care of a child (parental leave). Parental leave is also permitted when a child is adopted. Below is some information on maternity and parental leave:

- Maternity leave is either 17 or 18 weeks, depending on the province, and parental leave ranges from 12 to 52 weeks. Mothers who take both leaves must begin their parental leave immediately after their maternity leave.
- If you are on maternity or parental leave, you will not receive pay, but your job will be kept for you during this time. That is, it's "job-protected" time off.
- A woman may be eligible for maternity benefits. These are payments from the federal Employment Insurance (EI) program. For more information check with Human Resources and Social Development Canada or Service Canada (HRSDC).

Taking It Online

Website Name	Website Address
Compassionate Care Benefits	www.hrsdc.gc.ca/en/ei/types/compassionate_care.shtml
Service Canada	www.servicecanada.gc.ca

- To be eligible for pregnancy leave, a woman must have been hired by the employer at least 12 weeks to one year before the due date of the child—depending on where she lives—and she may need a medical certificate as well.
- After the birth, she or the other guardian can obtain the additional non-paid parental leave. The parent must give a written statement notifying his or her employer in advance. Both parents are eligible for parental leave within one year of a birth or adoption of a baby.
- Like maternity leave, parental leave is unpaid, but the employee may be eligible for EI payments and his or her job is protected.

Emergency Leave

Some employment contracts provide paid emergency leave. If yours doesn't and your workplace employs at least 50 regular employees, you may still have a right to receive unpaid, job-protected emergency leave.

Most jurisdictions allow for emergency time off, sometimes specifying whether it may be taken as sick leave, bereavement time, or to attend to family obligations. You must tell your employer about the need for emergency leave on the day of the emergency or as soon as possible afterwards. The leave does not need to be taken all at once.

This type of leave can often be negotiated even with employers who are not required by law to provide it.

Compassionate Care Leave

- Compassionate care leave, also sometimes called family medical leave or parental leave, is permitted in most provinces and territories so that an employee can care for members of their family who are seriously ill. Alberta and the Northwest Territories do not offer compassionate care leave, other than for federally regulated employees.
- This unpaid, job-protected leave can be taken in blocks of at least one week, usually up to eight weeks over a 26-week period. To obtain this leave, the employee has to provide a certificate from a qualified medical professional.
- Employees eligible for EI may qualify for EI benefits called Compassionate Care Benefits. To find out whether you're eligible, check with HRSDC or Service Canada.

Tip: By saving vacation days, or banking overtime hours, it is possible to makes leaves last longer.

13.6 Health and Safety Rules in the Workplace

Situation

Safety and health hazards can be found in all workplaces—some more than others. Canadian laws require safe working procedures, but even with the greatest care, accidents and illness can happen. What procedures must employers and employees follow to stay safe? What will happen if you're injured at the workplace?

Information

Employer and Employee Rights and Responsibilities

- Employers are required by law to establish safe working procedures and to give safety instructions to every employee.
- All businesses must be registered with the workers' **compensation** board or occupational health and safety board of the province or territory in which they operate.
- Employers must display a copy of the province or territory's occupational health and safety policy in the workplace.
- Every workplace must be monitored regularly by inspectors from the body which regulates its jurisdiction's occupational health and safety policies.
- To prevent injuries and occupational diseases on the job, employees are required to use personal protection equipment (eye protection, gloves, hard hats, etc.) and to follow safety procedures.

Is Your Job Too Dangerous?

- If you believe your job is too dangerous, you may legally refuse to do it, and any resulting time off must be paid by the employer.
- If an accident does happen, employees and the employer both have rights and responsibilities. These are outlined in the laws governing occupational health and safety in your province or territory.
  - To find these, search on the Internet using the keywords "workplace health and safety" and the name of your province or territory.
- If you are hurt at your workplace, you must immediately report to your supervisor.
- From that point, the employer must file a report as soon as possible (without undue delay—generally within three days) with the workers' compensation board. They must give you a copy of that report.

- The employer must pay your wages for the day you are injured and also for transportation to the hospital or to your home.

Applying for Compensation

If you have an injury related to your job, always apply to the workers' compensation board or commission for compensation. Do not let your employer give you sick pay instead of applying.

In most cases, the board or commission will pay you worker's compensation if your employer is registered. But if your employer is not registered, you also have rights to get benefits from your employer. Injuries covered by the board or commission include back problems, broken bones, heart attacks, asthma, deafness, and chronic pain.

The board or commission will decide whether or not you are covered. If you are in a union, ask your union representative.

Receiving Compensation

When you receive worker's compensation, you have to co-operate with the board or commission experts and with your employer. For example, you are required to tell the experts about any changes in your life that may affect your rights to receive benefits. These changes include changes in your health, income and medical expenses.

As a result of your report, your benefits may be increased, reduced, or even stopped. If you do not report changes in your life that would decrease your benefits, the board or commission may demand that you pay back any overpayment.

After Recovery

After you recover, your employer must offer you a job. If you are medically able to do your original job, the employer must offer you your original job or a similar one.

Sometimes you will be given your original job with "accommodation." This means using different equipment, making the work site easier to access, or changing the work schedule. If you do not agree with the board or your employer's decision, obtain help from a community legal clinic, the local workers' advisor's office, your union, or an injured workers' group.

Tip: Before starting a new job, ask your employer about the health and safety rules at the workplace.

13.7 Human Rights

Situation

After the Universal Declaration of Human Rights was proclaimed by the United Nations in 1948, many countries passed their own human rights laws; Canada was among them. As a result, your human rights are protected in the workplace. What are some of these rights and how are they protected?

Information

Canadian Human Rights Act and Canada Labour Code

The Canadian Human Rights Act and the Canada Labour Code both protect workers from harassment in the workplace. All employers are expected to have a clear anti-harassment policy and to make sure their employees understand it. Any work-related harassment is considered to be the employers' responsibility, as they are expected to provide safe and healthy work environments. This is true even if one of the parties involved is not an employee.

Any behaviour that demeans, humiliates, or embarrasses a person, and that a reasonable person should have known would be unwelcome, is considered harassment. This may be related to race, national or ethnic origin, colour, religion, age, sex, marital status, family status, disability, pardoned conviction, or sexual orientation.

Provincial and Territorial Human Rights Acts

Each province and territory has its own human rights act, code, or charter that outlines the rights and responsibilities of employers and employees in that jurisdiction. These acts will explain who you should contact if you experience harassment in the workplace.

Taking It Online	
Website Name	**Website Address**
Human Rights Commissions in Canada	www.infactcanada.ca/human_right_commission_and_fair.htm

What to Do if Your Rights are Violated

If you feel that you are the victim of workplace harassment, your first step should be to let the person who is harassing you know that you are uncomfortable or offended. If this doesn't resolve the situation, speak to your employer about the problem. Throughout this process, make notes of what the harassment involved, when and where it happened, and if there were any witnesses present.

If the harassment continues, you can file a formal complaint with your provincial or territorial human rights commission, the human rights tribunal in BC, or the fair practices officer in Nunavut.

Interviewing, Hiring, and Human Rights

At interviews, potential employers are not allowed to ask questions about any aspect of the interviewee's human rights. If you are being interviewed, you may refuse to answer questions about your religion, age, or ethnic origin. (For more information about human rights and interviews, see 10.8 and 10.9.)

An interviewer should also not ask if you are a Canadian citizen. You do need to have the legal right to work in Canada, but you do not have to be a citizen (citizenship can be obtained only after three years of permanent residence in this country).

Discrimination by Government Officials

If you feel that a government official has discriminated against you, you may appeal to your jurisdiction's ombudsperson—this is an independent officer appointed by Parliament who has the right to investigate citizen complaints.

Tip: Canada is a democratic country with strict legal protection; do not allow infringement of your rights.

13.8 Trade Unions in Canada

Situation
In Canada, as in many other countries, tradespeople and other workers are often protected by trade unions. What trade unions are in Canada and what are their duties? What advantages accompany becoming a member of a trade union?

Information
Trade Unions across Canada
- Trade unions have existed in Canada for more than a hundred years. Unions can currently be found across the country, with almost 3,000 local branch unions nationwide. The unions are all governed by their jurisdiction's labour relations act or labour relations code.
- The strongest and most numerous trade unions in Canada are found in the fields of manufacturing, office administration, education, construction, public health, and social service.
- Most trade union branches are united through the Canadian Labour Congress, which includes over three million workers.

Trade Union Duties
Trade unions have the duty of defending working people if employers are not giving them their rights. To do this, trade union representatives meet with employers to discuss employee working conditions and wages. These talks often lead to collective agreements about issues like wages, the duration of the workday, rules of dismissal, limitation of child labour, complaint procedures, and financial benefits for employees.

Trade unions work to make sure that employee wages relate to the cost of living and provide employees with enough money to live and support dependants (sufficient livelihood).

Conflict Resolution and Rights
Avoiding Conflict between Employers and Unions
Employers and trade unions try to avoid conflicts since conflicts can lead to strikes and therefore work and wage stoppages. Negotiation deadlines are set and both sides will work hard, sometimes late into the night, to reach an agreement before they expire.

The Strike Option

If an agreement is not reached during negotiations, both sides have the right to apply to the provincial or territorial ministry responsible for labour. Then, if there is still no agreement after the specified waiting period, the trade union can hold a strike vote.

If the workers do vote to strike, they will stop working at their workplace or not go to work at all. Strikers have the right to place pickets at their workplace, holding signs to tell the public about their complaints.

Workers in hospitals and nursing homes do not have the right to strike. This is true of any workers whose absence would endanger lives.

Employer Action against Strikes

Employers are permitted to take some action against strikers, such as a lock-out. If a conflict cannot be settled it is taken to court.

Should You Join a Union?

In some workplaces, all employees must become members of the trade union (these are called "union shops"). If your workplace is not a union shop, you have the choice of joining or not joining.

Depending on the jurisdiction, employees in non-union workplaces can either hold secret votes or sign cards stating that they want to join a union to decide whether to become unionized.

Becoming Unionized

If the majority of workers decide to become unionized, all workers must act according to the decisions of their trade union and pay union dues. This is because all workers (whether for or against having a union) receive the benefits of unionization.

Trade unions must be registered by the provincial or territorial labour relations board.

Taking It Online

Website Name	Website Address
Canadian Labour Congress	canadianlabour.ca/index.php/links_main
McMaster University Labour Studies Program	socserv.socsci.mcmaster.ca/maclabour/article.php?id=210

13.9 Termination of Employment

Situation
If you decide to leave a job to move on to another opportunity, certain procedures need to be followed under Canadian law. Legal requirements also govern situations where an employee is laid off or fired.

Information
In this chapter are some of the rules that apply if an employee is fired, laid off, or quits of their own free will. All three of these situations are called "termination." Note that when an employee is being terminated their employer must provide him or her with a Record of Employment (ROE) within five days (this document is also called a Separation Slip). Employees need this ROE to receive Employment Insurance (EI) payments.

Firing
In the first type of termination (firing), the employee is dismissed from the job without warning because of misconduct. The reasons for this might be, for example, ruining the employer's property on purpose, being late for work or leaving work earlier than the end of the workday without the employer's permission, arriving at work under the influence of alcohol or illegal drugs, stealing something, or refusing to obey the order of a manager with no good reason.

If you feel you were fired unlawfully, you may protest. For example, if you refused to work because of unsafe conditions and you were fired, you could appeal to your ministry of labour or take the employer to Small Claims Court.

Layoff
In the second type of termination (layoff), the employee is told to leave because of downsizing, bankruptcy, or market conditions—not because of anything the employee did wrong.

In this situation the employer must give the employee written notice at least two weeks before the day of layoff. If the employee does not receive enough notice, the employer must pay him termination pay (also called "severance pay"). The amount depends on how long the employee has worked for the firm. The employee should receive two days' pay for each year working for the company, with a minimum of five days' pay.

A temporary worker can be terminated without notice at the end of her period of employment. An employee on probation can also be terminated without notice during the three-month probation period if the employer decides that the employee is not suited for the job. An employee may also be laid off if the employer feels his qualifications in new technology are not strong enough to perform the job.

Quitting

In the third type of termination (quitting), the employee leaves the job of her own free will. An employee who quits may not receive Employment Insurance (EI) payments. So if you are having a problem at work, try to resolve it without quitting. If necessary, ask for legal advice. Even if you are not able to solve the problem you have to prove that you tried.

If you do not have "just cause" for leaving your job, you may not qualify to receive EI. For example, quitting to find a job that pays a higher salary or to go back to school would not be considered just cause. In these cases, EI could be withheld.

In many cases, however, people have good reasons to quit. Below are some reasons that are considered just cause:

- The employee's health becomes bad or worse.
- The employee encounters discrimination or has been sexually assaulted in the workplace.
- The family has to move.
- The employee did not know that the work would be dangerous.
- The employee has been given different duties than those that she was hired to do.
- There has been a decrease of salary.
- The manager has been unfair or hostile toward the employee without obvious reason.

Termination and Trade Unions

If your place of work is unionized, termination of employment is regulated by a collective agreement between the employer and the trade union.

Tip: If you have a serious problem at work that seems impossible to solve, send a registered letter to your employer describing the issue.

13.10 Employment Insurance

Problem
If you have worked in Canada for a long enough period of time and have become unemployed through no fault of your own, you will likely be able to receive Employment Insurance (EI) payments. What are the rules for receiving benefits?

Solution

Applying for Employment Insurance
Visit a Service Canada Centre to apply for Employment Insurance (EI) and take the following documents with you:

- Bring your Record of Employment (ROE) (also called a Separation Slip). The law requires that all employers give you a ROE within five days of your release. Do not hesitate to ask your employer for this slip. If you do not receive it within 14 days of your last day of work, submit your application without the ROE, but with some sort of proof of employment.
- Bring your Social Insurance Number (SIN) card. If your social insurance number begins with a "9," you will need to provide proof of your immigrant status and your work permit.
- Take your personal identification, such as a driver's licence or passport.
- Finally, bring bank account information as shown on a bank statement.

Length of Time You Must Have Worked
If the job you've just left or lost was your first job in Canada, or if you got the job after an interruption of two or more years, you must have worked not fewer than 910 hours during the last 12 months.

If you have worked between 420 and 700 hours without lengthy interruptions you may qualify for the benefit, depending on the level of unemployment in your field. The higher the level of unemployment, the fewer hours you will need to have worked in order to qualify for EI.

Benefits
- Most employees who obtain benefits receive 55 percent of their average insured earnings wage, up to $435 per week.
- If a couple has children, the combined income of both spouses is less than $25,921 a year, and they are receiving the Canada Child Tax Benefit, they may qualify for more money through the Family Supplement.

When Will You Receive Benefits?

If you qualify, you'll start receiving benefits within 28 days of receipt of your application. During the first two weeks (the waiting period), you will not receive EI.

Benefits will continue for up to 45 weeks, depending on unemployment rates in your area and the amount of insurable earnings you've accumulated. Any income earned during your waiting period will be deducted from the first three weeks of your benefits.

Rules for Receiving Benefits

- Service Canada will send you report cards every two weeks. You must fill them in accurately and return them to a Service Canada Centre promptly.
- While on EI, carefully save and collect all records of your job search. Make notes and store copies of all letters and resumes sent, as well as receipts, paycheque stubs, and correspondence related to your search.
- You are not required to accept *any* job you are offered. But you must seriously consider any job the Service Canada Centre offers. If you do not accept it, you must prove that this job is not suitable for you.
- If an EI staff person decides that you refused a suitable job, you may be disqualified from receiving benefits for a period of 7 to 12 weeks. If you disagree with their decision, you may appeal within 30 days. But you will have to live without that money until judgment is received.

Earning Money and Studying while on EI Benefits

You may earn a small amount of money while obtaining EI benefits. The level depends on where you live, but it's generally no more than $50 per week or the equivalent of 25 percent of benefits (whichever is higher). You may be able to earn $75 per week or the equivalent of 40 percent of your benefits if you live in a certain economic region. Everything over that limit will be deducted from your EI benefits.

If you do not report all of your income to EI staff, if you leave Canada while you are receiving EI benefits, or if you forge data in your ROE, you will have to return any money you should not have received. You may even be charged with the crime of fraud.

You are, however, allowed to study while on EI benefits. You may attend courses to increase your qualifications or to learn a new occupation. You must tell Service Canada if you are taking a course or training program, and they must not interfere with your job search. The Service Canada Centre may also enroll you in a Job Finding Club.

13.11 Unit Summary

Key Words

code: a set of rules for behaviour

compensation: money that you pay to somebody, especially because you have injured him/her or lost or damaged his/her property

legislation: a law or a group of laws

seniority: the rank or importance that a person has in a company, organization, etc. in relation to others, often related to how long he/she has worked there

time-and-a-half wage: one and one half times a person's usual hourly wage

Note: Entries taken or adapted from the Oxford ESL Dictionary.

Creating Your Canadian Experience

1. Find out what kind of holidays exist in your province.
    Tip: Search the Internet using keywords "[your province]" + "public holidays."

2. Once you know which holidays exist in your province, use a calendar and the description in 13.2 to figure out when each will occur throughout the year.

Holiday	2008 Date	2009 Date	2010 Date	2011 Date
New Year's Day	January 1	January 1	January 1	January 1

3. Research the employment standards in your province and fill in the boxes below.
   Tip: Search the Internet using keywords "employment laws" + "[your province]."

Work Hours:		Overtime:	
Minimum Wage:		Overtime Pay:	
Number of Days Off:		Vacations:	

4. Search the Internet for your province's human rights code or act. Read through it, write down some rights that are and aren't protected, and then find a friend to discuss your findings.

1. _____

2. _____

3. _____

4. _____

5. _____

5. Are you part of a union at your workplace? Find out by asking the Human Resources department or your co-workers. If you are part of a union, fill in the blanks below.

Union: _____

Dues (how much you pay to be a member): _____

Union representative: _____

Next union meeting: _____

Section 4

Provincial and Territorial Job Markets

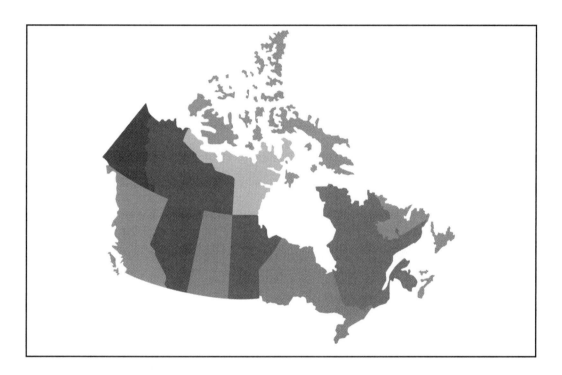

O Canada! Our home and native land!
True patriot love in all thy sons command.
With glowing hearts we see thee rise,
The True North strong and free!

Provincial and Territorial Job Markets

In This Unit

- The Canadian Provinces and Territories
- Canada's Major Cities
- Regional Employment Services

14.1 British Columbia

Life in British Columbia

British Columbia (BC) is the westernmost, and third largest, province in Canada (only Quebec and Ontario are larger). It also has the largest Chinese community in Canada. It became a province in 1871 and is now home to over 4.3 million people. What work opportunities does BC offer?

The Job Market

The unemployment rate in BC is 4.2 percent (as of 2008). Below is a list of some of BC's major industries.

Agriculture
- Livestock includes cattle ranching; pig, poultry, and dairy farming; and fish farming.
- Crops include grain, tree fruits, vegetables, berries, grapes, greenhouse vegetables, mushrooms, bulbs, and ornamental flowers and shrubs (www.britishcolumbia.com/information/details.as?id=31).

Natural Resources
- BC has the largest fishing industry in Canada. More than 80 species of finfish, shellfish, and marine plants are grown, harvested, and marketed by BC's seafood industry (www.britishcolumbia.com/information/details.asp?id=35).
- Forests cover half the province. Forest products include lumber, pulp, newsprint, paper products, and shingles (www.britishcolumbia.com/information/details.asp?id=36).
- The province has almost 20 operating mines that produce copper, coal, gold, silver, zinc, sulphur, lead, and others, including molybdenum.

Tourism and Film
- The Pacific coastline and beautiful mountains attract over 20 million visitors a year. This makes tourism BC's second-largest industry. BC is the third-largest film and television production centre in North America (after New York and Los Angeles).

Vancouver and Victoria

The capital city is Victoria, but the largest city is Vancouver. Greater Vancouver has a population of over 2.2 million. Vancouver's **port** is the largest in Canada and the second largest on North America's West Coast.

Newcomers in BC

BC welcomes newcomers, and over 40,000 immigrants arrive in the province each year. Most come from East and Southeast Asia, Bangladesh and Pakistan, and Britain and Western Europe. The top 10 languages spoken in BC are English, Chinese, Punjabi, German, French, Tagalog (spoken in the Philippines), Spanish, Italian, Korean, and Dutch.

BC's Provincial Nominee Program (www.ecdev.gov.bc.ca/ProgramsAndServices/PNP) offers accelerated immigration for skilled workers and experienced entrepreneurs who wish to settle in BC and become permanent residents. Skilled workers must fill positions that fall into Skill Levels O, A, and B of the National Occupational Classification (NOC) and must have a job offer from a BC employer. Entrepreneurs must plan to invest a minimum of $800,000 CAD for projects in Vancouver, or $300,000 CAD in the rest of the province.

If you are an internationally trained professional (ITP), you might benefit from the many programs being developed and adapted in BC (www.bcitp.net and www.sitebc.ca). They can help you have your credentials assessed and then receive training so you can practise your occupation in BC. MOSAIC Employment Programs for newcomers offer an Employment Access Program, a Career Connections Program (www.mosaicbc.com/programs_employment.asp).

Source: British Columbia.com.

Taking It Online

Website Name	Website Address
Business services	www.smallbusinessbc.ca
Career planning information	www.workfutures.bc.ca
Cost of living in Vancouver	www.canadaimmigrants.com/Vancouverliving.asp
Directory of ESL Courses	www.elsanet.org
Employment services	www1.servicecanada.gc.ca/en/gateways/where_you_live/regions/bc-yk.shtml
Government	www.gov.bc.ca
Job ads	www.bcjobs.ca
Newspapers with job ads	www.altstuff.com/newsbc.htm and www.nsnews.com

14.2 Vancouver

Life in Vancouver

About half the population of BC lives in Vancouver and its **metropolitan** area. This city, located between the Pacific Ocean and the Rocky Mountains, is also Canada's busiest port.

Located 40 km from the Canada–US border, Vancouver has a population of more than 600,000 (as of 2007). But the Lower Mainland, made up of the Greater Vancouver Regional District (GVRD) and the Fraser Valley Regional District (FVRD), has a population of more than 2.2 million. The mild climate makes Vancouver a very desirable location. And this city is almost always ranked as one of the top three in the world for livability.

Vancouver has two major daily newspapers, *The Vancouver Sun* and *The Province*. And the GVRD is home to a number of major universities, including Simon Fraser, with more than 25,000 students, and the University of British Columbia (UBC), with 4 campuses and more than 40,000 students. UBC is consistently ranked as one of the top 40 universities in the world.

The Job Market

Vancouver's unemployment rate is 4.7 percent (as of 2007). For job listings, see Vancouver's two major daily newspapers, *The Vancouver Sun* and *The Province*.

All Canadian trade with Japan, China, and other Pacific Rim countries goes through Vancouver's port, with its 50 steamship lines. Economic growth is happening in many sectors in Vancouver, especially in technology (new media, video games, telecommunications, and biotechnology); film and TV (200 movies are shot annually); the financial sector (including 30 foreign banks); the resource sector (forestry, mining, and petroleum products); and tourism (where 90,000 people are employed). There is also great demand for medical workers (for example, registered nurses, doctors, and lab technicians), and non-medical support workers (for example, cleaning, laundry, and food preparation) for hospitals and care facilities.

Other sectors on the rise include transportation and warehousing, the wholesale and retail trades (100,000 workers), banks and loan companies, and manufacturing (2,000 factories employ over 70,000 workers).

Newcomers in Vancouver

Vancouver has the second highest proportion of foreign-born citizens in Canada (38 percent). So it's not surprising that this city is a leader in providing immigrant services.

Newcomers in Vancouver include immigrants from China, Hong Kong, and other Southeast Asian nations. The South Asian population (from India, Pakistan, and Sri Lanka) is also growing quickly.

Information about assistance for newcomers can be found in *A Newcomer's Guide to Vancouver*. And organizations for newcomers include the Multicultural Helping House Society, the Progressive Intercultural Community Services Society, MOSAIC, Diverse*City*, Chilliwack Community Services (CCS), The BC Internationally Trained Professionals Network (BCITP Net), S.U.C.C.E.S.S. (a multi-service agency with almost 20 GRVD locations), and the Immigrant Services Society of BC (ISS)—the first multicultural immigrant-serving agency in Vancouver, with 7 large locations.

Taking It Online

Website Name	Website Address
A Newcomer's Guide to the City of Vancouver	vancouver.ca/commsvcs/socialplanning/ newtovancouver/sitemap.htm
Cost of living	www.canadaimmigrants.com/Vancouverliving.asp
Employment agencies	www.ucfv.ca/Jobs/Employment/OnlineResources/ VancouverAgencies.htm
Employment Resources for Newcomers	www.lmer.ca/federal.asp?Government=Federal&Region= *&Category=Programs%20for%20Immigrants
Immigrant Service Agencies	www.issbc.org
Bridge to Your Future	www.comserv.bc.ca/bridges
BC Internationally Trained Professionals Network	www.bcitp.net
Progressive Intercultural Community Services Society	www.pics.bc.ca
DIVERSEcity Community Resources Society	www.dcrs.ca
Multicultural Helping House Society	www.helpinghouse.org
S.U.C.C.E.S.S.	www.successbc.ca
Vancouver employment websites	www.vancouverjobs.com vancouver.ca/humanresources/jobs/index.htm

14.3 Alberta

Life in Alberta

Alberta, Canada's westernmost **Prairie province**, lies on the eastern side of the Rocky Mountains and includes part of the Rockies. Two-thirds of Alberta's 3.3 million residents are under the age of 40. With the highest incomes and the lowest unemployment rate in the country, Alberta offers plenty of employment opportunities.

Life in Alberta presents many advantages: the lowest taxes in Canada, a strong science and technology culture, excellent hospitals, schools, and post-secondary institutions, and world-class infrastructure (including transportation and telecommunications).

The Job Market

Over the past ten years, Alberta has had Canada's strongest economy and therefore a healthy job market. Approximately 500,000 new jobs were created during that time. And in 2007, Alberta's unemployment rate was the lowest in Canada at 3.3 percent. The strongest sectors of the provincial economy are farming, ranching, energy, forestry, and industrial products. More than 51 million acres are used for crop and livestock production.

Alberta is the world leader in oil sands development and one of the largest suppliers of natural gas on the planet. Described by *Time* magazine as "Canada's greatest buried energy treasure," the oil sands alone could meet the global demand for petroleum for the next hundred years.

With the highest minimum wage in Canada, Alberta even offers great survival jobs!

Job-Search Assistance

Labour Market Information Centres (LMICs) help people choose the right career in Alberta. These centres provide information about Alberta industries, occupations in demand, labour market trends and forecasts, career and education planning, education programs, and job-search techniques.

Many LMICs are equipped with computers, phones, fax machines, and photocopiers that can be used for job searching. They also have books, magazines, software, and audio/video materials for job hunters.

Below are some other Alberta job-search resources:

- The Edmontonjobs website—for jobs in Edmonton, Alberta's capital city (www.edmontonjobs.com).

- The Calgaryjobs website (www.calgaryjobs.com).
- The DiscoverAlberta website, which provides newspapers published in numerous Alberta cities (www.discoveralberta.com).
- The Human Resources and Social Development Canada (HRSDC) job bank site includes information about the Alberta labour market and resources for students about training, learning, and working.

Newcomers in Alberta

Alberta is working hard to attract immigrants. For information useful to newcomers, see the Alberta-Canada website. Click on Immigration on their index page. There you'll find topics like Canada's immigration laws and regulations, economic immigration program information, how to complete the immigration application, how to prepare for an interview with a visa officer, and how to find temporary work in Alberta.

The Alberta Provincial Nominee Program (APNP) allows the province to choose a limited number of immigrants to meet skill shortages defined as most critical by Alberta employers. People who apply to APNP must have a job offer from a pre-approved employer. (More information about this program can also be found on the Alberta-Canada website.)

Alberta Human Resources and Immigration Canada funds employment-readiness programs designed for new immigrants. It also offers counselling and workshops to help new immigrants understand Canadian workplace culture and find a job in Alberta.

Taking It Online

Website Name	Website Address
Resource Centre for New Canadians	www.ditpc.ca
Education	www.calcna.ab.ca/alberta/occupati/educatio/colleges.html
Government	www.gov.ab.ca/home/index.cfm
Immigration Information	www.alberta-canada.com
LMIC	www.hre.gov.ab.ca/cps/rde/xchg/hre/hs.xsl/3316.html
Newspapers	www.discoveralberta.com/BusinessIndex/Newspapers
The cost of living in Calgary	www.canadaimmigrants.com/Calgaryliving.asp

14.4 Calgary

Life in Calgary

Calgary is the petroleum capital of Canada and the largest city in Alberta. It is one of the fastest-growing cities in the country. It became a city in 1893 and now attracts many new immigrants because of its healthy employment and high wages.

Situated at the junction of the Bow and Elbow Rivers, Calgary is home to over one million people. The largest communities in the city are English, Scottish, German, Irish, Ukrainian, and French. And as of the 2001 Census, 2.3 percent of the residents were First Nations. The growing visible minority population (15 percent) is made up of people of Chinese, South Asian, Filipino, Black Canadian, and Latin American backgrounds.

Winter sports are a feature of life in Calgary, and mountain resorts are within easy driving distance.

The Job Market

Calgary's unemployment rate is 3.5 percent (as of 2007). For job listings, see Calgary's two daily newspapers: the *Calgary Herald* and the *Calgary Sun*.

Hundreds of oil, gas, and pipeline companies have their head offices in Calgary. A number of geological, geophysical, and surveying firms also have head offices there. Other major sources of employment include chemical companies, telecommunications firms, financing centres, electrical and electronic products, furniture, paper, and manufacturers of building materials. Among the top ten occupations in Calgary are business administration, natural and applied sciences, sales and service, trade and transportation, and management. Many engineers also find work in Calgary. Key Calgary employers include Calgary Health Region (the primary health service provider), Shaw Communications, the public school boards, and Canadian Pacific Railway Limited (provider of rail, freight, and transportation services).

Job-Search Assistance

The Calgary Labour Market Information Centre is a great source of information for you to use in making career and education planning decisions. It also sends mobile Career in Motion units across the province. On the Internet, information about the centre can be found on the Alberta Employment, Immigration and Industry website.

Newcomers in Calgary

Below are some noteworthy facts for newcomers thinking of living in Calgary:

- A list of organizations serving newcomers in the city can be found on the Calgary Public Library website (calgarypubliclibrary.com/multi/help. htm). The library also offers language training and settlement resources.
- In 1977, a Calgary citizens' group formed the Calgary Immigrant Aid Society to help new immigrants.
- In 1982, the Calgary Immigrant Women's Association (CIWA) was created to help immigrant and refugee women and their families (www. ciwa-online.com).
- The Centre for Newcomers (operated by the Calgary Mennonite Society Centre for Newcomers) was established in 2003. It was modelled after the Edmonton Mennonite Centre for Newcomers, which was founded in 1980 to help Southeast Asian refugees (www.cmcn.abn.ca).
- The Calgary Catholic Immigration Society (CCIS) offers settlement and employment services in more than 45 languages. Its mission is to provide diversity training and support for ethno-cultural groups and initiatives (www.ccis-calgary.ab.ca).
- The Calgary Multicultural Centre offers a wide range of volunteer opportunities.

Taking It Online

Website Name	Website Address
Alberta Employment, Immigration and Industry	www.employment.alberta.ca
Momentum Agencies	www.momentum.org
Calgary Jobs	calgaryjobs.net
Calgary Newcomer Phone Directory	www.afpa.com/hr/documents/ calgarynewcomerphonedirectory.pdf
Immigrant Services Calgary	www.calgaryimmigrantaid.ca
Jewish Immigrant Aid Services of Canada	www.jias.org/calvoc.htm
Cost of living	www.canadaimmigrants.com/Calgaryliving.asp
Employment	www.albertajobcentre.ca regionalhelpwanted.com/p/jobs_city/162/Calgary

14.5 Edmonton

Life in Edmonton

The capital of Alberta, Edmonton lies in the centre of the province. It connects the rich farm regions of the south with the natural resources of the north. The name "Edmonton" (originally Fort Edmonton) was chosen to honour Hudson's Bay Company Governor James Winter Lake, who was from the town of Edmonton, England.

Edmonton is now a sophisticated, modern city that hasn't lost its warm western hospitality. It's a great place to bring up a family, despite the cold of Edmonton's winters. (On average, for 28 days per year, temperatures drop below –20° C.) But it's also Canada's sunniest city. And with overhead walkways built since the 1970s, you can work and shop in downtown Edmonton without ever going outdoors. Shopping in Edmonton includes the world's largest shopping and entertainment complex—the West Edmonton Mall.

When Edmonton was a Hudson's Bay fort, most of the population was British and Irish. But from 1891 to 1914, 170,000 Ukrainians came to Canada, and many came to Edmonton. The city still has more Ukrainian residents than any other in Canada. Chinese and First Nations people make up the largest visible minorities, with the South Asian and Black communities growing quickly.

In 2006, the city was home to 730,000 residents, and the population of the metropolitan area was 1,035,000.

The Job Market

Edmonton's unemployment rate is extremely low, at 3.3 percent (as of 2007). For job listings, see the city's two major daily newspapers: the *Edmonton Journal* and the *Edmonton Sun*.

Edmonton's economy is now the second most diverse in Canada (according to the *Edmonton Economic Outlook*).The city's top industries include the health care, social assistance, manufacturing, and service industries. These include medical research and biotechnology; petroleum processing and refinery plants; chemical production operations; and food, plastics, and oil field supplies companies. Top occupations in Edmonton include information systems analysts and consultants; computer programmers and interactive media developers; and civil, chemical, and electrical engineers. Major employers in Edmonton include the video game developer BioWare; the Northern Alberta Institute of Technology (NAIT); Epcor Utilities; Canadian Western Bank, a chartered bank operating in the four western provinces; Focus Corp., a consulting firm involved in oil, gas, and oil sands; PCL Construction Group; and General Electric.

The University of Alberta, one of the country's largest universities, is also a major research centre. The National Institute for Nanotechnology was recently built on campus and the university has connections with the Alberta Research Council and Edmonton Research Park.

Job-Search Assistance

Alberta Job Corps (AJC) provides supportive training and work experience for people with poor work histories. Participants work on community projects and earn minimum wage from Alberta Employment, Immigration and Industry, in addition to pay from individual employers.

Newcomers in Edmonton

Employment programs and newcomer services are provided by such organizations as the Immigrant Services Association, Catholic Social Services, the Edmonton Mennonite Centre for Newcomers, Edmonton ASSIST, the Millwoods Welcome Centre for Immigrants, and Accès Emploi (for French-speaking immigrants).

Taking It Online

Website Name	Website Address
City site	www.edmonton.ca
Employment agencies	www.headhuntersdirectory.com/headhunters_recruiters/Alberta/Edmonton.htm
Edmonton newcomer phone directory	relocatecanada.com/pdfdocuments/edmontonyellow.pdf
Industry summary reports	www.edmonton.com/statistics/page.asp?page=1241
Job opportunities	www.edmontonjobshop.ca
Job opportunities for newcomers	www.movetoedmonton.com/working/jobbanks
Learning English	www.movetoedmonton.com/education/learningenglish
List of newcomer services	www.movetoedmonton.com/newcomer
Newcomer Agencies—Catholic Social Services	www.catholicsocialservices.ab.ca/services/immigration.asp
Edmonton Mennonite Centre for Newcomers	www.emcn.ab.ca
ASSIST Community Services Centre	www.assistcsc.org

14.6 Saskatchewan

Life in Saskatchewan

Saskatchewan is located in the centre of the Canadian prairies. The area was settled mostly by Germans, Ukrainians, Scandinavians, Danes, Poles, and Russians, and became part of Canada in 1905. Its population is just over a million people, making it one of the country's smaller provinces. About 95 percent of the people in Saskatchewan speak English.

Regina is Saskatchewan's capital (180,000 residents), and Saskatoon is its largest city (200,000 residents). Each has a world-class university, the University of Regina and the University of Saskatchewan, respectively. The province also has four skills-training campuses and numerous private schools and regional colleges.

The cost of living is lower in Saskatchewan than in most of the rest of Canada. A house that would cost $2 million in Toronto would cost less than a quarter-million in Saskatchewan.

The Job Market

Saskatchewan's unemployment rate is 4 percent (as of 2008), lower than the national average. For job listings, see newspapers such as Saskatoon's *The StarPhoenix* and Regina's *The Leader-Post*. The province's workforce is one of Canada's best educated. Nearly 60 percent of employees have at least some post-secondary education.

Saskatchewan is sometimes called "Canada's breadbasket" because its farmlands produce so much of the nation's wheat (54 percent of the wheat grown in Canada) and much of its barley, oats, flaxseed, and canola. Pig farming and cattle ranching are also important enterprises, and the province is home to many high-tech firms, such as the University of Saskatchewan.

Non-agricultural activities include high-tech firms (many of which are based in Saskatoon), the service sector, advanced technology, agri-value production and processing, forestry, manufacturing, and mining. The uranium mine at Key Lake is the world's largest, and potash mines in the south supply 49 percent of world demand. Saskatchewan exports over 80 percent of its manufactured goods. The province is also working hard to stimulate the growth of small businesses.

Job-Search Assistance

Saskatchewan Job Futures is a good source of employment information, structured according to the National Occupational Classification (NOC).

As well, browse the Saskatchewan Jobs site to view job openings by location and industry, and to see their Featured Jobs page.

Newcomers in Saskatchewan

The province of Saskatchewan is looking for immigrant businesspersons, farmers, and skilled workers who can help expand and diversify the growing economy. And the Saskatchewan Immigrant Nominee Program (SINP) is an excellent option for immigrants with the ability and resources to make a significant contribution to the provincial economy.

A small but growing number of settlement and integration services agencies can be found in Saskatoon, Regina, Prince Albert, and Moose Jaw to help newcomers. For contact information, visit the Government of Saskatchewan website (www.immigration.gov.sk.ca/going-to-sask).

Taking it Online

Website Name	Website Address
Saskatchewan Jobs	www.saskatchewan.jobopenings.net
Saskatchewan Jobs	www.saskjobs.com
SaskNetWork	www.sasknetwork.gov.sk.ca
The Career Centre	www.careers.gov.sk.ca
Working Canada	working.canada.com
Government	www.gov.sk.ca
Provincial Nominee Program and Immigrant Services	www.immigration.gov.sk.ca
Small business	canadabusiness.gc.ca/gol/cbec/site.nsf/en/index.html

14.7 Manitoba

Life in Manitoba

Manitoba is the easternmost of Canada's three Prairie provinces and has a population of 1,180,000 (as of 2006). Its area is twice that of the United Kingdom. Winnipeg, the capital city (population 700,000), lies at the geographical centre of the continent. Winnipeg has the most diverse economy of any major city in Canada and is well-known for its arts community and cultural diversity. It has two universities: the University of Manitoba and the University of Winnipeg. Other important cities within Manitoba are Brandon, Thompson, Portage-la-Prairie, Winkler, and Steinbach.

Manitoba has the highest proportion of First Nations people in the country, and many of the province's employment and cultural initiatives are directed toward this population.

The Job Market

Manitoba's unemployment rate is 4.2 percent (as of 2007). For job listings, see newspapers such as the *Winnipeg Free Press*, the *Winnipeg Sun*, and the *Brandon Sun*.

In Manitoba's diversified economy, the services sector is the most important. Manitoba also has the largest aerospace industry in Western Canada and is home to such world-class manufacturing and service firms as Boeing Technology Canada, Air Canada, Bristol Aerospace, Advanced Composite Structures, and Acsion Industries.

Mining is the second largest main resource industry in the province, including extraction of metals like copper, nickel, zinc, and gold and minerals like tantalum, cesium, dolomite, gypsum, and salt. The industrial electricity rates in Manitoba are lower than anywhere else in North America, and they're actually among the lowest in the world.

Manitoba produces a wide range of grain and cereal crops. One-third of the farmland is used for growing wheat for export. The food processing sector is the largest manufacturing sector in Manitoba. And the province is well known for its high-quality food products, including pork, eggs, and world-class frozen products for international markets. Pharmaceutical and agricultural biotechnologies are both major growth industries. Tourism is a vital industry, as the province has 2.5 million acres of parkland in 150 parks and numerous fishing and hunting resorts.

Job-Search Assistance

By entering the keywords "government" and "Manitoba" into a search engine, you'll find a page of government programs and services in Manitoba. This page will also give you a link to an excellent job futures site that includes wages and salaries, employment requirements, skills, education and training, course availability, and employment outlook.

Newcomers in Manitoba

Through the Manitoba Provincial Nominee Program (MPNP), Manitoba seeks immigrants to fill regional skill shortages and meet job market needs. If you are a skilled worker with training, experience, and language ability, this program provides an excellent way to become employed in Manitoba.

Manitoba also has many job preparation programs, English as an Additional Language (EAL) programs, settlement services, and volunteer work experience opportunities. The Immigration and Multiculturalism website has excellent information on these services.

Career Destination Manitoba for Newcomers features recent biographies of skilled immigrants who re-qualified in their professional fields and found jobs in regulated occupations. These immigrants describe their experiences and successes, to help other immigrants build their own success in Manitoba.

Taking It Online

Website Name	Website Address
Cost of living in Winnipeg	www.canadaimmigrants.com/Winnipegliving.asp
First weeks in Manitoba	www.gov.mb.ca/labour/immigrate/settlement/firstweeks.html
Information about small business	www.companiesoffice.gov.mb.ca/faqs.html
Job postings	www.manitobajobs.com and www.mbjobs.ca
Manitoba Job Market projections	www.mb.jobfutures.org
Manitoba newspapers	www.sunmedia.ca/Sunlib/mannews.html.
Provincial Nominee Program	www.gov.mb.ca/labour/immigrate/pnp/index.html
Immigration and Multiculturalism	www.immigratemanitoba.com

14.8 Ontario

Life in Ontario

More than half the immigrants arriving in Canada each year settle in the province of Ontario. It's the only province that borders the Great Lakes and it holds nearly 40 percent of the country's population (more than 12 million people).

Ontario is also Canada's most multicultural province. Newcomers have come to this province from 200 countries, and they speak 130 languages. Most have their own communities, associations, and local media.

The Job Market

Ontario's unemployment rate is 6.6 percent (as of 2007). For job listings, see the *Globe and Mail* and the *Toronto Star*, among many other newspapers.

Ontario is the centre of the Canadian economy, with many manufacturing and service industries. The head offices of most Canadian banks are located in Toronto, the province's capital city. Ontario's strong economy is based on the automobile industry, mining (gold, nickel, petroleum, and uranium), farm products (milk, beef, cattle, pigs, corn, chickens, and eggs), chemicals, electronic equipment, food and beverage products, forestry (wood and pulp and paper), and hunting and fishing.

The province is also rich in hydroelectric power (including power from Niagara Falls) and has numerous nuclear power plants. Ontario's service industry includes finance, insurance, real estate, education, health care, hospitality, and communications.

About 100 million tourists visit Ontario each year, some attracted by the province's more than 250,000 lakes and rivers.

Job-Search Assistance

Among the many sources of job-search assistance in Ontario, the Internet-based Ontario Job Futures provides statistics and advice on the job market, aiding you in your job search.

CareerBridge, operated by Career Edge Organization, offers paid 4, 6, 9, and 12 month internships for job-ready immigrants.

Newcomers in Ontario

In 2005, the governments of Ontario and Canada signed the first Canada-Ontario Immigration Agreement. Through this agreement, the federal government is providing $920 million over five years to help immigrants adapt to Ontario by expanding settlement and language training programs. The agreement also allows municipalities to work with the provincial and federal governments to serve immigrants throughout Ontario.

Meanwhile the Pilot Provincial Nominee Program (Pilot PNP, an Ontario government program) and a Temporary Foreign Worker agreement (developed by the federal and provincial governments) will help Ontario select newcomers who fit its economic and labour market requirements.

Other employment services for newcomers include Bridging Programs, Job Specific Language Training Programs, Job Search Workshops, Newcomer Information Centres, Mentoring Programs, and Immigrant Employment Loan Programs.

Job-search information for newcomers can also be found on the Provincial Ministry of Citizenship and Immigration website, the website of the Ontario Council of Agencies Serving Immigrants (OCASI).

You'll also find useful information and many valuable links in Canada's how-to magazine for new immigrants, *Canadian Newcomer Magazine*, which is available on the Internet. It is also free at settlement agencies, libraries, and retailers throughout Ontario.

Taking It Online

Website Name	Website Address
Canadian Newcomer Magazine	www.cnmag.ca
Career Bridge	www.careerbridge.ca
Immigrant Employment Loan Programs	www.maytree.com/index.asp?section=1&art=loanprogram
International Medical Graduates Program	www.imgo.ca
Ontario Immigration	www.ontarioimmigration.ca
Ontario Job Futures	www.ontariojobfutures.ca
Ontario regions	www.amo.on.ca/YLG/ylg/ontario.html
The OCASI information site	www.settlement.org

14.9 Toronto

Life in Toronto

Named in 1834 after the Mohawk word for "meeting place," Toronto is Canada's largest city and the capital of Ontario. It's also the industrial, financial, and cultural centre of the country, with a rich and diverse cultural and economic life.

Located on the north shore of Lake Ontario, Toronto's population is 2.6 million. But the Greater Toronto Area, which includes the suburbs Markham, Richmond Hill, Vaughan, Brampton, Mississauga, and Pickering, has a population of about 4.7 million.

Toronto has three universities: University of Toronto, York University, and Ryerson University, as well as many other educational institutions.

The Job Market

Toronto's unemployment rate is 5.8 percent (as of 2008). According to the City of Toronto website, the city's key industries include:

- Aerospace (commercial aircraft manufacturers)
- Biomedical and biotechnology (more than 100 medical/biotech companies)
- Business services (law and accounting, advertising and marketing, technical and design consultancies)
- Design (North America's third-largest design workforce)
- Financial services (Toronto is Canada's banking and investment capital)
- Food and beverages (Toronto is the second-largest and fastest-growing food processing centre in North America)
- Information and Communication Technology (ICT) (high-speed communications, IT, and New Media development)

Major Toronto employers (who have 2,500 to 5,000 employees) include Apotex Inc., Bombardier, Canadian Broadcasting Corporation (CBC), Canadian Tire Corporation, Hurley Corporation, IBM Canada Ltd., Manufacturers Life Insurance Company, Shoppers Drug Mart Inc., the Hospital For Sick Children, and the Workplace Safety and Insurance Board.

Job-Search Assistance

For Toronto's many employment agencies, employment resource centres, employment assessment centres, and job finding clubs, search the Internet using those phrases as keywords. Also look for the "Possibilities Online Employment Resource Centre."

Toronto job ads can be found on most of the major employment websites, including Workopolis, Eluta, Monster, and Torontojobs.

Newcomers in Toronto

Immigrant communities receive considerable attention in Toronto. This is partly because almost half of Toronto's residents were born in other countries. The city has 150 national groups speaking more than 100 languages. Here are some of the organizations serving newcomers:

- The YMCA offers many programs and services to help immigrants.
- COSTI operates from 14 locations in Toronto, York Region, and Peel, and provides services to over 42,000 individuals in more than 60 languages.
- JVS offers workshops, one-on-one counselling, support, and referrals to Canadian employers.
- Skills for Change, ACCES, Job Skills, and Microskills provide effective employment programs and services for immigrants and refugees.
- Most Toronto colleges, including George Brown, Seneca, Centennial, and Humber offer immigrant employment programs and workshops.

Taking It Online

Website Name	Website Address
City of Toronto	www.toronto.ca
College and University Employment Programs for Newcomers (YMCA)	www.employmentflyers.com
COSTI Immigrant Services	www.costi.org
JVS Toronto	www.jvstoronto.org
Skills for Change	www.skillsforchange.org
ACCES Employment Services	www.accestrain.com
Job Skills	www.jobskills.org
MicroSkills	www.microskills.ca
Eluta	www.eluta.ca
TorontoJobs	www.torontojobs.ca
Possibilities Online Employment Resource Centre	www.poss.ca

14.10 Ottawa and Eastern Ontario

Life in Eastern Ontario

Eastern Ontario runs from the eastern edge of the Greater Toronto Area to the Quebec border, and from the Ottawa River in the north to the Canada–US border and the St. Lawrence Seaway in the south. In this region of farms, forests, and important cities, businesses share excellent access to materials and to the many large Canadian and US markets nearby. Eastern Ontario's largest cities are Ottawa and Kingston.

Life in Ottawa

Located on the Ottawa River and right on the Ontario-Quebec border, Ottawa is the capital of Canada, with a population of nearly 780,000. Residents of Ottawa have easy access to outdoors activities such as skiing, skating (along the Rideau Canal), and sailing, and to cultural events at venues like the National Arts Centre. Ottawa is also one of Canada's youngest cities. Nearly half the population is under 35.

Life in Kingston

Kingston is located at the eastern edge of Lake Ontario where the lake meets the St. Lawrence River. The Kingston area has a population a little over 150,000 and is home to three post-graduate institutions: Queens University, the Royal Military College of Canada (RMC), and St Lawrence College. The area is also home to a large military presence as well as number of prisons.

The Job Market

For job listings, see the *Ottawa Citizen* and the *Kingston Whig-Standard*, among other newspapers.

Ontario's main economic sectors are agriculture, auto parts, food processing, information and communications technology, biotechnology and life sciences, logistics/distribution, plastics, and tourism.

In Ottawa

The largest employer in Ottawa is the Government of Canada (the federal government). To get a job with the federal government, a candidate must speak both English and French. Ottawa's workforce is divided as follows: 78,000 people in advanced technology, 73,000 people in the federal government, 70,000 people in health and education, and 57,000 people in trades.

Ottawa is surrounded by more farmland than any other city in Canada, and its farming revenues are more than those of Toronto, Montreal,

Vancouver, Edmonton, and Calgary combined. About 10,000 jobs in Ottawa are directly or indirectly associated with agriculture. Known as "Silicon Valley North," Ottawa has more than 800 high-technology companies. Tourism is also an important industry in Canada's capital.

In Kingston
The largest employer in Kingston is the Canadian Armed Forces. Kingston's industries include biotech/health sciences, tourism and culture, advanced materials, alternative energy, and environmental technology. The community is also home to many authors, actors, musicians, and academics.

Job-Search Assistance
In Ottawa
The four EFAC (Employment and Financial Assistance Centres) offer workshops on different aspects of job-searching as well as other career help.

Ottawajobs.com, a region specific part of canjobs.com is a good place to find job listings and post your resume.

In Kingston
KEYS (Kingston Employment & Youth Services) provides job-search help, including assistance with career planning, job-search techniques, interview skills, and resume building (www.keys.ca). It also has a job-posting board and access to the Internet, telephones, fax machines, and photocopiers for job searchers.

Newcomers in Eastern Ontario
In Ottawa
Ottawa is Ontario's second most popular destination for newcomers after the Greater Toronto Area. On average, 6,000 newcomers arrive in Ottawa each year, and about 25 percent of Ottawa's residents were born outside of Canada.

The Ottawa Community Immigrant Services Organization (OCISO) has been providing settlement and integration services to the community for almost 30 years (www.ociso.org).

In Kingston
Although a quaint, old city, it has not been a major destination for newcomers. Visible minorities make up less than 5 percent of the population.

The Kingston Newcomers Club offers events help. It may be a good place to learn more about the community and what it has to offer.

14.11 Ontario's Industrial Heartland

Life in Ontario's Industrial Heartland

Southern Ontario is home to more than 12 million people. They make up 94 percent of the province's population and more than one-third of Canada's population. The industrial heartland is generally located in the southwest and includes major urban centres such as Hamilton, Kitchener-Waterloo, London, and Windsor.

Auto manufacturing, agriculture, and high-technology industries are key to the region's economy.

The cities of Ontario's industrial heartland welcome immigrants, and they have the fastest-growing newcomer populations in Canada.

London

- London's population is 350,000, and its unemployment rate is 6.2 percent (as of 2007).
- The city is surrounded by productive farmland in the heart of southwestern Ontario.
- Industries in London include agriculture, financial sector, and medicine. The London Health Sciences Centre (LHSC) is one of Canada's largest acute-care teaching hospitals.
- About 75 percent of the city's workforce works in service industries.
- The well-regarded University of Western Ontario is located in London.

Kitchener-Waterloo and Cambridge

- The three cities of Kitchener, Waterloo, and Cambridge share municipal boundaries and have a combined population of over 400,000.
- They are sometimes referred to as "Canada's Technology Triangle" because of their focus on high-technology businesses.
- Waterloo has a service-oriented economy, including a health insurance sector and a strong technology sector, with hundreds of high-tech firms.
- There are two universities in Waterloo: Sir Wilfrid Laurier University and the University of Waterloo. The University of Waterloo is internationally recognized as a leader in Information Technolgy (IT).
- Newcomers can find help at the Kitchener-Waterloo Multicultural Centre and at YMCA Cross Cultural and Immigrant Services (www.kwymca.org/Contribute/immigrant/immigrant.asp).

Windsor

- Windsor, Canada's southernmost city, is across the river from Detroit.
- Three of its four largest employers are auto makers.

- Free job-search services are provided by a number of agencies, including the Windsor-Essex YMCA, the New Canadians' Centre of Excellence, and the Multicultural Council of Windsor and Essex County (MCC). These services include job-search workshops, computer courses, and Test of English as a Foreign Language (TOEFL) classes.

Hamilton
- The city of Hamilton is Canada's largest steel producer and a major Great Lakes port.
- Its population is 500,000, and its unemployment rate is 5.5 percent.
- In addition to the traditional steel and machinery industries, growth industries include environmental agencies, health sciences, advanced manufacturing, and port-related industries.
- The Myhamilton.ca website provides useful information on settlement services and on how to start a small business in Hamilton, among other things (www.myhamilton.ca).
- The city's high-level educational institutions include McMaster University and Mohawk College of Applied Arts and Technology. Each has more than 20,000 full time students.
- The largest organization serving newcomers in Hamilton is the Settlement and Integration Services Organization (SISO) (www.siso-ham.org.).

St. Catharines
- The population of St. Catharines is 133,000, and its unemployment rate is 6.4 percent.
- City industry includes mills, shipyards, metal and machinery manufacture, automobile production, canning factories, and the textile and clothing industries.
- Summer resorts with mineral springs attract thousands of tourists.

Niagara Falls
- Niagara Falls, Ontario (population 82,000) is known as the "Honeymoon Capital of the World" and attracts nearly 14 million tourists a year.
- Many electro-chemical and electro-metallurgical industries came here in the early to mid-20th century, attracted by the Falls' inexpensive hydroelectric power.
- Service and tourism are definitely the most important sectors of the region's economy. The largest employers are Casino Niagara and the Niagara Parks Commission.
- Fruit farming and wine making are important industries throughout the Niagara Peninsula.

14.12 Quebec (The Province)

Life in Quebec

Quebec has a population of 7.6 million (as of 2007), and it has the greatest land area of all the provinces. Settled by French immigrants in the 17th century, Quebec was taken over by the British in the 18th century. However, most of the population still speaks French, and a portion of the French-speaking population has always wanted to break away from Canada to form their own country. These people are called Separatists. The Parti Québécois represents their interests in the provincial Parliament.

Most of the population of Quebec lives in cities and speaks French. The capital is Quebec City (often called just "Quebec"), with 720,000 residents, but the largest city is Montreal, with more than 1 million residents.

Quebec has four French-language universities: Université de Montréal, Université du Québec, Université Laval, and Université de Sherbrooke. They also have three English-language universities: McGill University, Concordia University, and Bishop's University.

The Job Market

Quebec's unemployment rate is 6.9 percent (as of 2007)—higher than the Canadian average. For job listings, see *Le Devoir, Le Soleil,* and other newspapers. The service industry employs one-third of Quebec's residents in education, health care, and engineering, and in the fields of law, finance, insurance, real estate, and sports.

Quebec is one of North America's largest producers of hydroelectricity. This power is generated partly by the Great Lakes–St. Lawrence Seaway and partly by dams in the James Bay region. There are 32,000 farm businesses located along the St. Lawrence River. Milk and maple syrup are two of the many products produced in that area.

The province provides about one-quarter of all goods manufactured in Canada: food processing, aircraft, chemicals, plastic, newsprint, rubber, paper, aluminum, uranium, and transportation equipment. Northern Quebec has large deposits of iron ore, gold, copper, nickel, and titanium, while forests provide balsam, spruce, and other desirable softwoods.

About 10 million tourists visit Quebec every year, many of them visiting historic sites.

Government services in Quebec use both French and English, and there is a substantial English-speaking population, especially in Montreal. But newcomers who want to settle in Quebec should be able to communicate in French.

Newcomers in Quebec

- Since 1991, Quebec has controlled immigration to the province. Successful applicants receive a Quebec Selection Certificate issued by the Immigration et Communautés culturelles.
- Quebec also has responsibility for the cultural, economic, and linguistic adaptation and integration of newcomers.
- Each year, an average of 45,000 immigrants come to Quebec from about 100 countries.
- The main website for the Quebec immigration ministry describes possible immigrants according to six categories: permanent workers, business people, temporary workers, international students, sponsors and sponsored persons, and refugees.
- The Quebec Ministry of Immigration has published a guide for new immigrants, *Learning about Québec*. It includes information about how to learn French, where to find job-search resources, and more.
- In Montreal, many organizations work to provide recent immigrants with reception and support services, literacy training, French fluency, and defence of rights.
- The immigration website also offers a preliminary evaluation test to help potential immigrants determine their chances of being allowed to immigrate to Quebec. The test is based on criteria such as training and work experience; knowledge of French and English; any ties with, or visits to, Quebec; and similar information about the potential immigrant's spouse or common-law partner. It's also important to have an offer from a Quebec employer. The results of this test are not official, but they offer an idea of what the official response will likely be.

Taking It Online

Website Name	Website Address
Cost of living	www.canadaimmigrants.com/Montrealiving.asp
Quebec Jobs	www.Quebecjobs.com
Newcomer serving organizations	www.immigration-quebec.gouv.qc.ca/en/partners/services-offered.html
Quebec job trends	www150.hrdc-drhc.gc.ca/job-futures/accueil.asp?LastPage=-7
Quebec newspapers	www.onlinenewspapers.com/canadaqu.htm

14.13 Montreal

Life in Montreal

Founded in the 17th century, Montreal is now the largest French-speaking city in the world after Paris, and the second-largest city in Canada after Toronto.

Located on an island, Montreal is also a major port on the St. Lawrence River, which connects the Atlantic Ocean with the Great Lakes. Nearly 5,000 ships visit Montreal's port every year. The city has a population of over 1.8 million, but the metropolitan area includes more than 3.5 million people.

With its French and British roots, the Montreal region is **cosmopolitan**, attracting newcomers from around the world. More than half the city has French ancestry, but there are also large Italian, Greek, and Jewish communities. Most newcomers speak both of Canada's official languages (English and French). This is mostly because the Quebec Ministry of Immigration prefers newcomers to speak both.

Montreal is a modern, low-crime city with a rich cultural life. It also offers some of the best education in Canada. There are two English-language universities in the city and two French-language universities: McGill University (English), l'Université du Québec à Montréal (French), l'Université de Montréal (French), and Concordia University (English).

The Job Market

Montreal's unemployment rate is 7 percent (as of 2007). For job listings, see the *Montreal Gazette* (English) and *Le Devoir* (French), among other sources. There is also a wide range of newspapers in Spanish, Russian, and many other languages.

The most important industries in Montreal are aerospace, finance (international trade banks), food processing (canned goods), agriculture, manufacturing (5,000 factories), and telecommunications (computer software). According to the *Montreal Gazette*, the Mediacorp Top Ten List of Montreal Employers includes the following:

- Bell Canada (Canada's leading communications company)
- Business Development Bank of Canada (a bank owned by the Government of Canada)
- Cascades Inc. (a leader in the production, conversion, and marketing of packaging products)
- CGI Group Inc. (CGI is responsible for most information technology functions)
- Genetec Inc. (IP video surveillance and technology leader within the physical security industry)

- IMS Health Canada Ltd. (provider of market intelligence to the pharmaceutical and health-care industries)
- L'Oréal Canada Inc. (leader of the cosmetics industry in Canada)
- Laurentide Controls Ltd. (largest supplier of automation solutions in eastern Canada)
- Pfizer Canada Inc. (the world's largest pharmaceutical company)
- Yellow Pages Group (Canada's largest directory publisher)

The strongest career fields in Montreal are natural and applied sciences, health, art, culture, recreation and sports, and services.

Newcomers to Montreal

According to the 2006 census, 70 percent of individuals born abroad and living in Quebec are found in the Montreal region; they make up 28 percent of the total population of the region.

More than 120 cultural communities are represented in Montreal. Newcomers' main places of birth are Europe (37 percent), Asia (29.5 percent), US (21 percent), and Africa (12.4 percent).

Information sessions for immigrants are conducted by the Bibliothèque et Archives nationales du Québec.

Taking It Online

Website Name	Website Address
City site	www.montreal.com
Classified job ads	montreal.kijiji.ca
Cost of living	www.canadaimmigrants.com/Montrealiving.asp
Employment agencies list	www.yellowpages.ca/business/QC/Montreal/Employment+Agencies/00491400.html
Immigrant and settlement information	www.immq.gouv.qc.ca/en/settle/montreal.html#services
Information about Montreal ethnic communities	www.best-of-montreal.com/montreal_ethnic.html
Information about regulated professions and trades	www.immq.gouv.qc.ca/en/settle/sipmr.html
Montreal newcomer phone directory	relocatecanada.com/pdfdocuments/montrealyellow.pdf
Other employment sites	www.montrealjobs.com

14.14 New Brunswick

Life in New Brunswick

With a population of 750,000 (as of 2007), New Brunswick (NB) has two official languages: French and English. New Brunswick joined Nova Scotia, Quebec, and Ontario to form Canada in 1867.

The capital city is Fredericton (50,000), and the largest cities are Saint John (population 70,000) and Moncton (61,000). Approximately one-third of the population is French-speaking, and 97 percent of New Brunswick residents were born in Canada.

New Brunswick also has five internationally recognized universities, among those are the University of New Brunswick, and Mount Allison University.

The Job Market

New Brunswick's unemployment rate is 7.2 percent (as of 2007). For job listings, see the *Telegraph-Journal* and the *Times Globe* (Saint John), Fredericton's *The Daily Gleaner*, Moncton's *Times & Transcript*, and others.

The New Brunswick economy depends mostly on fishing, forestry, mining, agriculture, and tourism. Commercial fishing is a traditional NB industry that is still important today. More than 50 types of finfish and shellfish are harvested each year. The province is also a leader in forest management and has a steady production of solid wood products and pulp. Since the discovery of large base-metal ore deposits, mineral production has increased greatly. Metals mined include lead, zinc, copper, silver, and gold. Nonmetals include peat moss, silica, potash, sulphur, coal, lime, sand, gravel, and stone. Agriculture is also an important part of New Brunswick's economy. Potatoes, dairy products, eggs, and poultry account for over 60 percent of New Brunswick's farm income.

Of the four Atlantic Provinces, New Brunswick has the only nuclear station. Nuclear energy accounts for about one-third of the electricity generated in the province. New Brunswick also sells substantial amounts of electricity to other provinces and the US. At the same time, service industries and specialized manufacturing are growing in New Brunswick.

Job-Search Assistance

The New Brunswick Job Futures website provides information on wages and salaries, employment requirements, skills, education and training courses, future employment trends, and more.

New Brunswick's universities offer several degree programs with co-op work term options. These co-op options allow students to combine theoretical learning with practical, on-the-job experience.

Newcomers in New Brunswick

- High-quality literacy programs and English and French classes are available in large and small centres throughout New Brunswick—a great advantage for newcomers.
- The New Brunswick Provincial Nominee Program (PNP) measures applicants using factors like age, language skills, education, work experience, skill shortage (in the case of job offer applicants), and business experience (in the case of business plan applicants). As in most other provinces, PNP applicants need a guaranteed job offer or a business plan approved by the Department of Business New Brunswick.
- The New Brunswick Multicultural Council (NBMC), located in Fredericton, helps immigrants integrate into the province's workforce. NBMC offers such programs as Labour Market Integration, Enhanced Language Training, Prior Assessment and Recognition, Cultural Competency Training, and Research and Needs Assessment of Newcomers. These are available in French and English throughout the province.

Taking It Online

Website Name	Website Address
Career counselling and job placement services	www.diversityscope.ca/agencies.cfm
New Brunswick Job Futures	nb.jobfutures.org
Job finding resources	www.careerbeacon.com/bhn/index.html
NB newspapers	www.world-newspapers.com/new-brunswick.html
Newcomer programs and services including the Provincial Nominee Program	www.gnb.ca/immigration

14.15 Prince Edward Island

Life in Prince Edward Island

Prince Edward Island (PEI), with a population of 139,000 (as of 2007), is the smallest Canadian province. But it is also one of the most beautiful. If you like a busy urban environment, PEI is not for you, but it is a good place to settle because of its low crime rates, short commutes to work, tranquility, and clean air and water. It became Canada's seventh province in 1873 and is known locally as "the Island."Charlottetown is the capital city of PEI.

The Job Market

PEI's unemployment rate is 10.7 percent (as of 2007). For job ads, see the newspapers *The Guardian* (Charlottetown) and *The Journal Pioneer* (Summerside).

Agriculture is PEI's largest industry. The province has more than 2,000 farms, which grow about 30 percent of Canada's potatoes. Other crops include fruit, vegetables, and cereals. Tourism is the second-largest industry. The coast is lined with beaches that attract thousands of tourists every summer. Almost as many come to see Green Gables, the house that inspired the world-famous *Anne of Green Gables* books. Tourism has grown since the construction the 12.9 km Confederation Bridge, which connects the island to the province of New Brunswick. Fishing is the third-largest industry, based on catches of herring, tuna, cod, mackerel, mussels, oysters, and lobsters.

Over the past ten years, other sectors have developed considerably on the Island. Construction, food processing, aerospace, and other technology sectors have grown. In the service sectors, job opportunities have increased in information technology, health care, education and research, financial services, and retailing, as well as in various business and government management and support activities.

The greatest demand for job openings is in the following sectors: the aerospace industry, information technology, bioscience, television, data services, and gaming. The Island also has skill shortages in the medical field, so the following occupations are in demand: lab technologists, radiation and respiratory therapists, registered nurses, pharmacists, and doctors. There are also shortages of engineers (electrical and mechanical), construction workers (construction engineers, carpenters, plumbers), and tradespeople (welders, metal fabricators, long haul truck drivers, CNC/precision machinists, heavy duty mechanics, industrial electricians, manufacturing workers, and auto service technicians).

Job-Search Assistance

Prince Edward Island's Job Futures website provides information on current trends and the future outlook for over 80 occupations in PEI.

The Provincial Nominee Program is a partnership between the provincial and federal governments, administered by the province. There are four Nominee Program Categories: Professional and Skilled Workers (applicants with specialized skills and experience who may fill a job market gap), Immigrant Entrepreneurs (applicants who propose to establish a viable new business), Immigrant Partners (who invest in an existing PEI company), and Immigrant Connections (those invited by relatives living in PEI). More information is available on the PEI government website, or search the Internet using the keywords "PEI" and "PNP."

Newcomers in PEI

The PEI Association for Newcomers to Canada provides a wide range of services, including the Immigrant Settlement and Adaptation Program (ISAP), the Host program, and Employment Assistance Service. A newcomer's guide to PEI is available on the PEI government website. First go to Immigration, then click the link at the bottom of the page.

Taking It Online

Website Name	Website Address
Immigrant Services	www.peianc.com
InfoPEI: Labour Market	www.gov.pe.ca/infoipe/index.php3?number=13056&lang=E
Charlottetown Jobs	www.charlottetownjobs.com
PEI Employment and Jobs	www.buyitcanada.com/PEI/Employment
Job Market Trends	www.pei.jobfutures.org
PEI government website	www.gov.pe.ca
PEI newspapers	www.abyznewslinks.com/canadpe.htm
Small business information	www.peibusinessdevelopment.com/index.php3?number=63541&lang=E

14.16 Nova Scotia

Life in Nova Scotia

Nova Scotia (NS), with a population of almost a million people, was one of the four provinces that joined Confederation in 1867. Made up of a large peninsula (the mainland) and Cape Breton Island, NS has the highest tides in the world, scenic landscapes, and a rich history. The capital city, Halifax, has about 372,000 residents, and is an important Canadian seaport.

The universities in NS include Dalhousie University and Saint Mary's University (Halifax), Acadia University (Wolfville), and St. Francis Xavier University (Antigonish).

The Job Market

The unemployment rate in NS is 7.8 percent. In Halifax, it is 4.4 percent (as of 2007). For job listings, see the *Chronicle Herald* (Halifax), the *Cape Breton Post*, and the *Truro Daily News*.

Manufacturing and trade in NS have grown because of its peninsula location and excellent harbours. NS is also a leader in the Canadian fishing industry (haddock, lobster, scallops, and shellfish). And fishing fleet and fish processing factories provide work to many people in the province.

Thick forests cover much of the province, making forestry an important industry (lumber, pulp, paper mills, boatyards, and furniture factories). NS harvests almost 2 million Christmas trees each year. In the spring, it produces 100,000 litres of maple syrup. Mining in NS includes extraction of gypsum, stone, coal, natural gas, petroleum, and construction materials. Agriculture is also significant in NS, with operations in milk, hogs, chicken, eggs, fruit, vegetables, tobacco, cattle, and fur farming. NS ships frozen fruit and berries to over 40 countries and to other provinces in Canada.

As natural resources have waned over the last half century, tourism has grown, with more than 2 million visitors visiting NS every year for its beaches and coastal resorts, among other attractions. The economy is also diversifying and focusing more on information technology, the aerospace industry, medical research, ocean research, and the film industry.

Job-Search Assistance

The Nova Scotia Department of Education has an excellent website called Career Options. It provides information about labour market conditions, average earnings, and expected changes in employment, among other topics.

Service Canada's Nova Scotia Labour Market Information website lists potential employers. To find this information, click on the Who Hires link. Select a geographic area (for example, Halifax and surrounding areas), select Occupation Title and then enter a job title in the search box (for example, "civil engineer"). Once the different titles and their National Occupational Code (NOC) code numbers appear, click on the appropriate title to find the names and addresses of many companies that hire people in your field.

Newcomers in Nova Scotia

Immigrants are greatly needed to fill shortages in the permanent workforce. Through the Nova Scotia Nominee Program (NSNP), NS recruits and selects immigrants who meet the labour market and economic needs of the province. The most important factor is a guaranteed full-time job offer from an NS employer.

The YMCA Newcomer Centre, the Metropolitan Immigrant Settlement Association (MISA), and the Halifax Immigrant Learning Centre (HILC) help newcomers adapt to Nova Scotia's culture. MISA and HILC also offer a bridging program called Working in Nova Scotia (WINS).

Taking It Online

Website Name	Website Address
Career options	www.careeroptions.ednet.ns.ca
Educational institutions	www.novascotiaeducation.com
Government of Nova Scotia	www.gov.ns.ca
Guide to opening a business	www.cbsc.org/ns/images/connections.pdf
Labour Market Information	www.hrsdc.gc.ca/en/ns/lmi/labour_market.shtml
Nova Scotia Jobs	regionalhelpwanted.com/home/166.htm?SN=166&lang=1
The WORK Place	www.theworkplace.ca/page.asp?sect=19
Halifax Immigrant Learning Service	www.hilc.ns.ca
Metropolitan Immigrant Settlement Association	www.misa.ns.ca
Nova Scotia Office of Immigration	novascotiaimmigration.com
Provincial Nominee Program	novascotiaimmigration.com/en-page1040.aspx

14.17 Newfoundland and Labrador

Life in Newfoundland and Labrador

Newfoundland and Labrador (NL) has a population of 507,500 (as of 2007), and it is Canada's easternmost province. It joined Canada in 1949. The province consists of two sections, the island of Newfoundland bordering the Atlantic Ocean, and Labrador, on the mainland next to Quebec. The capital city, St. John's, has about 100,000 residents.

The Job Market

Unemployment in NL is 12.5 percent (as of 2007), the highest in Canada. For job listings, see *The Telegram* (St. John's) and other newspapers.

The economy of NL depends greatly on natural resources. The province's fishing grounds, the Grand Banks, were once the world's richest, and they made fishing the province's number one industry. But with fish stocks disappearing, this industry is currently in severe decline. Mining is also an important activity in NL, with operations extracting gold, limestone, gypsum, nickel, copper, cobalt, petroleum, gas, and iron ore. Forests cover one-third of the province, making forestry a significant industry. Many sawmills and pulp and paper mills are located in Corner Brook, Grand Falls, and Stephenville. The province's largest utility industry is electric power. Churchill Falls in Labrador is one of the largest hydro electric power plants in the world.

Goose Bay, in Labrador, has one of North America's best-known airports. It is a regular stop for aircraft going to international destinations and for mining/exploration companies flying to Canada's North. Agriculture is a small industry in NL and mostly serves the domestic market. But blueberries and furs are sold to markets outside the province. The service sector has grown over the last several years—especially the tourism industry. Nearly 500,000 people visit the province each year to enjoy the exceptional scenery.

The top employers located in St. John's include: IPSCO (western Canada's largest steel manufacturer), Co-op Heavy Oil Upgraders, Kalium Chemicals (potash mining), AgrEvo Inc. (agricultural chemicals), and Degelman Industries (agricultural implement manufacturing).

To learn about small business services, contact the Newfoundland and Labrador Business Service Centre.

The Provincial Nominee Program in NL

- The Provincial Nominee Program (PNP) in NL has three categories of immigrants.

  1. The Occupational/Skilled Worker Category includes applicants with specialized skills and experience that may fill needs in the provincial labour market.

     - Applicants in this category are required to have an offer of paid employment from a NL employer.
     - The applicant's job skills should be on the strategic sector list. To find this list (and self-assessment forms) search the Internet using the keywords "Newfoundland" and "strategic sector."

  2. The Entrepreneur Category includes applicants who intend to be self-employed and want to start a new business or purchase an existing business in the province.

     - Immigrant entrepreneurs who wish to apply in this category must show evidence of eligible business activity, experience, and investment in a new or existing business.
     - They should be prepared to submit a business plan, make an exploratory visit, and sign a performance agreement.

  3. The Partner Category is directed to prospective immigrants with business and entrepreneurial skills who want to form partnerships. To qualify, they must partner with up to three other prospective immigrants to establish a new business or expand an existing company in the province.

     - The Association for New Canadians offers career development and job-finding resources. These include employment assistance services for internationally educated skilled professionals or tradespeople, career placement programs connecting local businesses with job-ready international clients, occupation-specific language training, and job-search programs.

Taking It Online

Website Name	Website Address
Educational resources	www.ed.gov.nl.ca/edu/links.htm
Employment sites	www.lmiworks.nl.ca
Job Bank Canada	www.jobbank.gc.ca/prov_en.aspx?Student=No
Newspapers	www.world-newspapers.com/newfoundland.html
The Association for New Canadians	www.anc-nf.cc
Strategic sector list	www.nlpnp.ca/forms/strategicsectorlist.pdf

14.18 Canada's Territories

Life in Canada's Territories

Canada's North is made up of three territories: the Northwest Territories (NT), with a population of more than 43,000, the Yukon Territory (YT, or simply "the Yukon") in the northwest with population of 31,000, and Nunavut (NU), which also has a population of 31,000. Nunavut was once part of the NT, but it became a separate territory in 1999. It is now the largest of Canada's territories.

The territories receive their powers from the federal Parliament, but each has an elected assembly similar to those of the provincial governments. The NT's capital city, Yellowknife, is located 500 km south of the Arctic Circle and is home to about 20,000 people. Whitehorse, the capital of the YT, is located on the Yukon River and has a population of over 23,000. And Iqaluit (with just over 6,000 people) is the capital of NU. It is located on the southeast part of Baffin Island.

The Job Market

Throughout the Territories

Power corporations are studying the development of hydro power from northern rivers. This would reduce the North's costly dependence on diesel fuels. Using **state-of-the-art** technology to limit environmental impacts, the territories will likely generate much more hydroelectric power in the future—including power for export. This, in turn, will generate many new jobs and put the northern territories at the forefront of industrial development in Canada.

In all three northern capitals, the tourism industry is growing. Visitors to the territories are attracted by fishing, boating, sports facilities, and the scenery (including watching the Northern Lights).

In the Northwest Territories

- The unemployment rate for the NT is currently 5 percent (less than Canada's average). And in Yellowknife, unemployment is at 4.1 percent—one of the lowest rates in Canada.
- With two diamond mines and one currently under construction, Yellowknife now has the title, "Diamond Capital of North America." When all three diamond mines are in full production, the territory will be producing almost 15 percent of the world's diamonds.
- The NT also has large unexplored oil and gas reserves.

- Nearly 40 percent of employment is in government, administration, and health and education services.
- The tourism industry in the NT is worth just over $100 million per year.

In the Yukon Territory
- The Yukon's unemployment rate is 5.6 percent (lower than the national average).
- The Yukon River system was once a main transportation artery. But river travel was replaced to a great extent in the 20th century by airports, highways, and pipelines.
- The Yukon's economy is similar to that of the NT, with mining, tourism, and hydroelectricity as the major industries.

In Nunavut
- Most of NU's population is Inuit.
- The unemployment rate in Nunavut is over 20 per cent, but for non-aboriginal people, it's closer to 5 percent.

Job-Search Assistance
In the Northwest Territories
The NT has about 50 schools; some offer upgrading that could improve possibilities of employment. Aurora College (www.auroracollege.nt.ca), for example, provides further education, skill-based training, certificates, diplomas, and degrees. The college has campuses in Inuvik, Fort Smith, and Yellowknife.

In Nunavut
The Department of Human Resources of Nunavut runs a website that lists government jobs, including positions for registered nurses, health care workers, human resource specialists, social service workers, and family physicians.

Newcomers in the Territories
In the Northwest Territories
The growing diamond industry in the NT will need many highly skilled workers over the next decade (www.jobsnorth.ca). To help meet this demand, the governments of the NT and Canada have cooperated to speed up worker training through the immigration process. Internationally trained professionals working in the industry will train and guide Canadian diamond workers. The governments have also agreed to speed up immigration for skilled diamond artisans.

Key Words

cosmopolitan: containing people from all over the world

metropolitan: connected with a large city

port: an area where ships load and unload goods and passengers

Prairie province: the (Canadian) province of Manitoba, Saskatchewan, or Alberta

state-of-the-art: using the most modern knowledge or technology that is available

Note: Entries taken or adapted from the Oxford ESL Dictionary.

Creating Your Canadian Experience

1. What is most important to you about where you live? Write down the five biggest factors in choosing where you live.

    a. _____

    b. _____

    c. _____

    d. _____

    e. _____

2. Compare the pros and cons of three cities from different areas.
   Tip: Before deciding pros and cons, first review the chapter in Unit 14
   that is closest to each city, and then try looking on the city's main website
   or on the Job Futures website.

City	Province	Population	Pros	Cons

3. Search the Internet for the three biggest industries in your selected cities.
   Tip: Use the keywords "[your city]" + "[industry or economy]."

City	Top Three Industries		

4. Search the Internet for the newcomer settlement and employment
   organizations in each of the three cities.
   Tip: Search using keywords "[your city]" + "newcomer assistance"

City	Organization	Assistance Program
	1. _____ 2. _____	1. _____ 2. _____
	1. _____ 2. _____	1. _____ 2. _____
	1. _____ 2. _____	1. _____ 2. _____

5. Research the demographic (ethnic makeup) of the three cities.

City	Ethnic Makeup

6. Look on the Internet to find out if there is an ethnic organization that you could join in each of the three cities.
Tip: Try searching using the keywords "[your city]" + "[your nationality]"

City	Ethnic Organization	Contact Information

7. Do some research on the Internet about the education available in the three cities.
Tip: Search using keywords "[your city]" + "adult education" or "college and university"

City	Educational Institution	Programs Offered

8. Pick the city that you would most like to move to. Write down five reasons for your decision.

City: _____ Province: _____

Reason 1 _____

Reason 2 _____

Reason 3 _____

Reason 4 _____

Reason 5 _____

Note: If you are having trouble deciding on one city, do the above exercise for more than one place and compare your answers. Also, compare your answers in question 8 to your answers in question 1.

Authors' Final Thoughts

Well, your tour of the Canadian job market has come to an end. You should now have a better idea of the qualities and qualifications that are necessary for finding successful employment in Canada. We hope that our guide has helped you and has sped up your job-hunting process.

Throughout the book, we have tried to acquaint you with problems that newcomers typically face and have offered some effective solutions. If you have developed some of your own solutions along the way, we are sincerely happy—helping you effectively solve problems is one of our goals.

Before we say goodbye, we would like to remind you of the most important factors for your success in Canada.

The most valuable personality trait in Canada is a positive attitude. So be optimistic! Make up your mind to succeed, and do not despair about setbacks or give way to negative emotions.

Improve your English-language skills, because strong communication skills are a necessary tool when trying to overcome obstacles. If you don't understand 90 percent of what is going on around you, then your chances of success are reduced by 90 percent.

Network-building is also a very important factor. Psychologists say that the average person communicates with up to 2,000 other people—and all of those people can help with your job search. Contact your professional association. Your friends, relatives, and colleagues living in Canada can share their experiences and provide references. Create a circle of people who can help you to find a job.

A solid career plan will economize your actions and save you time, strength, and money. Career planning is the first important step in any job-search campaign. Know your present and future goals. Be realistic. Remember that looking for a job is a full-time job. Devote 40 hours per week to your job search and you will soon become an expert. And hopefully employed!

Be open-minded and ready to study. After becoming acquainted with your trade in Canada, you may see gaps in your education that keep you from attaining a fulfilling career. Graduation from a Canadian college or university is the best solution. Learn what you need to learn, and if that costs money, consider it as an investment in your future.

Finding a good job in Canada is not easy. Be ready to work hard but most importantly, be patient, persistent, and enthusiastic. Take advantage of the help that is offered to you in Canada, but most importantly, count on yourself. As Benjamin Franklin said, "He who waits upon fortune is never sure of dinner." And having found a good job, do not throw out this book; it will still be useful to you!

Welcome to the Canadian job market!

Efim Cheinis and Dale Sproule

Where Is Nina Now?

When Nina arrived in Canada in April 2007, she was eager to find a job but was unsure of how to tackle that task. Her decision to visit an immigrant employment centre helped to properly answer her questions about the Canadian job market. Nina's perseverance enabled her to adapt her resume and job-search methods to Canada's customs and conventions. Nina is now successfully employed in Canada, and is hoping to help other job seekers succeed: she is currently enrolled in the Career and Work Counsellor program at George Brown College with the aim of eventually assisting new immigrants with their job searches!

Where Is Peter Now?

Since immigrating to Canada in 2006, Peter has learned a lot about finding a job. His determination to start a good career meant that he was willing to learn and adapt to the different expectations and customs of the Canadian job market. He overcame his initial struggle with finding employment by making use of the tools offered at immigrant and employment centres. In April of 2007, Peter accepted a co-op position with Scotiabank, and by August he successfully earned a full-time contract position. At Scotiabank, he works on an International Banking System as a senior contract analyst. Peter enjoys his job and is doing well there!

About the Authors

Efim Cheinis is a Ph.D. who worked as a scientist for many years before immigrating to Canada 12 years ago. After immigrating, he studied the problems that newcomers most commonly face while looking for jobs. He found that the majority of newcomers are not prepared for the Canadian job market, and that their job search can last for months, or even years. As a result, many newcomers have faced feelings of confusion, uncertainty, and helplessness. After gaining experience in the Canadian employment services industry, Efim now works as a self-employed consultant and has published over 200 articles in the local press to help immigrants resolve their employment issues.

Dale Sproule is publisher of the bi-monthly *Canadian Newcomer Magazine* (www.cnmag.ca), and book, *The Canadian Newcomer Settlement Guide to Southern Ontario*. Born and raised in Canada, he recognized the growing demand for materials to welcome new immigrants and to help them integrate into Canadian society. With a BA in Creative Writing, more than 50 published stories and articles, and a wealth of media experience—including 15 years as an editor and publisher—Dale's specialty is communication.

Index

Boldface page numbers indicate definitions of key words

Immigrant Experiences
certification, 77, 195
cultural differences, 286
employability skills, 43
employment resource centre, 163
engineers, 59, 195, 219
first job, 285
job interviews, 231, 237, 242
job search, 151, 183
making cold calls, 149

networking, 145
public libraries, 52
reference letters, 17
resume bank scam, 153
resume writing, 200, 203
staying in original field, 7
studying English, 45, 87
upgrading credentials, 59
volunteer work, 61

Photo Credits

1 Blackred/iStock International Inc; 3 A330Pilot/iStock International Inc; 11 National Occupational Code 2132—Mechanical Engineers, http://www23.hrdc-drhc.gc.ca/2001/e/groups/2132.shtml, Human Resources and Social Development Canada, 2006. Reproduced with the permission of the Minister of Public Works and Government Services Canada, 2008; 17 Jason Tomassini; 33 Daniel Timiraos/iStock International Inc; 38 Service Canada website (http://www1.servicecanada.gc.ca/en/about/reports/sin/pdf/yoursin.pdf). Reproduced with the permission of the Minister of Public Works and Government Services, 2008; 39 Wish Canada; 39 Job Futures (www.jobfutures.ca/en/home.shtml); 52 Changzhi Qiu (Peter); 71 Chris Schmidt/iStock International Inc; 95 Skip O'Donnell/iStock International Inc; 117 Olga Lyubkina / Big Stock Photo; 119 Anne Stahl/iStock International Inc; 137 Willie B. Thomas/iStock International Inc; 159 Izvorinka Jankovic/iStock International Inc; 177 Chris Schmidt/iStock International Inc; 193 Foreign Credentials Referral Office (http://www.credentials.gc.ca); 199 Linda & Colin McKie/iStock International Inc; 229 Jacob Wackerhausen/iStock International Inc; 261 Blackred/iStock International Inc; 275 Diana Lundin/iStock International Inc; 277 David H. Lewis/iStock International Inc; 297 Lisa F. Young/iStock International Inc; 321 Alexander Gocotano/iStock International Inc; 323 Andrew Penner/iStock International Inc

Literary Credits

305 Human Resources and Social Development Canada (www.hrsdc.gc.ca/en/lp/spila/clli/eslc/table_minimumrequirements_vacations.pdf)

"Nina's Personal Experiences" written by Xiaowei Nie (Nina).

"Peter's Personal Experiences" written by Changzhi Qiu (Peter).